Dedicated to
Grandparents, faith
And love kindness
Resting in each one of us

Songs of Our Fathers

Songs of Our Fathers

Stanley Sackeyfio

Gulf Coast Publications
Texas

Songs of Our Fathers

Gulf Coast Publications
Dallas, TX

Gulf Coast Publishing

Songs of Our Fathers

ISBN 987-0-9883257-3-9
® TXu 1-156-231, 2004
® TXu 1-962-474, 2015

Printed in the United States of America

Acknowledgements

I grew up in Ghana, West Africa, where the oral tradition of storytelling is part of everyday life. These stories and the values they imparted helped me understand my friends and the people I met in chance encounters. They also helped my understand the universality of love, compassion, and need for understating, respect and acceptance of self and the difference we see in others.

I am grateful to my parents for using this tradition to pass on valuable life lessons to me. I am especially grateful to my father, mother, maternal grandmother and paternal grandmother, who reinforced these values as I grew up.

I am especially grateful to Mrs. Elizabeth Arkoful my first grade teacher who encouraged my sense of curiously and adventure. Mr. Walton and Rev. Acquaah who instructed me in Fantsi while I was a student at Mfantsipim Secondary School and helped me understand the maxims, proverbs, quips and symbols undergirding our Fantsi traditions, way of behaving and relating.

I am also grateful Mr. Tetteh my art teacher who opened my eyes to the notion of using words to paint pictures and to Mr. Fiagbozi for helping me understand the relationship between words and music.

I am grateful to Dr. Mary Jane Nelson of the University of Central Oklahoma for her unwavering encouragement and support while I was a graduate student at the university.

I am indebted to Linzi Sackeyfio, who cajoled me to undertake the projects and offering helpful hints and assistance.

I thank Valerie Gilley for typing the manuscript through its many revisions and Art Wilson for the print ready set up. I also highly value the sensitive and thorough editing performed by Sharon Adams and Stephanie Quinn.

Your support, encouragement, and patience made the undertaking of this project much easier than it would have been otherwise. Thank you!

Songs of Our Fathers

Table of Contents

Songs of Our Fathers

Introduction

Summer is the time of the year when school age children are let out of school for a long stretch of time to play and recreate without the demands of home work and grades. It is also a time when adults can take time away from the doldrums of everyday work and engage their children in fun and adventure or send them to spend time with grandparents or caring relatives. So it was the life in the Sackeyfio home when their parents sent their two boys to Apam, a small seaside town in Ghana for summer holidaying with other grandmother.

The story begins in Apam, where the widowed grandmother, Elizabeth Pratt lives a quiet life with her maid welcomes home her two grand teenage boys. The house comes alive when the boy's father drops off his children, Kwesi Sakyi and Ato, to holiday with their grandmother while he returns to lawyer cases in court at the town in which he lives. The father looks on his children's holidaying as an opportunity for them to spend time with their grandmother, be pampered, listen to her tell stories and learn from her experience. The strict, compassionate, and loving grandmother, who is deft in tradition, ceases situations as opportunities to teach and pass down cultural values and the traditional way of life to the youngsters. In a very real sense, *Songs of our Fathers* illustrates how older members of indigenous societies use life events to narrate stories and thereby pass down life lessons and traditional values to younger generations.

The coastal town with its silver shores and coconut mangroves provide a good backdrop, an escape from the stifling air of the big city—where privacy is paramount and eclectic from the small town – where everyone knows everyone and family secrets are topics for open discussion.

The two boys from middle class homes meet two native boys, from low socio-economic background. The local boys introduced their counterparts from out of town to life in the small town. They four boys embarked on adventures including trapping for crabs, dragging seine net, and joined in festival celebrations.

The story ends when Kwesi and Ato are picked up by their father and shepherded by him through a fort where slaves were exported to the Americas.

Songs of our Fathers, ever so gently gives a bird's eye view of transference of cultural heritage through storytelling. It informs us of some of the events that promulgated the slave trade and how the African Diaspora came to be. It reminds us of the unique rites and way of being that separate us as cultures and the common values of love, trust, care, compassion, acceptance that joins us as a people of world.

Songs of Our Fathers

Chapter 1

All days have the same appeal for children who believe in friendship, fun, and learning when the time is ripe. And so it was in the summer of the great corn harvest when Mr. Kofi Gyesi, my father's driver, drove Papa, my father, Kwesi Sakyi, my elder brother, and me in Papa's 1948 black-painted Ford touring car to Apam, a small coastal town in Ghana, West Africa. Mr. Gyesi and Papa were going to drop off my brother and me at Grandma Elizabeth Pratt's home to spend part of our holidays with her.

"Your Grandma Elizabeth was your Grandpa Sakyi's third and favorite wife," Papa said with a lilt that led one to infer that a man marrying for the third time had an epiphany into the secrets of matrimonial bliss when he chose her. But the lilt in Papa's voice lost its vivacity when I joyfully jumped up and down and piteously pleaded, "Please tell us more about the relationship between them."

"They were just ordinary," Papa replied in a voice of finality.

This led me to believe there were either some unpleasant truths about their relationship that he did not want to share, or a deep desire to preserve the pleasant memories he had of them. It also invoked the Akan tribal injunction against parental disavowal to mind. Either way, I believed he wanted to exercise prejudice in favor of the familiar while passing down cultural values and parts of our cultural heritage to us.

I was grateful for these exchanges because it helped me fill an essential part of who I was. For one thing, I did not meet Grandpa Sakyi because he died of a massive heart attack before I was born. Hence, the sparse recollection I have of him came from Papa's romanticized prism of the relationship he had with him. Indeed, I distantly recall Papa saying that Grandpa Sakyi was a successful cocoa merchant who was born in Tashie, a small coastal village situated on the southeastern part of Ghana, and settled in Apam. According to Papa, Grandpa Sakyi was a very shrewd and prudent businessman who invested his meager inheritance in cocoa farming and made an enormous fortune by trading with the British and Germans of his era. He used this fortune to educate his children and nephews in various British institutions of higher education. Papa studied law and was called to the bar in 1934. Grandpa Sakyi's nephew and Papa's cousin, Edmond Twit, studied medicine and graduated from medical school in 1929. "Your Uncle Edmond," Papa told us with an edge of bitterness, "did not return home to Ghana after his training. But Papa?....Here I am!" He said as he frisked our hair to denote affection.

As a Barrister at Law, Papa was an immensely gifted trial attorney with a keen mind and quick recall abilities of arcane legal points. His friends in the legal profession fondly called him "The Blade," in recognition of his legal prowess and courtroom antics. The number of clients and variety of cases he had to trial increased to a point where he was away from his family for several days at a time. So, whenever he was home, my brother and I clamored and vehemently competed for his attention like two emotionally deprived lap dogs in desperate need of petting.

We would stop playing outside before sunset, do our homework if we had any, have dinner without the customary whimper or groan, and go to bed with the chickens when Mama told us Papa was coming home. As was his usual practice, Papa gave us undivided attention after he was settled in and well-rested.

But this morning was different. It was the first day of summer vacation and we were especially eager to wake up and ready ourselves to ride with Papa to spend some of our vacation time with Grandmother Elizabeth, who lived in Apam.

Mama woke us up at exactly five o'clock in the morning when the alarm clock rang and advised us to hurry through our toiletries. "Wash your face and brush your teeth," she hallowed as we stumbled out of bed, counted to three, and made a mad dash to the bathroom to comply with her directives. "And use the sliced lemon halves to deodorize your armpits after you bathe," she added as if it were an afterthought. And as if that was not enough, she hollered, "Wear your Sunday best!" But then, Mama always talked like one who was going through a mental checklist.

"Once again the Sunday best," I snickered as I began to go through the routine of debating with myself about the virtues of dressing up for a public that is basically preoccupied with itself and the need to dress only to be cooped up in a car just to see our grandmother, or to attend church on Sundays when what God really needed from us is to "love our neighbors as ourselves," as I often heard preachers proclaim from pulpits. But, as always, I kept my thoughts to myself because I did not want to subject them to adult scrutiny or ridicule. I had learned this from observing some children my age withdraw from group interaction under intense and continual adult inquiry of the positions they held, and I was not about to become one of that statistic.

All in all, I was happy for the change in atmosphere but not overjoyed to leave Mama in order to visit Grandma. In fact, I wished Grandma lived in the same town as we did or close by so we could visit more frequently. But the hard reality is that she did not live close to us and we could not be in two places at the same time, nor could I choose the affection I had for one over the other. I loved them both but in different ways. For my sibling and me, Mama was simply that—our mother. We did not call her Auntie Effe or refer to her maiden name as some of our neighbors did, nor did we call her any of the endearing names we overheard Papa use in addressing her when he was in a good mood or feigning endearment. We always called her "Mama." We loved all five feet four inches of her. We loved her oval face, dark brown welcoming eyes, engaging smile, effusiveness, and affectionate embraces. She was the go-to person when we were hurt and needed comforting; the person we could count on to show up at school for parent-teacher conferences; the person we complained to when we had a bad day at school, did not like our food, wanted new clothes, or our clothes needed mending. We did not appraise her through the lenses of other people or judge her conduct against any social performance scale. Those external considerations were as irrelevant to our daily interactions with her as extemporaneous thoughts to a hungry baby. She was our mother—our Rock of Gibraltar—and that was all that mattered to us.

Therefore, to leave her, even for a short time, was like losing a part of me to a town and a place that did not fully embrace all she is, and that was not easy for me to do. But I was comforted by the fact that I was leaving her to live with someone who would be equally kind to me.

"Hurry up and get dressed, kids," Mama yelled as she saw Papa stroll out of his office to the verandah. "Your father has to return for a court hearing this afternoon, and doesn't want to be late," she tersely added.

"There she goes again," I remarked to Kwesi. "She's always yelling about one thing or another as if we are hard of hearing."

"Oh, yes," Kwesi agreed, "it is yell, yell, yell! I do not believe she knows the difference between yelling and normal talking."

I paused briefly from the discussions with Kwesi over Mama's mannerisms to listen for Papa's footsteps.

"Did you hear the crunching footsteps?" Kwesi whispered.

"Hush," I commanded. I listened attentively and heard Papa's leather-sole shoes crunching the sand on the asphalt verandah as he strolled.

"Let's hurry," I urged.

We hurriedly put on our Sunday best as instructed, punched one another as he tried to squeeze through the door to our bedroom at the same time as me, and broke into a trot once out of the doorway to see who would be first to catch up with Papa.

"Stop running around," Papa counseled as we rushed toward him. "Slow down, both of you!" he commanded. Kwesi Sakyi and I exchanged glances and slowed to a walk. I was tempted to run toward Papa but held down my impulse. Then, Kwesi Sakyi suddenly elbowed my right ribcage as we walked side by side toward the kitchen and close to Papa.

"Ouch!" I screamed and tried to retaliate by vehemently shoving him off, but Papa stopped me before I could deliver the push.

"Stop that!" he said, "I do not want to see the two of you fight this morning."

"Settle down," Mama said in support of Papa's edict.

Kwesi Sakyi defiantly shook his right fist at me when neither Papa nor Mama was watching.

"I will knock your head off," he murmured between his clenched teeth.

"You dare not," I challenged in full knowledge that neither of my parents would stand by while he pummeled me.

You see, like most boys our age, Kwesi Sakyi and I bickered and got into fistfights over one thing or the other. Our parents called us by our full names and with emphasis on every syllable when we were summoned to answer for our misdeeds. Otherwise, both of my parents affectionately called my elder brother Kwesi and called me Ato for short.

Papa did not like to witness our hostile and unfriendly exchanges. Above all, he did not like us to stamp our feet in the dust, spit and cover our sputum with dust, throw rocks, or call each other spiteful names before or after the fights. In fact, Papa did not want us to treat each other disrespectfully at any time. So, to ensure a peaceful ride, he directed Kwesi to sit with him on the back seat of the car and for me to sit on the passenger side of the front seat for the journey to Grandma's home. That was how we always traveled.

"You boys must behave during your visit," Mama began. "I do not want either of you to give your Grandma any trouble because, as both of you know, your Grandma is no spring chicken who can chase after you. She is frail and deserves better, especially from her grandchildren," Mama said, as we got ready to take our seats in the car. "I will call and check on you from time to time."

"But what about breakfast?" I asked.

"Indeed, where is breakfast? I am famished," Kwesi asked between a half smile.

"Your Grandmother will have breakfast ready for you when you arrive," Mama replied in a calm, reassuring voice, and topped it with goodbye hugs. "Don't forget to send my love to your Grandmother," she said in a tone that once again questioned our hearing abilities.

"We will," Kwesi and I replied in unison.

Papa's driver Kofi Gyesi was dressed in well-pressed light brown khaki shorts, a white, short–sleeved uniform shirt, and a polished pair of brown shoes when we arrived at the front of the house. He was wearing a white cap banded with yellow ribbon and a crest of crafted-bronze birds pinned to the front of the rim, ringing the cap. He removed his cap and placed it on the roof of the car, loaded our red and white striped aluminum suitcases into the trunk of the car, and closed the trunk. Then, he pressed down on the trunk until it clicked and pulled up with his fingers on the latch to verify it was securely locked.

After that he opened the right rear door of the car for Kwesi to sit down, shut the door after Kwesi was seated, and verified it was securely closed. He repeated the routine for me on the passenger side of the car, and then on the back seat behind me for Papa. The driver gingerly closed the door after Papa was seated. Then he picked up his cap from the roof, put it on, took his seat behind the steering wheel, and adjusted his hat. He closed his door, started the engine, honked the car's horn to denote departure, and pulled away from the house. We were whisking past rows of mud homes and open space dotted with tufts of bush at about thirty miles per hour through the town as we made our way to Grandma Elizabeth's home.

We had hardly traveled ten miles out of town when the rhythmic roll of the car tires on the granite and tar road coaxed me to sleep. I grudgingly woke up from sleep when I heard voices of roadside vendors hawking yams, cocoyams, cassava, pineapples, oranges, tangerines, and vegetables, trying to attract the attention of the driver, who had stopped the car on the shoulder of the road and was at the point of getting out of the car.

Papa leaned forward from the back of the car and gave him money to buy some fruits and vegetables.

"The usual assortment of fruits and vegetables," Papa said. "A bunch of bananas, a load of cassava, some plantains, and so on. Just use your discretion," Papa concluded offhandedly as he handed him the money and reclined in his seat.

The fact of the matter is driver Kofi Gyesi and Papa have made this journey several times. They have been travelling together for more than five years, know each other's tendencies quite well, and had settled issues of preferences in vegetable and fruit selection long ago before we joined the ride. Above all, I was convinced that Grandma would gladly accept the gifts and desist from looking at them with scrutiny.

The driver accepted the money from Papa, stepped out of the car when he was sure there was no coming traffic, and walked to the rear of the car with the vegetable vendors swarming around him to haggle over prices. A disheveled man, who looked liked a trapper, held high a pair of giant dead ground pangolins for the driver to examine and buy. But the driver ignored the disheveled hawker and his pangolins carcasses and proceeded to select the fruits and vegetables he wanted to buy. He paid for them and opened the trunk of the car for the vendors to empty the fruits and vegetables he had purchased. He rearranged the vegetables and fruits that had been poured into the trunk, walked briskly to assume his seat behind the steering wheel, and resumed driving.

As we drove on, I began to wonder whether Grandmother Elizabeth was poor and if Papa needed to buy the foodstuff to assure we would have enough to eat during our stay, so I asked him, "Papa, why did we have to stop and buy that foodstuff for Grandma?"

"Your Grandmother is not poor," Papa responded as if he knew my mind, and continued, "I buy the foodstuff for her on my visits as a token of my deep appreciation for all the days she fed and clothed me when I was a youngster like you. Indeed, your grandmother has grown used to this and will be miffed if I don't bring anything to her. And while we are on this subject, I would like both of you to note that bringing token presents to people you visit is part of our cultural heritage. It denotes to your host that you were thinking about them and don't take their kindness for granted."

After a few tidbits about tradition and lessons in cultural values from Papa, I fell asleep for the second time only to wake when we arrived at our destination and saw the driver ready to help me out of the car. He then opened the car's rear door for Papa and repeated the exercise for Kwesi. We got out of the car, stretched our legs and arms, and began to walk toward Grandma.

In the meantime, the driver offloaded the fruits and vegetables we bought for her, as well as our steel travelling suit cases from the trunk of the car. He carried the fruits and vegetables to the kitchen, and our travel suitcases upstairs. Then, he returned to the car to wait for Papa.

Kwesi took Papa's right hand and walked in lock step with him. I hurried to join them and held Papa's left hand when I did. As we walked on, I began to wonder if Grandma would receive us as kindly as she usually did and took refuge behind Papa's back to ward off any unpleasant surprises.

Grandma Elizabeth promptly got up from her soft wood-carved stool and started walking towards us. She was in her mid-fifties, and not as frail as Mama had led me to believe. She looked about five feet and a few inches tall, weighed about one hundred and twenty pounds, and had a quiet presence. The tropical heat had creased her forehead and dimmed her vision. Her hair was covered with a tie-dyed kerchief with visible speckles of gray on her sideburns. She squinted when she looked at close objects or examined people's features. Otherwise, she looked average in her black wrap-around cloth with a matching blouse and shoulder-cover.

She hugged Papa and kissed him on both cheeks and let him go. Then, she leaned forward and tried to pluck Kwesi from Papa's hand, but Kwesi wiggled away with eel-like swiftness into the open, dusty compound and looked askance at her. Grandma took a few nervous steps toward him and abandoned the chase. She reached out and grabbed me from the refuge I had taken, wrapped both of her arms around me, and hilariously declared, "I have got you." Then with cheerfulness in her face, she lifted all sixty pounds of me, and instantaneously set me down like a slice of hot yam and momentarily caressed my belly. She took a half step backward, looked at me from head to toe, and exclaimed between shallow heavy breaths, "Boy, you are heavy!" She paused to catch her breath and with her eyes still set on me, continued, "look how you have grown. It was only yesterday, I recall, when I saw you crawling in your diaper and eating anything you could lay your hands on. And now here you are, quite a handsome little boy." She reached out and cradled my face in her palms, kissed me on the forehead, and gently let go of me with a gentle pat on the head.

I enjoyed the praise and the sweet embrace. I felt special!

Grandma Elizabeth turned to look for Papa, but he had already made his way to the corrugated covered kitchen and was talking with the maid. He stopped talking and embraced Grandma Elizabeth when she reached him. He let go of her and stepped to her right and clasped her left fingers into his as they walked the compound and up the staircase onto the second floor of the two-story family home where Papa was born. Kwesi and I brought up the rear.

We snickered and whispered our observations of Papa and Grandmother Elizabeth's show of affection. I wondered why I did not see such demonstration of affection around town if that was normal. Notwithstanding my apprehension, I made a mental note to replicate the example with my own children.

While engaged in these thoughts, Kwesi gently poked me in my ribcage with the first finger of his right hand to attract my attention and inquired,

"Why did the Old Lady," referring to Grandmother Elizabeth, "want to hug and kiss me? She is too old. Her hands are withered and her palms appeared hard and rubbery," Kwesi said in a tone that was mixed with inquiry and uncertainty. He paused and disdainfully added, "She is not my type."

The kind of woman Kwesi had in mind was beyond me. For all I cared, I could not imagine her being the baby-snatching type. Indeed, Grandma was much older than either of us and grew up in an era of small townships, intimate friendships, and closer family ties where trust was paramount and rife. She had a maternal responsibility with a tint of tolerant freedom towards us. Hence, I thought it was crassly absurd of Kwesi, who was fourteen, and two years my senior, to expect the same budding friendship he had with two girls in his middle school class who lived in our neighborhood, visited frequently, and stayed for hours when Papa was out of town on a case. It was not unusual for Mama to send me after him at sunset when dusk turned into darkness and the night blanketed our neighborhood. I often wondered what amorous chitchats held him in their company for such long periods and asked him that much one day, to which he simply replied, "You do not understand," as if there were some mystery to it.

But Papa understood the hold enough to be concerned about the impact the time away from his books had on his grades. So, early one morning, Papa called him on the carpet and lowered the boom on him. "Kwesi Sakyi," He began in elevated tones, "I do not like you to spend so much more time with the 'chicks,'" as he called the young girls, "than you do with your studies and homework assignments. You cannot realize your full potential if you do not spend the required time with your studies. You must apply yourself and use your given talents to obtain an education that leads to a portable profession that guarantees self-employment and positions you to open your own office wherever you go. It is absolutely naïve and very shortsighted to expect the young girls you see to grow up and take care of you. You have to put yourself in a position to take care of yourself and the children you may bring into the world. The best these young girls can do, financially speaking, is to possibly help you take care of the children both of you bring into the world, if you are lucky enough to have one who has a job and is not caught in the traditional trap of looking up to her male partner to meet all her needs.

"My life experience has taught me that romance and love do not feed families. They do not bring up children, buy diapers, or clothe them. Sometimes young girls, and for that matter some boys too, lust after the opposite sex who have money in their pockets and can entertain. They like to be pampered and spoiled with gifts and remain in puppy love as long as the spending and adoration continue and abandon the 'love object' like bees do to a flower when the nectar is completely sapped and has lost its savor. Their friendship, if you could call it that, breaks down like friable rock for the wind to carry away at the end of financial support. Occasionally, you may find one who will genuinely love you and go through life's labyrinth with you. But such pure and committed love is few and far between. Young man," Papa continued, "your way out of the fog of lustful love and unreliable friendships they ferment is through your books. Sow your seed in knowledge, set your foot on the rock of wisdom, invest in yourself through education, and the rewards will follow you throughout your life." With that, Papa gave Kwesi a list of books to read and told him to submit a written report for discussion at their next meeting.

I listened to Kwesi as he narrated the lecturing he received from Papa and chuckled in disbelief when he got to the part about the chicks. Thereupon, he nodded and invited me to concur with his account of events, but I declined his invitation. He was my brother and must be told the truth. Falsehood, I told myself, is abhorrent, particularly when it comes from family members that share in our daily living and love you.

The conversation palled and fell silent until Kwesi remarked, "You must admit Grandma Elizabeth's fingers look terrible," he insisted when grandmother was preoccupied. "They look as shriveled as an orange peel."

I continued listening without falling victim to his veiled invitation to join with him in condemning Grandma, who was not present to speak for herself. Besides, I didn't want to reinforce his tendency to stretch the truth ever so slightly to fit his reality or rendition of events. I clearly remember an incident where he passed the buck to me when Papa caught him eating a big, sun-yellowed, but unripe mango.

"What are you eating?" Papa asked in an elevated, angry tone.

"A mango," he replied listlessly.

"How could you be eating mangoes when they are not in season?" Papa asked skeptically.

"Ato Kwamena gave it to me. I am only taking a bite to validate its ripeness."

"So you are not sure whether it is ripe or not?"

"No, I am not."

"And you are only trying to find out."

"Yes, I am," he tersely replied.

For a moment, I thought Kwesi was in a witness box being cross-examined to uncover latent truth. But then, that was how Papa often asked us about things, because for some unknown reason, he could not put his training aside when it came to discovering truth among family members. So, I felt gangs of fright when Papa turned to me and asked, "How did he come by the mango."

"It was Kwesi who knocked it down from the mango tree standing across the street of our home with a catapult," I replied in a calm and controlled voice.

Without saying a word, Papa snatched the half-eaten mango from

Kwesi, examined the indentation of teeth, and sighed, "It is definitely big, but unripe. You could have left it to ripen into a juicy, tasteful fruit. You did not. Instead, you chose to catapult it down, eat it while it is still unripe, and lied to me when asked. Your behavior is dishonorable and deplorable. You remind me of the poor, emaciated hungry people I see around town who beg you for money to buy food to feed their children and feign anger when you do not buy into their story of misery. Nobody, absolutely nobody, asked them to have children they could not support. They could have left those children where they were instead of bringing them into the world and begging for help and support from the public. We are not poor in that way and do not want to see either of you going about town and getting involved in any low down shenanigans of the kind we just talked about. Let this be your last warning. I do not want to see either of you do this again. Is that clear?" Papa chided.

I kept mum and walked away solemn and crestfallen because time and observation had taught me to stay out of Papa's line of fire when he was hot under the collar. Besides, I could not see the advantage to be gained from further discussion. So I stealthily stepped out of the house to perch in the branch of a tree that hung over a stream flowing at the back of our house to sit and aimlessly throw pebbles into the stream that flowed below to soothe my dejected senses.

When I returned home at dusk, Kwesi was still pouting from his scolding and declined to talk to me. This went on for days, so I kept my distance from fear of saying something that might set him off and thereby lose his friendship for a longer period. I surmised that with time his emotional wounds would heal; he would appreciate the good intentions behind Papa's retributions; things would return to normal between the two of us; and we would become closer at a more mature level. We did as the days wore on, and remained so up to the time we left home to visit Grandmother.

"What are you two talking about?" inquired Papa as he turned around away from conversing with Grandma and looked at us.

"Nothing," Kwesi replied.

Then, after Papa turned his head, Kwesi looked at me and asked me to "hush" by putting his finger on his mouth.

I stopped jiggling and tiptoed up the wooden stairway. When we got to the top, Papa signaled us to follow him into the living room that was situated to the right of the stairway. Grandma Elizabeth invited us to sit in a soft, bird-feather stuffed cushion on her mahogany sofa. Papa and Grandmother Elizabeth sat on an upholstered sofa facing us. Papa waved us to keep quiet while he talked with Grandma, and we did as told for a moment. Then, our childhood instincts suddenly took over and we started whispering inquiringly to one another about the large, imposing photograph of a black man in a suit and tie hanging from the wall of the living room.

"What are you two talking about? Can't you keep quiet for just one moment?" asked Papa.

"Just leave them alone," interceded Grandma Elizabeth, who added, "they are just doing what kids do. Kids are entitled to the privacy of their reflections and expressions in much the same way as we adults are, so long as these reflections and expressions do not harm either themselves or society. Children develop better decision-making and coping abilities when they observe parents practice decision-making and are allowed to do the same in the safety of their homes. We, as parents and loved ones, must create that crucible, that safety cradle, which allows them to develop confidence and the sensitively structured restraints, the need for risk taking, growth, and adult to adult interactions."

Papa waited until Grandma was through and then insisted Kwesi should explain our behavior, but Kwesi Sakyi stood defiantly silent. He knew that Papa would not be harsh with him in the presence of Grandma. Indeed, he had watched Grandma intervene with Papa over some discipline issues with us. So, after a short silence, which seemed like an age, Papa turned to me for explanation. "Ato Kwamena," he cajoled, "tell me what all the whispering was about."

I told Papa what we were discussing.

"You kids could have asked instead of giggling and carrying on like a pair of cackling cocks."

"Sorry," I replied weakly.

Papa took in a deep breath and unbuttoned the stiff collar of his white shirt to loosen the bow tie clipped to its lapel. He looked at the hanging picture and proudly announced, "That is the picture of Papa Sakyi, my father and your Grandpa, whom you are named after." Then he paused, took in a deep breath, breathed out slowly, and said, "Let me see. Let me see," he continued with a scratch of his forehead, "this is nineteen fifty.... that makes it twelve years ago when he died?"

"What did he die of?" inquired Kwesi in a demurred tone.

"He died of a stroke. You see, in those days, not that it would have mattered, we did not have enough doctors to go around. We did not have a single doctor in this town. Most of the doctors in the country were stationed in the capital cities like Accra, Cape Coast, Takoradi, and Kumasi, but not in Apam because it did not have adequate political influence or resources to attract large commercial enterprises or government investment. So, Grandpa Sakyi passed away a few days after the stroke. All in all, I believe he took a quick way out. Indeed, your Grandma would have found it difficult to care for him day after day, week after week in a semi-vegetable state, taking labored breaths with the same inescapable result—his death."

Just as Papa got to the end of the story about Grandpapa Sakyi's death, the maid came to tell us breakfast was ready. Papa and Grandma got up to go to the dining room. Grandma led the way with Papa at her side. Kwesi and I dutifully brought up the rear.

Papa sat at the head of the table and asked Kwesi and me to sit in the two middle seats of the six-seat, oval-shaped dining table. Kwesi wanted to sit in the chair facing me from the opposite side of the table, but Papa stopped him in his tracks and reiterated that Kwesi should sit next to me, and advised us not to change seats once it was assigned by a host or hostess.

After we were seated, Kwesi tried to reach across the table to grab the orange marmalade, only to be reprimanded by Papa for the nth time about spreading across a table to reach condiments or other things.

"Don't let me see you spread yourself across the table to reach any food or condiment again. Always ask the person who is closest to the item you want to pass it over to you. Is that clear?" Papa sternly concluded as he passed on another lesson in table manners and social conduct to us.

"Yes, Papa," Kwesi replied.

In the meantime, Grandma Elizabeth scooped up two big wooden spoonfuls of toasted corn porridge into a deep porcelain soup bowl and handed it to Papa. Papa got up from his seat, reached for the bowl, and set it down on the dinner plate in front of him. He thanked Grandma and sat down in his seat. Then, Grandma Elizabeth used the same wooden spoon to scoop two spoonfuls of porridge into two separate earthenware bowls and handed one to Kwesi and the other to me. We thanked her. Then, she passed a plate filled with slices of toasted white flour bread around for us to help ourselves and followed it with a plate full of scrambled eggs. Papa picked out two slices of the toasted white bread, put them on his side plate, and passed it to Kwesi, instructing us to take two slices of toasted bread apiece. Kwesi took two slices as instructed and passed the plate to me. Papa was not watching so I helped myself to three slices, ate one slice before he could turn his eyes, and put the remaining two slices on the plate in front of me.

Next, Grandmother Elizabeth passed around a bowl containing bananas, huckleberries, yellow berries, avocado, grapefruits, lemon, and lime. Papa picked a medley of fruits from the bowl and passed the rest around for us to help ourselves. Papa asked Grandma if he could have a slice of the pineapple in a bowl on top of the glass door cupboard.

"Of course," Grandmother Elizabeth replied, getting up from her chair. She took a few nimble steps, picked up the pineapple, and called for the maid.

The maid came and stood quietly at the doorway.

"Skin and slice this pineapple," grandma said, handling it to her.

"Yes, Madam," the maid responded. She entered the dining room and took the pineapple from Grandma Elizabeth and vanished down the stairway.

Papa took the opportunity to tell us a short story about his childhood. He narrated one of his exploits when he visited Grandpa Sakyi's cocoa plantation while he was on summer holiday from his secondary school at Mfantsipim. He told us how he snuck out to harvest coco-yam tubers that grew under the cocoa plants and roasted them in a pit fire made of dried twigs and dead branches. He had hardly started narrating a second incident about trapping deer in mangroves when the maid brought in a plate of peeled and sliced pineapple. Papa thanked her for her efforts, took two huge slices from the plate, and again passed the remainder to us to help ourselves. We took a slice each and bit it. Juice from the slices oozed down our arms towards the floor. I watched Kwesi stick out his tongue and partially succeed in licking the dripping juice at his elbow before it reached the floor. Once again, Papa admonished him for his rascally conduct and thus soured the end to an otherwise pleasant breakfast.

Papa rushed out after breakfast to fulfill his left docket hearing, which was scheduled that afternoon at the Region's High Court. We accompanied him to his car to wave our sad goodbyes. Papa hugged Grandma Elizabeth and returned to the rear seat he occupied during the inbound journey and warned Kwesi as follows, "I do not want to hear that you dragged your younger brother all over the place and coaxed him into mischief. Do you hear me?" he inquired haughtily.

"Yes Papa," Kwesi flatly replied.

The driver saluted after Papa was seated, shut the rear car door, and shook it to verify it was securely closed. He took his seat behind the steering wheel, started the car's engine, went through his usual checking routine, and eased the car to the gate of the house. Then, he turned the retractable car signal to indicate he was turning left and eased out of the compound. Kwesi and I ran out of the compound to catch a glimpse of Papa, but only saw rust-colored dust rise from the unpaved road to mask the car as it sped away. The maid closed and bolted the gate to the compound after the car had left.

We returned into the arms of Grandma Elizabeth, who was waiting to soothe our sadness at Papa's departure. She escorted us up the stairs into her bedroom where the maid had earlier stuck our suitcases. We undressed and hung our traveling suits to air out. We opened our suitcases and changed into our red shorts and white short-sleeved shirts with green stripes and walked downstairs barefoot. We were eager to see the world outside the confines of the compound and rushed towards the gate.

"Not so fast!" Grandma Elizabeth said as she took measured steps down the stairways to the ground.

She assumed her seat under the shade of the big neem tree that stood close to the kitchen and asked us to tell her about school. We sat in seats located under the tree to narrate stories about what went on at school during the last term. Kwesi took the lead and told her about the friends he made in his new school and the many different things he did during the school year. I told her about Ms. Brown, my class instructor, who was a fat, strict teacher from hell. You see, Ms. Brown was a no-nonsense teacher who did not like adults to contradict her about homework or children to ignore her pleas for self-restraint.

One day during the school year, she gave six lashes to one of the most popular boys in the class for spitting on the grass. She explained she did so to deter the boy from spitting on public thoroughfares. My personal feeling was that Ms. Brown was simply a fat and unhappy spinster who took out her unhappiness on children for being who they were. But then, my views did not count in a school system where teachers rule over the children like masters and mistresses over a serfdom of evil, conniving children that are steeped in mischief and up to no good.

But before we could get out of the house, Grandmother stood in the middle of the compound and looked at the length of her shadow on the on red-dust soil to measure time and declared, '"It will soon be time for lunch."

"That is good news," I said to myself as I heard rumblings in my stomach.

I got off my stool and went to the kitchen to check out what the maid was already cooking over the open-pit fire and discovered she was making palm nut soup with assorted dried fish and other meats. I stood and watched the fish and assorted meat somersault in the boiling soup. Kwesi left to wait for lunch at a small wooden table and spied as the maid picked up a wooden spoon to stir the soup and occasionally tasted it. He tapped the table a few times and pounded it when the pangs of hunger got severe.

The maid, a rather small-framed girl in her early teens, turned her head in response to the pounding and looked askance at him. She picked up the pot containing the soup from the open pit-fire and put it on a charcoal fire, which was next to the open-pit fire, to simmer.

Then, she set an earthenware pot, which was filled with cassava, plantains, and water, to cook over the open-pit fire. She stoked the fire to increase its intensity and sat down in a seat close to the fire to watch it cook. From time to time, she looked at Kwesi and me and asked if we were hungry.

"Yes, of course," Kwesi replied.

"And how about you?" she inquired.

"Not really," I answered, more to be kind than truthful.

"Food will be ready soon enough," she said assuredly.

Grandma Elizabeth remained seated in the shade of the neem tree and called on Kwesi and me to rejoin her. Occasionally, both Kwesi and I looked in the direction of the open kitchen for clues of the food's progress, but there were none, so we waited some more with continual glances at the kitchen. I spied the maid as she opened the cooking cassava and plantains, poked one of the boiling vegetables with her first finger of her right hand, and put the finger into her mouth and licked it to cool. She repeated her effort, re-stoked the fire, and cheerfully said, "The vegetables will soon be ready."

Kwesi looked at me and nodded. I responded in kind.

In the meantime, the maid took the lid off the cooking vegetables and set it on a small wooden table. She picked up the hot earthenware pot from the open-pit fire and poured the steaming medley of vegetables into an earthenware credenza to drain and cool.

After the vegetables had cooled, the maid grouped them into cassavas, plantains, and cocoyams. She picked up a six-foot tall, two-inch diameter wooden stick for pounding fufu and poured the cassavas into a four-inch deep and twelve-inch diameter wooden receptacle to pound. She fetched tap water from a faucet, which was adjacent to the kitchen, and set it by the wooden receptacle. She sat in a stool behind the wooden receptacle and recruited Kwesi to help pound the cooked cassava into fufu. She turned the cassava in the wooden receptacle up and down and from side to side, and intermittently sprinkled it with water as Kwesi pounded away. Kwesi broke a sweat and panted from exhaustion with the passing moments. I was excused from the chore because of my age and, for the first time, I counted one in the air with my first finger to mark the advantages brats like me had over mischievous teenage tyrants like my elder brother.

Lunch was ready about an hour after draining and pounding the vegetables. Grandma Elizabeth dipped her fingers into standing fresh tap water and used them to slice some of the fufu into an earthenware bowl. She repeated the process for herself, Kwesi, and the maid. Grandma ate at the table with us while the maid sat on a short stool and ate alone in a dark corner of the kitchen.

As I looked at the maid eating alone, I thought about her youth and hard work. I imagined how forlorn, drab, and walled in she felt at a place where she had no toys for play or playmates to have fun with. I imagined how she felt about her social position in a home where she was a mere footnote—an appendage—and given the remnants of all that she either cooked alone or helped to cook. I imagined several skills she was missing from not attending school and associations she could not build with children of her age group and was sad.

I thought about how funny it would be to have her as a playmate and attempted to include her in our activities, but each time I tried, Grandma Elizabeth either surreptitiously or directly undermined these efforts. She either increased the maid's workload or beckoned me to come on for a lame reason. I soon inferred that Grandma Elizabeth did not want my brother and me to associate with the maid, and was afraid to say so directly to us. She successfully used a careful mixture of manipulation and planned interventions to enforce the inviolable rule that sets the pecking order by steering me to accept the lower social status she had assigned to the maid.

I felt pitted against towing Grandma's discriminatory line against the maid as a matter of family solidarity and objecting to her unspoken edict as a matter of principle. Sadly, I chose the former. I was a child and did not know how to intervene effectively to change the maid's circumstance.

The end of lunch coincided with dusk and sunset, so we did not have dinner. Instead, we helped the maid wash, dry, and put up the earthenware pots, porcelain cups, saucers, and dishes we had used. Grandma Elizabeth asked the maid to fetch the kerosene lantern from its peg on the kitchen wall and ready it for the night. The maid fetched the lantern and popped out of its soot-covered oval bulb to clean it. She sprinkled the inner portion of the bulb with ash from the day's burnt firewood, and used a tattered cloth to rub off the soot inside the bulb. She reset the bulb in its holder and filled the lantern's tank with kerosene. She trimmed the lamp's wick with a pair of scissors and then opened a small matchbox, picked out one of the matchsticks, and scratched it against the rough surfaced of a nearby stone to light it. She lit the lantern's wick with the burning matchstick, set the bulb into its holder, and used the lever to lower the bulb into its mount. Then she shook the holder to verify if the bulb was securely set and brought the lit kerosene lantern to Grandma's room and left the bedroom we were sharing. As she left, I began to wonder where she was going and how she would spend the night. I wanted to ask Grandmother to help me understand the maid's status with the family, but I was afraid, so I decided to sleep on my concerns and air them at a better time.

Kwesi and I undressed, spread our thin reed mats on the hard wooden floor, and lay down to sleep. We covered ourselves with our wrap-around cloths and slept after exchanging a few thoughts about the journey and our day's experiences with our Grandmother. Fatigue clouded my mind. The food I had eaten put the *coup de grace* on my tired body and induced it into a dreamless sleep. I woke up the next morning to the twitting and shifting jubilee of assorted tropical sparrows in the trees behind the window of our shared room.

I was ready for the summer holidays to begin. I went out of the room to survey the compound with help of the beaming sun and noted that the compound was quiet except for a lonely black cat that casually strutted on its way. I returned to the room and lay down to wait for the rest of the household to wake up.

Kwesi woke up much later, when the morning was about spent. He stretched out his body, rubbed his eyes with the back of one of his fingers, and mumbled a few incoherent words. I asked him to repeat what he had said, but he did not. I lay down quietly and watched him rub his eyes again, contort and stretch his body with the ritual resemblance of a worm, and spring to life.

"What do you want to do today?" he asked when he was fully awake.

"I have no idea," I replied.

He asked me to get ready for us to go downstairs. We folded our flimsy reed mats and placed them in one corner of the room facing the door and took cautious steps down the stairs. When we arrived downstairs, I noted that the maid was already awake. She had just finished making the charcoal fire and was waiting on breakfast instructions from Grandma. Grandmother was already seated on her large ashy stool. She enjoined us to do our toiletries and get ready for breakfast.

"What are we having?" I inquired.

"You just get ready and you will find out," she responded with a beckon for us to proceed.

We returned promptly to the kitchen. When we arrived, we noted that the maid had laid the table, and readied water for us to wash our hands. Kwesi and I washed our hands with a bar of soap in a large bowl of water and dried them on a hand towel. We sat down at a small soft wood table facing each other and waited on Grandma to invite us to breakfast which he did in a very short order by serving us the prepared cooked oats in flower decorated porcelain bowls. We made sandwiches of fried tomatoes and onions and scrambled eggs on toasted bread and ate it with the oats the maid had cooked. Then we complemented the entrée with assorted tropical fruits. Kwesi and I made short work of the food, got up from the table, and washed our hands in a fresh supply of water. We dried them with our table napkins folded the wet napkins, and casually tossed them onto the table. Then we looked at each other for want of something constructive to do or say.

"What next?" Kwesi asked me while I was looking at Grandma.

Grandma took the cue and responded, "You kids can go out and play. Be careful not to hurt other children or yourselves."

With that mixture of encouragement and admonition, Kwesi unbolted the compound gate. We stepped out of the compound into the world outside and looked at the large expanse of sky and the opportunities for both good and mischief that faced us. We looked at each other again, smiled, and started walking away without knowing where the road would lead us, as the maid bolted the door behind us.

Footnote: Akan is the largest tribal group in Ghana.

Chapter 2

The will to live and the will to thrive are sometimes as inseparable as thought is from expression, and for bendable minds these notions often appear to be the same. And so it was for us when we stepped on the unpaved street in front of Grandma Elizabeth's home and saw the sun a quarter of its daily travel across the azure tropical sky. I made a mental note of landmarks to use as reference points on our way back as I trudged behind Kwesi from Grandma Elizabeth's home and joined the people from all walks of life going about their daily affairs. I was intrigued to see young girls about my age and, possibly older, carrying babies on their backs and walking with intermittent breaks for play. From time to time, the young girls adjusted the babies on their backs into a different position with the lengthy side of a wrap-around cloth or towel tucked just below the neck, and the bottom part just under their buttocks. The young girls tied two bows with the remaining cloth or towel: one just above their breasts and the other close to their hips to tighten the hold and keep the babies from slipping. The heads of the babies were laid to one side or the other on the backs of the young girls to keep them comfortable. I was totally taken in when I observed a short young girl in a cream-colored chemise with a baby tied to her back balance a calabash of water on her head while stringing beads.

"Look at those boys over there!" said Kwesi with an exclamation that jolted my stupor.

I turned around but could not see what he was talking about.

"Look," he repeated with abated excitement while pointing his right hand in the direction of the boys. I followed the direction he was pointing to and sharply inquired, "What is the matter?"

"Do you see what they are doing?"

I still could not see what he was talking about, and said so.

"Look! Look at those two boys," he repeated in strident, emphatic tones while wagging his right forefinger, as was his habit. "Look at them. They are kicking around a rat."

He grabbed my left wrist and started trotting toward the boys before I could ask him to explain why that should matter to me. I reluctantly towed behind him and let go of me when he sensed my pull, broke into a run. "Come on," he yelled as he sped way toward the boys. I paused to catch my breath and celebrate my freedom from his forceful grip. I looked over my wrist to see if I was bruised from his grip but found none. I collected my composure and sprinted at full speed with the intent of outrunning him, but could not, as he was much faster than I was and caught up with the boys before I could.

He started tiptoeing behind the two boys when he got closer...like a wounded dog that had received a severe beating from its owner. I joined him in the pusillanimous approach. Then, he urged me to peek over the shoulder of the shorter boy and spy on what they were doing when I got closer. I peeked over the shorter boy's shoulder as he had suggested and whispered to him that the boys were kicking a tennis ball that had lost its fluffy-woolen coat from either abuse or overuse and not a rat, as he had thought. Upon hearing the news, he mustered courage and gently tapped the left shoulder of the taller boy, who appeared to be in his age group, and asked if we could join them at their play.

"Sure," the taller boy responded, and proceeded to introduce himself. "By the way, my name is Kobina Amuah, and this is my cousin, Kofi Mbrah, but is popularly known by his nickname, Danger." We shook hands with Kobina Amuah and Danger.

"Join us," Kobina Amuah invited.

Kwesi joined them without much ado. I paused, appraisingly looked at the two boys and my elder brother kicking the ball, and decided it would be all right to join the game. After awhile, Kobina Amuah held up his hand and asked us to stop kicking the ball. We stopped to listen to what he had to say:

"Danger and I are going to the market," he declared. "You may come with us if you like."

"Yes, we will," Kwesi replied, since we saw it as an opportunity to learn and make new friends.

I tagged along without knowing what to expect. We were the new boys in town who did not know the local customs nor had friends to instruct us in them. It was summer; the schools were closed for holiday and we had plenty of time on our hands to do what we pleased. Therefore, I did not see what harm my brother and I would cause by joining the two boys in the market. Besides, there was every possibility we would meet and make more friends.

Along the way, we chattered about a host of school activities that included lessons and classmates. Kwesi excitedly informed the boys that our father was a barrister. He shared his aspiration to be an accountant. Kobina Amuah shared information about his school with us and expressed his desire to be a renowned carpenter. "I want to be a carpenter because I want to make beautiful furniture for people," he said.

As I listened to the older boys talk of their dreams, and concluded that they were not extraordinarily talented but just middle-of-the-road, average students. I pondered what those professions meant, and how much schooling was required to achieve the goals they had set. I wondered whether my brother would look the same as an accountant or wear a white wig and black robe like Papa did for his court appearances. I had a vague idea what carpenters did from the stories Papa told about Jesus' father and from observing the carpenter two houses away measure and shave off cuts of boards to roof houses and build chairs, boxes, and cabinets. I could not wrap my head around the idea of a black Joseph in the role of Jesus' father or the second coming of Jesus in my part of the world, where paganism was rife and belief in a spiritual being was not an article of faith. I did not believe the people of the town were spiritual enough for the second coming of Jesus—a Semite of Palestinian and Jewish descent who was not accepted by either group—to emerge in their midst. I also did not know enough about the politics of Jesus' era to appreciate the legal authority of Pontius Pilate, the rationale for his decision, and its unintended results for that society or posterity. Equally, I did not care for my elder brother and Kobina Amuah's impressive sounding sentences about careers and professions. What mattered was for me to have an exciting, unencumbered summer vacation devoid of homework, report cards, grades, lessons, assignments, quick breakfasts, and hot dusty trots to school. Careers, or lack thereof, lay in a foggy future. My desire was to have joyful frolics—my reality was living in the moment, and so was Danger's. Dreams and future aspirations were simply too far-fetched and unreal for me to either contemplate or discuss.

All of a sudden, Danger unceremoniously announced, "Here we are!" when we arrived at a relatively small market stall measuring about four-foot walls on three sides that served as an eatery for customers. The stall contained two small tables with four chairs each. There was a slightly taller table in front of the stall that was long, and big enough to hold a large aluminum tray containing the wrapped balls of ken-key that was covered with a heavy calico cloth and a small wood box with clear glass displaying assorted fried fish.

Danger's mother, a plump lady and appeared to be in her early forties with an engaging smile, was engaged in a conversation with a lady in the next stall. She stopped talking as we entered her stall and asked Danger, "Who are these kids?"

"They are two new friends we made on our way here."

"What did you say?" inquired Danger's mom.

"I said these are two friends we made on our way here," Danger repeated with a tinge of frustration in his voice.

"Hi, boys, what are your names?"

"Ato Kwamena" I replied amiably.

"And yours?" she asked, looking at my elder brother.

"Kwesi Sakyi," my brother replied tersely.

"My name is Ayah," said Danger's mother.

"Thanks," I responded, and started to tell her about our journey to Apam, but Kobina Amuah took over my narration. He told Ayah that we had come from the Cape Coast and had arrived in town only yesterday and did not know any children in town. He told Ayah about our father being a big-time lawyer and all that jazz that did not have anything to do with who we really were. He also told Ayah that we were living with my Grandmother.

"Are you Madam Elizabeth's grandchildren?" Ayah inquired in a surprised voice.

"Yes," Kwesi enthusiastically replied in a tone that indicated he was associating with children from a respectable home.

"Oh, I know your Grandmother. In fact, I have known her since my childhood. My mother and she are friends. We all belong to the same church's female singing group."

Ayah's acquaintance with our grandmother encouraged Kwesi to give a synoptic rendition of what we did at Cape Coast during holidays and how much we looked forward to spending our holidays with Grandmother. A petite lady customer in her early twenties stopped at Ayah's stall to buy ken-key and fried anchovies and shrimp.

Ayah stopped listening to Kwesi momentarily to sell the young lady what she wanted, and turned her attention to us after the lady left her stall. She served a medium-sized ball of ken-key wrapped in a boiled dried banana leaf that had been cooked over an open cauldron to Kobina Amuah and Danger. She gave them generous servings of fried herrings and fried shrimp, and dabbed the serving fish with a stew of coarsely ground cayenne pepper, ginger, dehydrated ground shrimp, and other spices.

"Are you kids hungry?" she asked after Danger and Kobina were served and encouraged us to breakfast as well. "Don't be bashful. There is plenty to share," she urged.

"No." Kwesi affirmatively declined her offer for both of us because we had just breakfasted. And, even if we were hungry, we still would have turned down her offer because prior to leaving home for vacation, Mama impressed upon us to decline food offered from people we did not know.

"It may be cooked under unhygienic conditions," she said. So we looked on while Kobina Amuah and Danger made themselves comfortable in one corner of Ayah's eatery and breakfasted, methodically unwrapped the ken-key and used the wet banana leaf, which was wrapped around it to cook it, as a plate, and ate with relish.

Danger grunted loudly after the meal and clicked his tongue a few times to underscore his satisfaction. Then, both Danger and Kobina washed their hands with bar Lifebuoy soap and a bowl of water Ayah had readied for them and dried their hands by whisking them in the air. They washed down the meal with water they poured from an earthenware cistern standing in the opposite corner of Ayah's stall after rinsing their mouths. And wrapped the uneaten shrimp heads and skeletal remains of the fish they had scrapped on one of the cooked banana plates to pitch in a heap of garbage that was secluded at the back of the market.

"Are you boys full?" Ayah asked after they had finished their meal and Danger had burped and slapped his stomach with both hands.

"Yes," they responded in unison.

Ayah patted Kwesi and me on our heads and told all of us to be careful out there.

We left Ayah's stall feeling elated and ready to have fun with the world.

Chapter 3

We had hardly left the market when Danger signaled us to come along. "Come on," he screamed as he jubilantly jumped, bounced, half-skipped, and snaked his way through the clutter of houses that surrounded the market to an open prairie dotted with tufts of bush and secluded bungalows.

Once in the open prairie Danger pivoted his arms on the grass and gleefully somersaulted. The two edges of cloth that were tied together to drape him inverted to reveal his private anatomical parts with each somersault and blissful scream. Kobina Amuah joined Danger and so did my elder brother, but I did not. Instead, I looked for crawling insects on the ground and found a small anthill with ants trouping in and out of a hole in the ground with whatever they carried. I observed some of the ants trouping alone with their loads while others carried their loads in groups. I picked up a twig close by and poked the hill. The ants started to come out of their underground chambers and began to scamper for cover. More came out with each successive poke until they began to crawl over my hand holding the twig and my feet. One or two of them stung me. I instinctively threw away the twig and tried to shake off the ants from my feet by repeatedly stamping my feet to the ground and simultaneously using my free arm to brush the ants off the other arm. I took to my heels and slowed down into an uneasy walk when I felt a bite on my right cheek. I brushed off the vicious ant with my palm into the surrounding grass and took short leisurely steps to recover from the ant molestation episode. Then I gradually steadied my walk to a regular pace toward my brother and newfound friends.

I stooped, uprooted one of the common wide plants growing on the prairie, and began to methodically and deliberately break off its prickly leaves limb by limb. I chewed the stem and threw away the remaining roots when I was done with it. I soon realized that my preoccupation with the plant was keeping me further behind the gang, so I spat out the partly chewed stem and hopped and jogged to join the three, who were screaming like wild hogs that had just escaped the butcher's knife.

"Stop! Stop, you guys," Danger demanded in an urgent tone.

Kobina Amuah stopped instantly. But, neither my elder brother nor I followed suit as were in caught up felling the freedom of the blowing wind and unaware of the request to stop.

Kobina Amuah took a few deliberate steps closer to where my brother and I were standing and echoed Danger's call. We heard his call and stopped.

"Look!" Danger urged.

"Look down the ridge," Danger enthusiastically pointed. "Can you see the sea?" he said, pointing to the Atlantic Ocean. "Can you hear its roar?" he inquired.

Kwesi and I were too wrapped up in inhaling the cool, fresh-scented air of the sea to hear the roar of the ocean and realize how close we were to it.

Suddenly a cattle egret flew across the sky and cried plaintively to jolt the tranquil air. We looked at the sky for the source of the noise and observed the bird gracefully flap its white-feathered wings as it gradually flew away toward its destination. We walked in the direction of Danger's pointed finger and played a game of wit and raillery as we walked on.

"What is the difference between a dog and a bog?" Danger started.

"One is a four-legged animal and the other is a marshland," I replied.

"You are wrong," Danger replied with a mischievous smirk. "There is no difference. Both are three letter words that end with the same 'g' sound."

"Why do kittens play with cotton balls?" Kobina Amuah asked.

"Because they want to sharpen their claws," Danger replied with a sense of conviction.

"Wrong again," Kobina Amuah replied. "Silly, don't you remember, because they are getting ready for the hunt."

"Why do dogs wag their tails when they see their owners?" Kwesi asked.

"Because they want to show their love," Danger enthusiastically replied.

"Wrong!!" Kobina Amuah replied. "Because they want to have treats and sweets from their owners," he concluded.

"What is the first word in the English dictionary?" Danger asked.

"'A,'" I replied.

"'A' is not a word, knuckle head. It is aardvark," Danger replied.

And so we did, talking and teasing each other as we walked on until we descended the ridge joining the grassland with the sandy embankment to arrive at the seashore. As we waded in the sand we saw two teams of about thirty people each, made up of fifteen men, six women, and the rest children of varied ages dragging a rope from the ocean. One of the teams was close to us and the other was a half mile or so away. A woman on the line that was close to us was carrying a baby on her back. She, along with the members of her team, was recovering a tethering rope of a seine dragnet from the ocean to an assortment of indigenous melodious songs and harmonizing the refrains to ease the boredom of the repetitive work motions. An older man in a tattered shirt and a pair of patched pantaloons coiled the recovered rope as it was dragged up to ready it for the next net casting.

A few children, who were either too young or reticent to partake in the dragging, sat quietly in the dry sand close to the line but away from the group recovering the tethering rope of the seine dragnet. Other children used the moist sand to build sand turrets, which the uncoiling waves of the roaring sea either washed away or broke down when they ended their journey on the shoreline. A few beach visitors waded in the foreshore waters, sprinted to kick the white surf left at the soggy shoreline as waves receded, or stooped to pick up kelp and weeds. Others simply paused and gazed at the bubbling sands the waves left as they receded.

"Let's join them!" urged Danger.

On this urging, we trekked through the deep, cream-colored, sandy beach toward one of the net recovering teams. Kobina Amuah, Kwesi, and Danger joined the team without waiting for a formal invitation to do so. I looked at the ocean and saw seaweeds sluggishly floating on the waves toward the shore. I rushed toward the fluffy surf at the end of a wave, fully intending to kick it, but it fizzled before I could reach it. I scrambled back from the shoreline and joined my brother and our newfound friends. They adjusted their hold and made room for me on the line. I grabbed the rope and soon found myself humming along as we recovered the dragnet from the ocean. My palms began to redden and burn after a few trips up and down the rope. The team that was on the other rope of the net was going through similar recovery motions. The ocean breeze blew the song of the distant team to us, but the sea breeze carried the sounds to us in such a discordant hum that we could not echo the effective refrain customarily required of us.

After three to four hours of net recovery and scampering from left to right along the beach to secure our end of the teetering, large, dragnet rope, a trawl containing the catch came to view. Seagulls hovered and futilely dove to snatch some of the catch from the holding trawl. The professional fishermen of both teams shouted frantic and sometimes conflicting instructions, as we wrestled to join the tail end of the two ropes to secure the catch. With a little help from the ocean and brute force from the entire team, we wrapped the two ends of the dragnet ropes together and successfully brought in the attached trawl containing the catch to the shoreline. We dragged the partially torn seine and trawl further up the shoreline and gathered to inspect the catch. One of the fishermen opened the trawl to expose a shoal of assorted fish and shrimp fervently gasping for breath only to give up the ghost within ten twinklings of the eye. Another directed his crew to untangle the seine dragnet and ready it for the next casting. Another combed a small part of the catch that stretched in front of him with his fingers. As he did, a sea snake slinked out of the trawl, bore into the soggy sand, and vanished. I marveled at its agility and wondered what I would do when faced with similar circumstances.

Yet another fisherman with a gruff domineering voice, possibly the lead fisherman, directed one of his compatriots to fetch a measuring pan hidden under a pile of clothing a few feet away. The compatriot complied with the directive. The lead fisherman used the pan, which measured about six inches deep and ten inches in diameter, to scoop the shoal of fish into approximately equally sized heaps on the dry sand further up from the shoreline. Then he invited the fishmongers to pick out a heap and bid on them. The lead fisherman gave me two big, gray-blue herrings for my trouble, three medium-sized red snappers that looked pinker than red to Kwesi, four silver-colored eels to Danger, and four dark blue-gray mid-sized mackerels with light gray bellies to Kobina Amuah.

We left the torn seine for the fishermen to mend and trudged on the edge of the tide where the firmer sand met the soft shore sand towards a coconut mangrove farther up shore. We examined our rewards along the way, and debated the fairness of the lead fisherman's reward to us. We also picked up some seashells and weeds lying on the shore, rigorously examined them for signs of life, and found none. Kobina Amuah picked up a smooth pebble and whisked it *tout de force* toward the prairie. The pebble sailed through the air, gradually lost speed, and sank into the thick green grass that carpeted the prairie.

Upon reaching the mangrove, we dug a shallow hole in the sand and buried our fish to secure it from potential predators. We gathered fallen coconut branches for mats and lay down to rest under the shade of the coconut trees and the salt tang breeze of the sea. The sea's ceaseless anodyne waves erected a wall between us and the buzz of the nearby town as we gradually eased into a serene siesta. We were enjoying the quietude until Kwesi disrupted it with this unexpected juvenile demand. "I am hungry," he cried out.

"We do not have any food to eat except the raw fish, and none of us has a grill to roast it on or a pot to cook it in. Besides, nobody here is your Mama," Danger emphatically replied.

After a pause, Kobina Amuah asked in a conciliatory tone, "So what shall we do?"

"Let Ato Kwamena climb one of the coconut trees. He is small and light enough for the job at hand," Danger suggested.

"Why me? I am only a small boy," I asserted, as I tried to get out of the climbing.

Egged on by Kobina Amuah, Danger insisted I climb the tree and pluck down some coconuts for the gang.

"But I have never climbed a coconut tree before," I protested.

"So what?" replied Danger, with a sense of sarcasm. "There is a first time for everything."

"You are a virgin only once in your life," Kobina Amuah said. "Besides," he continued, "what is the point in keeping one's virginity when life is more pleasurable without it?"

"Yes, indeed," I agreed, "there is a first time for everything. But I do not want this to be my first time. Besides, I cannot trust any of you to take care of me if I fall or hurt myself."

"Chicken," taunted Kwesi. "You are just too timid to try anything new. Just get on with it and everything will be fine."

Kwesi's concordance with the two boys made it clear to me that there were no mitigating excuses left for me to hang on to. I was at the end of my rope and had to accept their irrational edict or face certain expulsion from the group.

After overcoming my skittishness, I got up from the sand, pulled off my shirt and forcefully flung it on the sand to register my displeasure as the rest of the gang who were looked on with abject indifference, "Let's go for it," I said defiantly.

We scrambled around the mangrove in search of a short coconut tree with lots of fruit. Danger found one close to where we had rested. Kobina Amuah, the tallest of the four, clasped his fingers tightly into a platform and asked me to step into it. Then, with help from the remaining members of the gang, I was hoisted and pushed as far up the coconut tree as they could reach. Their efforts got me half way up the tree. Danger instructed me to pivot the arc of my foot against the rungs of the tree and push my body up while using my hands to grip the trunk of the tree for support to continue the climb. I meticulously followed his directives, climbing four or so rungs at a time, and ascended the tree, spurred on by their words of encouragement.

Kobina Amuah insisted I desist from clutching the branches that were closest to me as I made my final ascent into the branches of the tree. "Those close-by branches have reached maturity and are liable to fall off from heavy weights set against them, including your weight," he explained. So I maneuvered my right hand, which is the stronger of my two hands, to one of the second tier branches and pulled myself up the tree. I found a secure mooring once I reached the top and used the heel of my left foot to knock down the coconut fruit one at a time onto the soft beach sand. The gang got giddy and giggled with each fruit fall.

Suddenly, a distant voice rose above the uncontrolled gabble and asked, "Who is there?"

I looked up and saw clouds, tenuous as smoke drifting and dissolving into the limitless blue sky. For a moment, I thought the voice was coming from the heavens. I stopped the plucking to listen. Then Kwesi unceremoniously shattered my thoughts.

"Stop! Stop and listen. There is someone coming," Kwesi whispered with a sense of urgency. I was transfixed and ready to hear either God or the voice of one of His angels. Since I was a sinner, a voice from any angel would be a good consolation and harbinger of good things, but the gang on the ground was of a different mind. They fell onto the sand and faked sleep. I surveyed the landscape and saw a man walking on a footpath that passed by where we were located. I whispered my observation to the gang and took cover behind the canopy of the coconut's tall cone branch. I continued to watch the man from that vantage point until the image of the person who emitted the question got closer and clearer. As it neared, I noted that it was a bare-footed and bare-chested man in tight, gray, tattered pantaloons toting a pouch over his shoulder and tottering to the rhythmic movements of the waves down the narrow pathway through the surrounding green grass. I suspected from his manner of walking that he had imbibed more than his fair share of *Akpeteshi*, the local hundred-percent-proof alcoholic beverage that was condensed from fermented sugar cane syrup, but I was not in a position to verify my suspicion and would not if I were. From my way of thinking, everyone has a right to live a manner of his or her choosing so long as that lifestyle does not affect others or break the law.

Be that as it may, he passed without incident. I resumed kicking down coconuts with my heel to the very last of the cluster. In all, I kicked down twelve coconuts. After that, I cautiously picked my way around the fronds of the coconut tree and hugged its trunk to make my descent. Gravity aided my descent so fast that I lacerated my chest at several spots. I looked at the lacerations after reaching the ground and wondered why I did not heed my instinct to wear my shirt for the job. I also wondered why none of the gang offered helpful hints to aid my descent and concluded that no amount of brooding would return lost innocence or restore my chest to its unblemished state, so I resolved to let bygones be bygones and share in the spoil.

Kobina Amuah took the lead in distributing the booty. He mixed the small-sized ones with the big ones and shared the harvest three apiece. I took my share and pounded the coconuts, one at a time, against the trunk of a conveniently located coconut tree in the grove. Like the other members of the gang, I did this to remove the husk and fiber to reach the coconut shell. Three members of the gang held their fresh coconut shells in one hand at a time and cracked either the bottom or top with a medium-sized stone. They gingerly removed the cracked shell to reach the fruit juice and drank it. After that, they searched for a bigger rock to place the shell containing the coconut meat on, and used a medium-sized stone to crack the shell and reach the meat.

I used a different approach to solve the conundrum by searching the ground for a sturdy twig to do the job. I found one lying in the grass nearby and rushed to the ocean for the sea's brine to wash off any contaminant. Then I held the first pick of my share firmly between my thighs, set the cleaned twig into one of the coconut's three eyes, and used a granite stone with sharp edges to drill the eye until it punctured it and the juice began to flow. After setting my drilling bits aside, I sucked the juice of the coconut fruit to the lees. I placed the shell containing the meat on a large stone and cracked it open into two unequal parts with a medium-sized rock. I forced my right thumb between the coconut's meat and one side of the broken shell, separated the meat from the shell, scooped out the soft coconut meat, and half-sloughed, half-chewed it, tossing the empty shell on the grounds of the mangrove. I repeated this exercise with the remaining two coconuts until I had eaten my portion of the spoils and was full beyond measure.

We sat in the shade of the coconut mangrove for a time to rest our engorged stomachs. From time to time, we emptied our bladders at the base of one of many coconut trunks of our choosing. We chattered a little more about school, cohorts of the dragline, the people we saw afar as we made our way to the beach, and anything else that suited our fancy.

"What are you kids doing?" asked a passerby.

"Nothing!" Danger replied.

"Well, it is getting dark and you must be on your way home."

"He is right," echoed Kobina Amuah. "We must go home before your Grandma and my Mom begin to worry."

We got up one by one and unearthed our fish. Then we stripped one of the leaves of the coconut stems and coiled them into strings, tied a nut at one end, and threaded the fish through the gills and mouth to string it. We repeated the process until all our fish were strung one on top of the other and fully balanced on the strings. Each one of us slung his reward of fish over his shoulder and got ready for the homebound journey.

"Are you ready?" Danger inquired.

"Yes," we responded in unison.

And with that, Danger led us out of the mangrove to the grassland and searched for a path that would lead us home. We found one and joyously started to journey towards town.

As we walked home, Danger told us of a persistent rumor. He said that over the years, the fishermen that lived in the huts close to the ocean gagged, bound, and killed children between the ages of six and thirteen who were loitering at the shoreline after sunset. The fishermen, he continued, removed the hearts of these children and buried the remaining carcass at sea. Then they roasted the hearts they harvested over a big bonfire in sacrifice to their pagan god of the sea. He said that an old man in town told him this story and that the sea god preferred the spirits of virgin male children to adults of either sex. The fishermen did this in a belief that these pure and unblemished children had better supplications with the gods than older children who are patently mischievous and schooled in the ways of the world. Danger said the fishermen believed that the pagan god of the sea would assure bigger catch as a result of the favorable supplication. The fishermen also believed that the size of the catch would continually decline for them until the children reached adulthood in the world of the dead. Since the supplication would go on longer in the afterlife if the child were younger, it was better for the fishermen to sacrifice children who were closer to six with good verbal acuity than those that fell away from that age in either direction. Danger concluded by inviting us to listen to the continuous, rhythmic drumbeat and hum of pagan incantations coming from the hamlets built from coconut branches by the seashore where most of the fishermen lived. "They are truly menacing!" he concluded.

Looking back, I saw blue smoke billowing from one of the hamlets and was frightened. I began to believe that the fishermen were possibly engaged in the ritual Danger had just described. I felt I was a prime candidate for the holocaust, and I was not going to be foolhardy enough to test the validity of his assertions. Therefore, I was elated to be out in the open field where someone could hear my cry, if attacked, and tested the range and reach of my vocal cords for range and amplitude.

"Halloo!" I yelled.

"What is wrong?" inquired Kwesi.

"I was just testing my vocal cords," I slyly replied.

"And for what, may I inquire?" asked Kobina Amuah.

"Just because I wanted to," I replied, in the hope of dropping the subject.

"Not so quickly, smarty pants," said Danger, who continued, "Were you thinking about the rituals and all the other stories I told you?"

"Yes," I replied squeamishly.

"Well," he continued, "you do not have to be afraid. You have three of us to protect you. Besides, we are not alone. Look over there," he said as he pointed with his right index finger. "There are all those people going in the same direction we are. We will make enough noise for them to hear and rush to our aid if attacked."

We continued our journey toward home on that tepid reassurance and hastened our walk to keep in step with the other people who were walking further to our right in the same direction. I looked back and saw the sun use its rays to color the ocean solid gold as it began its dip below the horizon to start the day for people living in other parts of the world.

From time to time, we cast suspicious glances toward the hamlets under the mangrove for signs of being followed, but found none. We walked on in this watchful manner until we reached the town and breathed a sigh of relief to cap an end to that day's adventure.

Danger and Kobina Amuah guided us home since we did not know our way around town.

"Thank you," Kwesi and I said as we reached home. "We hope to see you again tomorrow," I said cordially.

"In fact, we will see you tomorrow," Kwesi affirmed with a sense of invincibility.

We parted company on that note.

Chapter 4

Generally speaking, I value being home with Mama and Dad and even my elder brother because, in some mysterious way, they make me feel secure and loved. I can truly express who I am and not worry about social approval or lack thereof. Therefore, I was very surprised when Grandma Elizabeth confronted us in this line of questioning when we arrived home. "Where have you been all day?" she began as we crossed the threshold of the gate into the house's compound.

"We were just walking about town and looking at a few pleasant places," replied Kwesi Sakyi in a casual tone.

"And where exactly may these be? Tell me! Tell me!" she demanded, but we did not answer. Then, after what seemed like a millennium, she continued her demand for an explanation in a high-pitched ranting voice. "I do not want you kids to go out there and get into trouble. Your father, who is an officer of the court, would not want any of it, nor would your mother." She paused, looked at the fish dangling at the end of string made of the coconut leaf, which we had lowered from our shoulders, and asked in her normal tone of voice, "And where did you get that fish?"

"From some fishermen at the beach," I replied, and attempted to continue. "We…." But as I uttered the word, Kwesi stepped on my heel and elbowed my ribcage to indicate his displeasure with my approach and took over the conversation with this response, "We went to the beach with two lovely boys we met on the prairie this morning."

"Which two boys? And where do they come from?" inquired Grandma haughtily.

"Danger and Kobina Amuah," Kwesi replied. He narrated how we met and accompanied them to the market to see Ayah and ended at the beach. He gave her a very cursory recap of our adventure and left the part about my coconut climbing experience entirely out of his account.

Grandma Elizabeth looked me in the eyes for confirmation of Kwesi's account of events. I looked away and shamefully nodded to affirm his story.

"Give me the fish," Grandma commanded, and half-snatched them from me.

Kwesi gave his fish to her without waiting on her to ask for it. "Here you are, Grandma," he said nonchalantly.

"You must be sweaty after being in the sun all day," she conjectured.

"Indeed we are," replied Kwesi in an agreeable tone.

"Then get with it and have a bath and dinner before going to bed."

"Yes, Grandma," I replied in a flat tone.

While we were walking away to bathe in a makeshift bathroom, I overheard Grandma calling the maid to prepare the fish for grilling and frying. She wanted to use one half of the catch in making soup and the remaining half for fish over tomato stew the next day.

As we bathed, Kwesi and I took turns recounting highlights of the day's activities to one another. He applauded me for supporting his version of events to the Old Lady, as he called Grandma, and co-opted my complicity in his future responses. Suddenly, Kwesi paused, looked me squarely in the eyes, and crowned our pact with these remarks, "The Old Lady is not there with us and does not need to know exactly what happens or what we do with our friends."

"That does not mean we should not tell her the truth," I rejoined.

Kwesi proceeded as if he had not heard a word I said with these remarks. "In fact," he continued, "I doubt whether she will want to be there with us. She is old and cannot keep pace with us. She has no other choice than to accept our account as gospel until proven otherwise. Therefore, an abridged edition, or a little fib here and there should be sufficient to appease and satisfy her curiosity. And don't you dare contradict any of what I say to her," he warned in a slightly elevated voice, and concluded with the threat, "Otherwise, I will cease to claim you as my brother."

Losing him as a brother and playmate was not a happy prospect, so I quickly conceded to his demand despite my misgivings and promised I would not. I continued bathing, but bathing was rather difficult for me that evening. The cold water gave me a burning sensation when it reached my lacerated chest. I shivered momentarily but continued bathing. After the bath, I wrapped myself in the top, smaller size of Grandma Elizabeth's two-piece cloth and stepped into a pair of beach sandals. Kwesi wrapped himself in the bottom part of the two-piece wrap-around cloth, which was larger, and stepped into a larger pair of similarly colored beach sandals Grandma had availed to us.

We made our way out of the bathroom and joined Grandma, who was already seated at the dining table and waiting for us. We dined on fried red snapper, topped with a stew made of tomato paste, fried onion, ginger, and cayenne pepper, complemented by fish stew with slices of balled ken-key.

We took heavy steps up the stairs after dinner to ready ourselves for sleep. After fetching and spreading our thin reed mats on the wooden floor, we assumed fetal positions to await sleep. Grandma walked into the room just as we were comfortably positioned and ready to sleep and began, "Are you asleep?" she inquired.

"No," we responded.

"Then wait. Don't go to sleep yet," she pleaded. "I have something to tell you."

On that plea, Grandma got behind the door to our room and removed the two-piece cloth she had been wearing all day, folded them nicely, and placed then on top of a stack of steel trunks. She wrapped a larger piece of cloth around herself and tied it just above her drooping breast, climbed into her cotton-stuffed bed, and faced the wall to which her bed was moored. She untied the knot of the cloth, got comfortable in her bed and proceeded.

"Ato," she began, "I noticed you looked away when I talked with you this evening about your day's activities. Why did you do that?" she pointedly inquired.

I faked deafness when she asked the question on the first go-around, so she repeated her question. Once again, I did not respond because I felt trapped between telling the truth, and thereby reneging on my promise to my brother, or keeping quiet and postponing the inevitable. I chose the latter.

The crux of the matter is, I was mentally unprepared to face her scrutiny. I was also cowed by the prospect of facing my elder brother's wrath the next morning and thought my silence would buy valuable time until dawn when traditional norms allowed serious counseling, but my presumption was mislaid. Grandma Elizabeth did not interpret my silence in the manner I had hoped. After all, how could she? She was not a mind reader, nor should I have expected her to be. Her mind was made up on what she wanted to talk about. She was old and culturally privileged to talk about what she wanted to talk about, when she wanted to, and nothing was going to impede her from exercising that option.

Grandma concluded that I would not respond and began the first of her bedtime stories as a way of instruction. She crafted her story around the things we did in the daytime. "On the seventh day after your births," she began, "your parents invited family members and a few close friends to witness your child naming, or out-dooring, which is the Akan ritual of welcoming newborns into the community. Under normal circumstances, your grandfather would have performed the ceremony. But since he was dead, the honor fell to your uncle, Kobina Abakan, your mother's elder brother. As is the tradition, he half-filled a glass with gin and poured libation to invoke the presence of your extended family in the following order: First, to your clan; second, to the elders of the family from both sides who have passed on; third, the spirit of well-wishers who have passed on, and finally to God who, according to Akan belief, is not seen and supposedly lives high in the infinite sky. This is done to invoke their help, protection, and guidance as you grow up.

"Then he dipped the middle finger of his right hand into the water contained in the glass and touched your lips with it and mentioned your name, which your father had chosen for you to reflect your connection to his lineage. He invoked you 'to affirm you have tasted water when asked, and if, indeed, you have.' He repeated the process with a glass containing the gin and summoned you to 'affirm you have tasted gin if, indeed, you have done so.' After that, he filled the glass that had been used, took a sip, and mentioned your name. Then he passed the glass filled with gin to the guests and invited them to sip and repeat your name and give any advice they might have to guide you as you grew up. Nowadays *bon vivant* families prefer imported gin to the local fermented sugar alcohol *Akpeteshi*.

"The question is, why does our cultural heritage prescribe using water and gin for this ceremony? Why did our ancestors use two liquids that are colorless, crystal clear, and appear the same to the naked eye, when in reality one is alcoholic and the other is not? There are two plausible explanations. First, our ancestors wanted the custodians of our heritage to develop a capacity for discerning truth from lies, separate fiction from nonfiction no matter their similarities, and maintain self-discipline and personal integrity at all times. Discomforting situations, like the peaks and valleys of life, give way to flatlands, comfort, and other travails of life. Truth, no matter how long it is submerged, will pop to the surface to reveal its glory like cocks do. Therefore, there is no justification for you or anyone who shares in our cultural heritage to take solace in the temporary comfort of lies or falsehood when time will expose lies to the light of day!

"Above all, it is much better to direct the beam of your inner light to shine on truth, and support honest conduct and chastity at all times in whatever manifestation. These qualities of truth, honesty, and integrity transcend time. They form the bedrock of fidelity and honest relationships even among people of divergent views. I hope you will learn the virtue of these lessons as you continue your vacation and journey through life."

On that note, Grandma Elizabeth bade us good night and went to sleep.

I closed my eyes and tossed and turned as I lay. Then I heard Grandma's bed squeak. I opened my eyes and looked askance at her bed and spied her turning to shake the mosquito netting covering the window close to her bed to assure it was fully secured. She got out of bed and picked up a white ewer stored under her bed. Using the light provided by the dimmed lantern sitting on top of the stacked steel trunks to guide her, she tip-toed over our reed mats toward the back of the slightly ajar bedroom door. She held the ewer under her genitalia with one hand, covered her head with a bedding cover that she held in the other, and relieved herself into the ewer. She returned the ewer to its place under her bed and returned to bed. She tossed and turned and settled into a quiet, easy breathing to denote she was asleep. I turned to see what my elder brother was doing and noticed he was fast asleep. I stayed up to ponder what Grandma had said, but a mixed melody of cricket chirrs, wailing bats, hooting owls, and calls of other nocturnal creatures soon lured me to sleep.

Chapter 5

I woke up to the usual chirping of sparrows and bobbing bulbuls that nestled in the tall, bushy hibiscus tree behind Grandma's opened mosquito-netted window. The cock crowed its clarion cock-a-doodle-doo. I opened my eyes to his call and stretched out to celebrate the dawn of a new day. I was a child on holiday, immune from job demands, socially unadjusted, and malingering on a thin, reed-mat.

"Time to eat," yelled Kwesi, who appeared ready for the day.

"I will be right down," I responded as he disappeared around the bend towards the staircase.

I got up, rolled up my sleeping mat, and put it in the corner where Grandma had instructed us to stow it. I folded the shoulder cloth, which Grandma gave me to sleep under, and placed it at the foot of Grandma's bed to use when I went to bed. I changed into my khaki shorts and a red and white-striped short-sleeved shirt. Then, taking a page from Grandma's aversion to bad oral hygiene and its adverse implications for social intercourse, I picked up my chewing stick from its storage at the windowsill, moistened it with saliva, excised the wet part with my incisive teeth, and slightly chewed the top part of the remaining stick to brush my teeth as I went down the staircase. I poured water into a hemi-calabash, rinsed my mouth, and spat out the water onto the dusty compound. I returned the toothbrush and the empty calabash to storage and joined my elder brother and Grandma Elizabeth, who were already seated at the small softwood table, for a breakfast of toasted ground-corn porridge, a medley of tropical fruits, toasted white bread, fried eggs, fried ripe tomatoes, and fried onions. Grandma gave each of us a tablespoon of quinine to prevent malaria infection, a tablet of cod liver oil to boost our resistance to rickets, and a teaspoonful of mineral supplement to make up mineral deficiencies in our diet.

"Why should we take all this medicine?" asked Kwesi after experiencing the bitter aftertaste of the quinine. "I do not like it one little bit," he emphasized.

"Because it is for your own good," Grandma responded, adding, "You must count yourselves very lucky. I know of kids in this town who thrive on half the food you eat in this house. Their parents struggle every day to put bread on the table and can't afford to give them preventive medicine like quinine tablets to fight off malaria or the nutritional supplement you complain about and take for granted."

I swallowed my share of the medication Grandma had dispensed as I observed the exchange between her and my elder brother. I made a mental note to desist from discussing the virtues of primitive medical care or class stratification with her.

After breakfast we hugged Grandma goodbye and left to search for Danger and Kobina Amuah. I stepped out of the entrance gate, stumbled on a protruding rock on the unpaved road in front of our home, and decided to use it as a landmark for our return journey. I looked to our home to log the vector of the rock in relationship to Grandma Elizabeth's home on my mind. As I turned, I saw the maid coming out of Grandma's home to empty the white ewer into the open gutter that ran in front of the house. I was distressed to see the maid emptying the pee because I thought it was reprehensible for her to clean up after a fully-grown woman like Grandma. Indeed, I couldn't imagine how Grandma, who was God fearing and church going, could be so odiously insensitive as to assign such a menial task to her. To me, the maid deserved to be treated with as much dignity as any person in the household, and not be assigned the task of cleaning up another person's excrement. But the maid was a person of meager means, a mere vessel of service and an instrument of Grandma's will, who was indentured to do as told and not question the rationale of the people she was indentured to serve. For me, the fundamental question was whether her indentured servitude made her sub-human, and therefore a subject of derision.

Furthermore, I didn't believe that her low social status granted Grandma or anybody else the right or moral authority to either emotionally maltreat or physically abuse her. But morality and justice as aspects of cultural norms, as I have heard it said, are built on evolving social relationships that are not anchored in legal precedence or permanency.

I was sad to see that she did not have any friends in her age group to play or form relationship with. The relationship she was in, if you could call how she related to Grandma a relationship, was premised on moral tradition of a stratified society, which for the moment barred her from any meaningful intercourse with the family she served and turned her into mere chattel—a vessel of service. It diminished her relevance and contributions in the country of her birth and had no advocate to assert her human rights or recognize the fullness of her existence.

Grandma's indifference to these indignities drove me to question the broader meaning of love and its underlying assumptions of compassion, commitment, freedom, fortitude, discipline, discretion, and responsibility. I also began to question how the rich, like Grandma, could develop the gall and establish a moral basis for exploiting other human beings from dawn to dusk and times in between like a galley slave owner. I wondered how members of Grandma's social class adequately justified the rightness of taking maids from their circumstances and providing them with meager meals, shelter, clothing, and paltry stipends. I pondered why the Creator, who is ubiquitously present, could, in His infinite wisdom, allow maids and the less endowed of societies to be subjected to such crass abuse, exploitation and indignity. Much as I tried, I couldn't find a logical explanation for these social or economic forces that led the maid to surrender her dignity and freedom and cow-tow to such unbridled humiliation. I couldn't find anything noble, right, or kind in either the inane actions of the rich or the passivity of the deprived.

In a surreal sense, both groups were venally poor; the rich for using their social position as permit to oppress the poor, and the poor for want of courage to seek fulfillment of their destinies. I decided to hold my tongue and observe the situation, because as a child of limited life experience and resources, I could not change the maid's station in life despite my burning desire to do so.

I trotted to my elder brother who was walking away toward the market to begin the search for our newfound friends. As this was Wednesday and market day, a mass of the town's dwellers was making their way to hunt for bargains at the market. We mingled with the moving mass to tread the unpaved dusty road that joined Grandma's home to the market and beyond. We stopped and looked at a nanny dwarf goat and two newly born kids with dangling, fresh umbilical cords attempting to take their first steps of life and fall. They got up, tried again, and fell again, but succeeded on the sixth attempt. They bleated to denote their success and instinctively started to suck milk from the nanny goat that gave birth to them. A forest goat, with a gapped goatee appeared out of nowhere and stopped at the heels of the nanny and bobbed his head as if to say "congratulations" to the nanny goat. He looked quizzically at the kids, stomped his feet four times in the dusty road, tucked in his hooves, and half-walked, half-trotted away. The nanny goat stopped in the middle of the milling crowd to nurse her growing offspring and continued to stroll after the feeding. She scavenged a grain of corn that had fallen in the sand to begin rebuilding the blood she lost during childbirth.

The forest goats and the Nungua blackhead sheep scattered black droppings as they meandered through the moving mass of people. A duck followed by a half dozen yellow, fluffy ducklings limbered in single file along the sidewalk towards the market. I looked at the broken walls of the sand-filled open gutter, which lay on the left side of the street running with torpid water, and saw a hen scavenging for food in a pile of garbage that was dumped there. She crackled a finding to her chicks, which were otherwise engaged in their individual scavenging for food. The chicks abandoned their search and rushed to peck with the hen, only to return and forage for floating food remnants and other edibles after the joint pecking was done. I dashed for one of the chicks and ended up scattering the flock. It dawned on me how agile the domesticated chicks were when compared with their commercial cousins who are kept in hatcheries and fattened for sale. I turned to record the progress the ducks and her ducklings had made towards their destination and found them jumping into the gutter to join the hen and chickens who were scavenging for food. I slowed my pace as I thought about the mindset that directed animals to fend for themselves and find their way back to their pens, corrals, and fences at dusk and concluded that nature is an unfathomable mystery.

I turned from my reverie and found my brother had walked farther away from me toward Danger's mother's stall. I doubled my pace to catch up with him and was tempted to discuss my observations with him when I did, but I noted that he was preoccupied with his thoughts and contented myself with silently walking beside him. We walked in that manner until we arrived at Ayah's stall. We exchanged pleasantries with Ayah upon arrival and asked of the whereabouts of Danger and Kobina Amuah, to which Ayah replied, "They have not made it in yet, but you are welcome to stay and wait for them if you like. I am sure they will be here soon."

"We definitely will!" we answered in unison.

We had the time and an open agenda. Besides, we would not know what meaningful things to fill our day with. We sat on the stools Ayah provided and watched marketers go by and stop to buy the things they wanted and continue on their merry ways.

After a while, we grew bored and restless with waiting and decided to visit other market stalls and find out more about the market. We passed a woman who had a baby tied to her back like we have seen wherever we go, but I was amazed to see her balance a short wicker basket containing assorted species of chicken on her head at the same time. The chickens made small, uneasy crackling noises as we passed by. Perhaps our presence disturbed them. We soon came upon a barefooted lanky man in a white gown, desperately trying to corral his dwarf goats with a long staff but passed him without incident.

Distant, intermittent, pounding sounds attracted our attention. We traced the source to an asphalt-constructed house close to the rear gate to the market. The house was painted white and measured about one hundred fifty feet wide and one hundred twelve feet long. It was roofed with corrugated iron sheets and had two average-sized windows with mosquito netting. We looked around and tried to find out what purpose it served or what was going on inside its walls.

"What is that house for?" I asked a young girl of about twelve who was a passerby in a hurry to God knows where.

"Just go in and find out," she snapped as she hurriedly walked away.

We followed her suggestion and decided to satisfy our curiosity by opening its half solid wood and half mosquito-netting door to enter it. The base of the door scratched the cement-paved floor of the room as it opened. We quickly closed it behind us to keep out the buzzing houseflies that hovered around it. We looked up and saw four men wearing blood-spattered calico aprons standing behind a long wooden counter. The counter was about four inches thick, ten feet long, and four and a half feet tall. We saw carcasses of dwarf goats, sheep, and various cuts of meat hanging free from overhead steel pegs and presumed that the men behind the counter were butchers. We also presumed that the house was the municipality's butcher shop. The butchers had the decapitated heads of a dwarf goat, a sheep, and a bull displayed on a shelf that stood behind them. The eyes of the butchers were sad and deeply set in their sockets.

A medium-sized woman in a dark, oversized dress suddenly opened the door and came into the shop. She shuffled her feet as she strolled in, stopped in front of the tall, husky butcher standing behind the counter, and slowly raised her right arm to point to a cut of the goat's carcass she wanted to buy. The butcher picked off the meat from the peg, sharpened his cleave knife on a small grindstone, and carved the meat she wanted. He put the part of the meat containing the bone on the chopping board and hacked it with a small axe he held in one hand. Then he removed a long knife from its sheath, pulled out a leather strip hanging from his waist, and sharpened the knife to complete cutting off the hacked meat and bones into manageable portions. The butcher put each portion in a smooth green leaf, folded the leaf over the meat and broken bones, and handed the packet to the lady. The lady placed the folded leaf containing the meat at the bottom of her shopping basket she was carrying and walked away after paying for it.

I couldn't hear the full conversation or see which part of the carcass the customer had requested the butcher to cut and could not care less. The only thing that interested me was to learn about how the butchers got the meat into the shop.

Kwesi was also interested in the same subject and took the lead in this inquiry. So, I decided to lay back and watch the exchange between Kwesi and the butchers because over the years I come to believe that he was a better diplomat than I was. Above all, he didn't trust me to question the tall husky butchers behind the counter without either botching the questioning or annoying them.

"Where did you get the meat from?" He pointedly asked the only butcher in the group who was wearing a white Turkish turban.

"We bought it from the tribal herdsmen," the butcher replied.

"And where did the tribal herdsmen get the herd of goats, sheep, or cows from?"

The butcher in the Turkish turban explained how the tribesmen, mostly of Hausa or Dagbani descent, husbanded the animals over years. They fed them dried grass if housed and wet grass when grazed, corn on occasion, commercial chicken feed, and the skin of unripe plantains when available. He told us that the goats, sheep, and cattle were selected for slaughter when they got older or became udderless. He added that sometimes they slaughtered calf for special occasions like weddings, and traditional celebrations like the feast of Ramadan, because of its tender meat. He added that selected animals were slaughtered at dawn, skinned, disemboweled, and their carcass brought to market first thing in the morning since the butchers' shop didn't have refrigeration. This allowed the carcasses to remain fresh for a long time in the tropical heat. He also said that they stretched the animal skins inside out and pinned them to the ground with four-inch nails or wooden pegs to dry in the sun. He explained how they removed the drying animal pelt at sunset and returned them outdoors only to re-peg them to the ground at sunrise to continue drying. He said they repeated this process over several days until the pelts were completely dry and usable as prayer mats, doeskin for gloves or membrane for Ewe Drums.

He explained how the butchers used to disembowel the sheep, goats, and cattle and retrieve their intestines to make kebabs. He said that slaughtering sheep and goats was a group job with task assignments based on years of experience and apprenticeship status. Butchers did the slaughtering, disemboweling, and skinning of selected animals. The butchers' apprentice scrubbed and cleaned the intestines and marinated them with assorted dried and fresh-ground ginger, dried and fresh cayenne, dried thyme, oregano, and special spices and strung them way up the kebab stick for grilling.

The apprentice made a large charcoal fire, spread the fire on the ground to cover about a four-foot diameter, and fed the fire with hickory wood. Then they planted the empty portion of the stick, which was about a third of the stick's entire length, into the ground close to the fire to grill the uncooked meat on the top two-thirds of the stick into tender '*kyi kyinga,*' the local kebab. They grouped the sheep, goats, and cattle intestine kebabs and arranged them on a large aluminum plate ready for sale. He added that they continually seasoned the unsold kebab with the same marinating spices as curative. The best kebab, he told us, was made of chopped cow liver.

He said they sold the unsold meat at reduced prices to "*chop bars,*" community based restaurants that cook and serve indigenous foods like palm, garden eggs, and peanut butter soups on cassava, yam, or coco yam fufu; cooked powdered cassava; and cooked and mashed rolls of rice in earthenware bowls. Sometimes they served yam, stew of palm oil, or cayenne pepper and coco-yam leaves as side orders. The "*chop bars*" are often located close to lorry stations, open markets, and alleys leading to major road arteries. The butchers grill and sell the leftover meat, which the "*chop bar*" owners and cooks would not buy as "*suya.*" This portion of meat is usually a sirloin cut of goat meat—boneless, marinated, and cured in a special blend of spices and sold by the slice.

We thanked the butcher for satisfying our curiosity and left to link up with Danger and Kobina Amuah.

We saw a flock of hooded vultures squawking with one another close to the butchers' shop as we stepped out. The vultures momentarily stopped hissing and slapping their wings against each other over cast off meat and bones the butchers in the shop had tossed out for them to feed on. We took our eyes off their squabble, resumed our journey and soon came upon a row of women roasting ripe plantains over a charcoal fire and selling roasted peanuts as complements to the plantain. We also passed by a couple of women dressed in colorful dashikis, selling black and brown tiger nuts. According to Ghana folklore, black tiger nut juice increases male virility and sperm count.

We continued our return journey to Ayah's stall and found that the boys had still not come in when we arrived. So, once again, Ayah offered us the stools that our two friends had sat on for their breakfast the previous day and invited us to wait for them. We settled in and resumed watching shoppers go by until Danger and Kobina Amuah eventually arrived.

We quickly got reacquainted and recognized that Kobina Amuah looked disheveled and unhappy. His torn dark shorts were dirtied with dead grass and the space between his toes crammed with thick black mud.

"Where have you been?" I asked suppliantly.

"I went to pick up a tattered jute bag containing red crab traps I loaned to my cousin."

"And where are the traps?"

"I dropped them off at the house before coming here," he responded drily.

I had never seen crab traps and asked Kobina Amuah if I could see them.

"Sure! I will show them to you tomorrow."

"I would like to see them too," joined Kwesi.

Ayah interrupted our conversation and summoned Kobina Amuah and Danger to the standard breakfast of ken-key and fish. Once again, she asked if we were hungry and wanted something to eat, and once again, we responded no and passed up the meal.

After breakfast, Kobina Amuah asked, "What do you guys want to do?"

"We have no plans," Kwesi answered.

Danger and Kobina Amuah consulted for a fleeting moment and asked us to follow them to a nearby orchard.

"Whose orchard is it?" I asked apprehensively.

"Just come on. Let's go,"Danger yelled. "You will find out soon enough. Cowards sit on their hands and watch the world go by because they mistakenly believe that life, with its endless possibilities, is only an absurd proposition. The brave, on the other hand, fully believe in the infinite good of people and all they represent. They are eager to get up at dawn and celebrate each moment of life with unfettered joy and gusto. Come on and let's have some fun. So far we have not gotten you into any trouble, have we?" he asked rhetorically, as he beckoned us to follow him and Kobina Amuah.

We followed them and passed a gaggle of agile children between the ages of six and eight engaged in devouring a roasted bird and horsing around. A pair of young girls carrying water on their heads that they had fetched from a community spigot raced passed us. They did not spill any water.

"I guess that is a pigeon," I said in an attempt to solicit the opinion of Danger and Kobina Amuah on the children's meal.

"Your guess could be wrong," Kobina Amuah replied without breaking his pace.

We carried on and soon crossed the open prairie, walked past a row of well-built bungalows and thatch-roofed hamlets tucked behind tufts of scattered bush and trees, and entered a thickly wooded forest whose leaves blanketed the sun and exchanged a gray haze for daylight. I was overcome by the eerie silence that enveloped the forest. An eagle owl spread its wings and listlessly landed on a tree limb a furlong or so away. I looked down and treaded softly to avoid stepping on any creeping creature that lived in the sallow, fallen leaves that were decomposing from lack of sunshine. I saw a snail sliding along a protruding plank. A bushy rabbit bobbed from what appeared to be a rabbit warren and hopped away. A scorpion with raised tail at the ready wallowed away on the moist decaying leaves. I waited for them to pass and continued with my watchful advance.

Suddenly and unexpectedly, the crickets began to chirr their mating calls. I looked yonder and saw the sun's ray streaming through the forest's rustling leaves to dance on the sere leaves that were awaiting interment. A large cone of light exposed a coiled brownish snake that lay a few yards away. I shuddered, became stiff and immobile with fright, and opened my mouth to cry out for help, but was so petrified that the cry stuck in my throat.

"Come on!" Kwesi said harshly.

I heard his egging but I did not respond because I did not want to wake the snake from its slumber. I gingerly inched my way away from the brown-skinned snake into safety.

"Be quiet," urged Danger as he saw the snake. "We do not want to announce our presence."

I mustered courage and ran through tassels of spider webs dangling from between trees and stepped over broken, decaying tree limbs and twigs that covered the floor of the forest. I ran until I was out of breadth; stopped to catch my breath and looked back to see if my compatriots were tailing me and was gratified to learn they were. I heaved a heavy sigh of relief and slowed into an easy trot and without a sense of urgency until I emerged at the other end of the forest. I looked around for more creeping creatures and found none but was shocked to see blood trickling from my elbow and oozing through my shirt. I examined my legs for any cuts and noted they were lacerated at various points and had embedded thorns here and there. I slowly picked out the thorns with my fingers and ran my palms over my legs and concluded they were all right. I felt blood trickling down my shoulders and removed my shirt to ascertain the depth of the cut. I took a look at the fresh wound and again concluded it was superficial and probably came from whisking by a thorn, brush, or shrub. The blood gradually clotted. So, I put my shirt on again and thought it was extraordinary that I did not feel the cuts when they occurred. Perhaps in my desire to escape the perceived danger, the sharpness of the cuts and my sense of pain was numbed. I turned and looked at my companions and saw them going through similar motions and concluded that ritual was part of the human condition and accepted it is as normal.

"I want to go back home," I plaintively declared.

"So do I," Danger responded in kind.

"And so do I," echoed Kwesi.

"I do not want to," contradicted Kobina Amuah. "What is the point? We have to go forward and accomplish our mission."

"What mission?" inquired Kwesi.

"Yes, we did not tell you. We are going to Mr. Minoo's orchard."

"For what?" I asked rather anxiously.

"To pick up some fruits. Just a few," Kobina Amuah replied with a shrug of the shoulders to underline the petty nature of the crime they were leading us to commit.

Kobina Amuah's "few fruits" set off the alarm bells in my head and made me leery of the whole thing. So far, we had been lucky enough to pick up a few coconuts and avoided detection or apprehension. Sooner or later, the odds would go against us, our luck would run out, and we would be caught in the act. Having thought this, I was afraid to share these thoughts with the other boys because I believed they would consider me a traitor and a deserter if I bowed out of the adventure. True enough I would save my skin from any fallout if I did not join them. I also faced the real prospect of social isolation and of losing them as friends during the holidays if I did not partake in the scheme. Peer pressure and inclusion? or preservation of the self and alienation? I debated between choosing social isolation and joining the illegal scheme, and chose isolation.

"I do not want to be a part of this," I declared, and indignantly continued, "We have no business going into other folk's homes and stealing their things. It is wrong, wrong, wrong!"

"Nobody is forcing you to," Kobina Amuah replied. "You know how you got here and you can surely find your way back home."

"Yes, you can," Kwesi supportively added.

I got up and searched for a path back to the town and found none in the vicinity. I decided to look farther and mapped a path I believed would get me back to the town. I walked the route a few yards and hit the forest wall. I tried another route and came to the same end. I tried one more time with the same results. I felt defeated. My sense of belonging won over my desire for isolation and what it entailed. I abandoned my intentions to break away from the group and reluctantly returned to the gang.

When I returned, the boys were sitting on the grass listening to Kobina Amuah. He wanted to know whether they wanted to proceed with the banditry or return home. I sat within hearing distance and listened to the deliberations.

"Would you like to go to the orchard?" Kobina Amuah asked Danger.

"Yes, I would," Danger replied affirmatively.

He asked the same question of my elder brother who also responded he wanted to join in the illegal visit.

Finally, he asked, "Are you here to stay, or just to sit and listen to our discussion?"

"I am here to stay," I replied.

"Does it mean you will join us in going to the orchard?" he asked as he looked for affirmation.

"Yes, I will join you," I reluctantly agreed.

We got up on the unanimous consent vote in favor of the aberrant behavior. We brushed grass from our behinds and started to ascend the hill in front of us. A stretch of corrugated roofing appeared to denote we were close to a home or homes. Soon, a mud-constructed building came into full view. It had peeling, white paint and looked deserted and unoccupied. A broken wooden window in the home that was hanging on one hinge oscillated with the force of the wind.

"Tread softly," implored Danger.

We looked at each other's face for signs of weakness and reassurance. We stopped tip-toeing, paused, and looked around to see if there were signs of human life but found none. Instead, we found an emaciated black and white cropped coated dog, resting under the shelter that was projected by a palm tree in front of the house. It was chained and had a white, chipped porcelain drinking bowl lying by it. It did not bark or whimper, but momentarily woke up and returned to sleep. I tapped on Danger's shoulder to alert him to the presence of the dog. "It is asleep," Danger whispered. He shared his observation of the dog with the other boys who continued to tip-toe on the Bermuda grass surrounding the house in order to avoid waking anybody that might be asleep in the house. We arrived at the fruit orchard behind the home and noticed that it was fenced with a tall, barbed wire and an unlatched, slightly open gate. I held the gate and attempted to gently open it wider.

"Stop and leave the gate alone," Kobina Amuah commanded, "we don't want the owner to detect anything different from how he left it." So we left the gate and crawled under the barbed wire fencing to reach the orchard.

The fruit orchard was about ten to fifteen square acres and filled with rows of oranges, tangerines, mangoes, avocados, cherimoyas, guavas, grapefruits, lemons, limes, papayas, and carambola. Their leaves provided shelter from the hot sun. The ground was unevenly carpeted with an assortment of fallen rustic yellow-colored leaves, rotting fruits, and decaying twigs. Sparrows flew away when they heard us. I intermittently heard the soft landing of seared leaves as they fell while we combed the grounds for fallen fruit. We picked up a few mangos, guava, and oranges here and there and pulled the front of our shirts into sacks to stack the fruit we considered edible. We summarily discarded those we could not eat (because they were either insect-infested or overripe) and searched for replacements. The drying and dried leaves crunched under the weight of our footsteps as we combed and scrambled for the fallen fruit. I found a firm, ripe mango, picked it up, and bit into it, finding it as juicy as it looked. I also found a ripe guava, but I was not equally lucky when I picked it up and examined it. It was worm infested, so I threw it away as fast as I picked it and inched toward a cherimoya tree that was in view. I searched under the tree for fallen cherimoyas and found none, so I took a few steps back and examined its branches for any ripe cherimoyas.

I found one hanging down and decided to climb the tree to pick it. However, I could not find the fruit I had sighted from the ground after climbing the tree. I forged my way up a different branch of the tree and found a fruit that looked much smaller than the one I saw from the ground. It looked as green and unripe as the big cherimoya fruit. I reached for it, squeezed it, and found it to be soft and ready to eat. I plucked it off the branch, peeled off its green skin, and ate the white juicy meat, while picking and throwing away its large brown seeds.

I descended to the ground and continued with the fruit hunt. I saw a papaya tree with a long stick under it and used the stick to yank one of the fruits from its anchor on the trunk of the tree. I threw away the stick and attempted to catch the papaya before it could hit the ground but failed. The papaya fell with a big thud and broke into several dust-filled pieces, but I managed to scoop a handful of the scattered remnants for my efforts.

Looking around, I found my elder brother high up in the avocado tree. Danger was making his way up a guava tree, and Kobina Amuah was still searching for fruit among the fallen leaves. He took deliberate steps and bent down from time to time to pick up a fruit or two, bite into it and either eat it or throw the bitten pieces away. We climbed up and down the fruit trees and ate the ripe fruit we picked as we went through the orchard from one end toward the other.

"Listen! Listen to the hurried steps coming our way," Danger alerted as we approached the other end.

We took to our heels toward the nearest barbed wire with enough space from the ground for us to crawl through. We hurriedly let go of the temporary sacks we had made and their contents, threw away the fruits in our hands, and trouped out of the fruit orchard with military alacrity. Kobina Amuah got stuck under the barbed wire like a fly in oil. He successfully freed himself after a few attempts and ran away with all speed. But then, who would not? Not I. To begin with, I did not want to partake in the looting and, now that it was done, I certainly did not want to be caught and expose my identity. I wanted to remain as anonymous as I was to the fruit trees. Most of all, I wanted to protect my family's reputation and preserve my freedom to roam the fields in search of adventure and new experiences.

We took cover in the middle of a nearby bushy ravine, looked back at the fruit orchard from this vantage point, and saw a short man limping towards the point of our exit. The lean, emaciated dog was wobbling behind him. The man and dog looked well matched and suited to each other. The man stooped and picked up what looked like a piece of torn cloth. Carefully folded the cloth, he put it in his pocket, and started limping back toward the house. We watched him disappear and emerged from our hiding place to look for a footpath that would lead us back home. Then, we picked our way through the tall grass and boulders until we found footprints that seemed to belong to a dog.

"Let's follow it," I urged, not knowing where it would lead.

The group followed my lead, possibly to make me feel like part of the team. Luckily, it led to an unpaved road that wound down a hill. We walked in the large dry ditch for runoff water from the street but ran for cover when we heard pedestrian footsteps. We stayed in this watchful mode until the road became flat and one with the grassland and bent away to take a downhill slope. A distant cock-doodle-do that was echoed by closer one told us we were at the edge of town.

We looked at the length of our shadows and decided it was close to five p.m. We said our goodbyes and promised to meet again the next day.

"You are in early," said Grandma as we entered the compound. "And how was your day?" she inquired.

Kwesi responded to her question while I looked on. Grandma noted my silence and wanted to know if I had something to say.

"What is going on with you?" she started. "You are so quiet. Do you have something to add to what your brother is saying?"

"No, not at all," I responded rather pusillanimously, and added, "I think he has pretty much covered our activities for the day." The truth of the matter: I did not feel like talking about the day's adventures for fear of jinxing our good luck.

We had our dinner, our baths, and went to bed early that day. Grandma went through her rituals with the ewer and the mosquito netting. She lowered the wick in the lantern to dim the light and coiled into a position to sleep. I thought how lonely she must feel.

I covered my head and lay down to reflect on the things we had done that day. For an unknown reason, I felt sad and guilty when I came to that part about plucking the cherimoya. My conscience told me that I had degenerated from an unwilling, unwitting prankster into a full-fledged crook. It dawned on me that it was one thing to pick up fruit that had fallen and would rot anyway, and another to pick one from its tree without permission or giving the first rights to its rightful owner. I debated the concatenation of unplanned events that cascaded to transform me from an innocent child into a bandit and wondered how many of my actions emanated from volition and how many were induced by peer pressure. I could not come up with a suitable formula to apportion blame. I concluded that I was not coerced into participating in the looting. Hence, the blame lay squarely on my shoulders. I knelt down on my bed and covered my body with my sleeping cloth to pray for forgiveness. I asked God to consider my youth and inexperience in ranking my sin and assessing punishment. I told God I was not a common criminal and had not killed anybody in my life. Therefore, my sin was not venal and asked God to be merciful. "I am a coward who wanted to belong," I prayed. "Forgive me my sins, oh God. You know my heart and know I would not hurt a fly or a bird except to eat them to nourish my body. You have given us humans dominion over all things including the fruit in Mr. Minoo's orchard and given him the wisdom to plant and care for those fruits as You have given us the vision and appetite to eat them to nourish our bodies for Your glory. God, You are the only one who knows and truly understands that. Neither Mr. Minoo nor any of Your children can take any fruit as a possession to the grave, nor can I, so forgive me for plundering the fruit and bless me as I grow to be a testament of Your will and creation. Amen."

I felt relieved after the prayer, lay down on my reed mat, and slept like a log.

Chapter 6

I woke up the next morning elated to be alive. I did not pass on to purgatory for rehabilitation and preparation for final rest in Heaven nor to the den of the damned during my sleep. The Creator had overlooked my sin and extended my lease on life to enjoy all the wonderful things the world had to offer: the good and the bad: the beautiful and the ugly: the sweet and the sour. And I was going to bask in the bounty of the Creator.

I began the next phase of my journey by strutting to the toilet to do my ablutions. I bathed as expected and ardently gorged on Grandma's breakfast of porridge and fruits to fill the stomach vacuum the excessive excretion had created. My brother Kwesi and I kissed Grandma goodbye on her cheeks and left home to link up with our friends at Ayah's market stall to map out another day of adventure and fun-filled activities.

The walk from our home to Ayah's stall was filled with a fare of the usual marketers, roaming goats, sheep and a throng of people going about their daily affairs. The light blue sky was cloudless, but the rising sun was lukewarm against a backdrop of the cool breeze from the ocean. The air of the marketers reeked of sweat. We passed a pair of haggard beggars. One of the beggars was a frail, elderly man in a dirty brown smock with a long and unkempt gray goatee in his early forties sitting on a small, thin reed mat close to the entrance to the market. His face was weather-beaten: his forehead deeply lined; his cheeks prematurely wrinkled. He had a small straw basket in front of him for people to drop alms into. Otherwise, he was oblivious to the throng of passers-by. The other one, a barefooted, lanky little girl in a dingy, oversized brown chemise, who appeared to be about six or seven years old, moved nimbly among the milling crowd accosting passers-by for alms. She continually adjusted her chemise and held it from falling off her. We eased by the two beggars without incident and soon arrived at Ayah's stall.

For the second time, Kobina Amuah and Danger had not made it to the market so Ayah invited us to take a pair of stools in her stall to wait for them, while she attended to a customer.

"I hope they come soon," Ayah said after completing the sale.

"We hope so too. We need them here to plan our day," Kwesi remarked anxiously.

Indeed, Kwesi had lots of ideas that either violated social norms when acted on, or assigned us to the ranks of petty criminals and chiefdom of unscrupulous urchins. I began to be afraid that sooner or later our evil acts would catch up with us; someone would catch us in the commission of a crime and either report us to our folks or make a citizen's arrest and march us to the police station for the law to deal with. I strongly believed that we needed a drastic change in our behavior to stay out of jail and blow a whiff of our scandalous actions through town. We had a social duty to obey the law and moral obligation to respect people's rights to live in peace and enjoy their property as they saw fit.

As these thoughts raced through my mind, Kobina Amuah arrived at the stall. He was wearing a loose pair of purple pantaloons and an oversized khaki shirt that looked like a hand-me-down from an older relative or a cheap buy from one of several used clothing displayed on counters at the market. He looked sullen and held a bulky jute bag that dangled and clanged on his back in lockstep with his movements and again when he changed the hold from one hand to another. He grimaced and looked down with a sense of shame.

"What is the matter?" Kwesi anxiously inquired.

"Nothing," he limply replied.

"Really?" I continued with a sense of disbelief as I looked at the pitiful figure of a friend who, I believed ,was invulnerable.

"Yes, really," he denied.

"You must tell us if something is the matter," urged Danger.

"And why should I?" Kobina Amuah responded wearily.

"Because we are your friends," I replied.

"Well," he started in a low voice, piteously looked at me, and continued, "I will if I must. But you must promise not to tell another soul as long as you live," he pleaded.

The echo of Kobina Amuah's request for secrecy on what he was about to share pitted two conflicting thoughts in my mind: my obligation to respect, keep, and protect his personal safety pitted against my commitment for candor and personal integrity in my interactions with my "extended" family. I could not reconcile the two commitments for openness and secrecy. Indeed, my commitment to a friend in need of support and understanding was as important to me as my need to maintain open and honest communication with my parents and Grandma Elizabeth. But my scant religious understanding and a search of my partially-developed sense of identity provided a poor compass for solving the moral dilemma that confronted me. I gave up the struggle and hesitantly promised I would not betray his trust. I crossed by heart, separated my right first finger from the second, whipped the separated fingers to the upper right portion of my chest, and said, "Scout's honor," to affirm my promise. The rest of the gang followed suit with the sign which became our secret code for keeping promises. I looked at Kobina Amuah and asked him, in encouraging tones, to tell us what was on his mind. Kobina Amuah sighed, took a deep breath, and laconically started to explain.

"Well," Kobina Amuah pursed his lips as if he were ready to whistle, but did not, gave a strange half-laugh and continued, "You see, when I woke up this morning, my Mom was upset with me for ripping her cloth. While she was expressing her disappointment over the tear, the Old Fox, Mr. Minoo, walked into our home with the torn piece of cloth that had been caught in the barbed wire as we made our escape. He pulled the torn cloth out of the left pocket of his shorts and showed it to Mom with the flair of a circus performer.

'Well, Mrs. Abena Emifa, I am bringing this torn piece of cloth to you because I remember seeing your boy walking with you and wearing something similar at the market sometime ago.'

'Yes indeed, it belongs to my boy. 'In fact,' Mom continued, 'I was just talking to him about it when you arrived.'

"Mr. Minoo narrated the incident in his orchard and how we escaped by crawling under the barbed wire in his old and raspy stentorian voice. Mom patiently listened to him vent his anger and apologized for our shenanigans and promised to make sure we did not go uninvited to his orchard again. She ended with the remark, 'I can't fathom what goes on in the heads of our youngsters. They are not as concerned about other people's property and respect for the law as we when we were younger. I do not like to hear such unpleasant reports floating around my neighborhood about any child, least of all my own. I will knock some sense into him and make sure he never repeats the offence.'

"Mr. Minoo sensed the palpable anger in Mom's voice and affirmed his observation saying, 'I see you are as concerned and committed to the right moral development of our children as I am. I am confident that in working with you and like-minded parents and concerned citizens in this town, we could influence these kids to abandon their wicked, irresponsible ways and grow up to be useful and law abiding citizens. In fact, I am hopeful that they will grow up to be the kind of citizens who will cherish the good values we imbue and transmit them to their children.' Mr. Minoo paused for acknowledgement, but my Mom did not offer any.

"Mr. Minoo inferred from the silence that Mom did not want to discuss the matter any further, so, he began to ask the usual socially acceptable questions about our family and the goings-on with Mom's sister Auntie Adoma Suma and her children. He particularly wanted to know how my

Auntie Adoma Suma's oldest child, Mona, who is a third year university student, was doing. My mother nonchalantly responded that she was doing just fine. Mr. Minoo made his bow to end his report and left.

"Hardly had the Old Fox made his exit when Mom locked the compound gate and changed her mildly pleasant expression, reserved for visitors, to deep anger and fury. She raised her voice about two octaves higher, ranted and stamped her bare feet in the dusty compound to register her displeasure while repeating some of Mr. Minoo's incendiary phrases, "You snuck your way into his orchard, thinking no one was home and you ransacked the fallen fruit without permission. Then, you ate what you could and threw away what you did not want and ran away like a well-schooled coward when the owner showed up. You and your friends are unprincipled, despicable, shameless thieves." She said as she raised her voice to a fever pitch. And as if the talk-down was not enough, she untied a dried vine holding together a load of firewood resting close to the kitchen wall, stretched it to full wobbly length and belted my buttocks, back, and anywhere else her raging, undirected vine could land on my body.

"'I do not want you to set foot in that man's orchard ever again!' She screamed between lashes. 'I will personally march you to the authorities if you do. I do not know what goes on in the heads of you young people. You do not want to get a decent job or put in a fair day's work when you are offered a job. Decent, honest work is honorable. Nobody dies putting in a fair day's work for a fair day's wage. Hard work is respectable and ennobling. Do something productive with your hands and stay away from trouble because trouble, simply put, is social cancer. It destroys the family it touches with a bitter payoff. It decays every social norm and cherished value it touches. It maims and destroys families, and I am not going to sit idly by while you destroy this family with your wanton, reckless, crassly irresponsible and anti-social acts.'"

"Why didn't you run away?" Inquired Kwesi, in elevated tones, "I would have."

"That is easier said than done. I couldn't. Remember the compound door was locked. Besides, she got angrier, chased after me, and lashed me more intensely when she caught up with me. Above all, there was nobody at home to persuade her to see the situation differently or to intercede for mercy. To her, I had committed an unpardonable sin and brought shame and dishonor to the family and she was determined to beat me back onto the straight and narrow path. After a few fits and starts, I uttered a squeal of pain and stopped groaning altogether. I concluded it was easier to stand still and stoically take the beating than to attempt a futile escape. For that reason, I am bruised and sore all over. I feel as hot to the touch as when I came down with malaria some time ago. Except that this time, I was beaten into feverish submission by a twisted, dried vine instead of a band of bloodsucking anopheles mosquitoes with the sole mission of spreading unease," Kobina Amuah concluded and lifted his head which was mostly downcast during the narration.

I was saddened to see Kobina Amuah stand with his head down, dispirited and full of self-doubt, like a steamed spinach leaf. I could not help but contrast his current status with the confidence he exuded at the start of our summer holidays when he was vibrant and full of energy, and I wanted to soothe him, and make him feel better – like his old self. I lifted my arms and leaned forward to hug him but an unidentified force pulled me back so I ended up with an empathetic look into his eyes as I watched him go through the pain and anguish. There was a moment of silence after his account as we searched for words to console our bruised comrade.

Meanwhile, I pondered the rationale parents, loved ones, and significant grown-ups use to justify beating children in the name of "love" and "appropriate social behavior." I wondered whether all the beating was truly done to absolve and redeem heathenish children from evil or to soothe parents' anger and reassert their power over helpless children who look up to them as role models and for emotional sustenance. I also thought about how these people could claim to want children to grow up to love their neighbors and live in peace with the world when they do not negotiate through love, but use violence to resolve simple perceptual or value differences and wondered whether grace and forbearance could coexist with evil and dishonor in the same person.

Then I pondered the unsavory rationale that powerful countries use to justify war as an instrument of peace to spread political ideology or control commerce. I simply could not understand why countries and their leaders kill, maim, and exploit innocent people and end wars by suing for peace. In time, I concluded, the Creator is the only one who knows the hearts of all men. He is the only one who can heal hurt minds and souls, and soothe the pain of injured children and swage spiritual poverty among adults. The Creator has a way of revealing all truths, even to the unborn. My aim was just to live life fully and celebrate each person's life in my own.

"So, what are we going to do?" I inquired of the gang.

"So, what shall we do?" mimicked Danger.

Suddenly, Kobina Amuah, shrugged his shoulders, vigorously clapped his hands and snapped out of his self-pity. "We only live once," he passionately proclaimed and added, "Yes, we will not go to that man's orchard, but there are other things that are equally exciting to do. Summer is here and absolutely nobody is going to douse our spirits and deny us fun and adventure. For starters, you can help me lay these red crab traps."

"What traps?" I inquired apprehensively.

"The ones on my shoulder," Kobina Amuah replied.

"Can I see them?" I asked.

"Yes, but only after we arrive at the crabs' habitat." "Come on fellows, follow me!" he yelled!

The fun of the holidays was resumed on that call. We hurried toward the habitat of the crabs at a lagoon on the outskirts of town stopping to catch our breath from the brisk pace. A gentle sea breeze wafted in from the Atlantic and restored us. We wound our journey around the corner to a slew of deserted houses and came upon two teenage girls in see-through muslin chemises, playing hopscotch close to one of the crumbling houses. We stopped to watch the girls jump around the boxes that had been claimed by the other competitor. Kobina Amuah drew our attention to the shorter of the two, whose breasts bobbed up and down like rolling tennis balls with nipples when she jumped from one hopscotch box to the next. Smallpox scars marked her face, legs, and arms. She was not a raving beauty but voluptuously attractive. She appeared to be well mannered. The other girl was tall, awkwardly clumsy with a distended stomach and a gaunt face common of kwashiorkor sufferers. Her skinny, long legs wobbled slightly when she skipped the hopscotch boxes.

A stray, emaciated dog of unspecified breed with a brown coat sprang from the surrounding tuft of grass and started yapping fiercely at us as if to tell us it was time for us to get going. A thick blue-black smoke rose from the gap between the roof and the wall of one of the hovels to tell us the air would soon be fouled with putrid smoke.

"Let's go. We need to be on the way if we want to be back by sunset," Danger beckoned as he attempted to refocus our attention to the task at hand.

"Let's go!" Kobina Amuah echoed with a sense of urgency.

We searched for a pathway that led from the hovel to the edge of the lagoon and found one. On arrival, I noticed that the lagoon was big and tranquil: mosquito larvae wiggled in the ford; the debris of twigs and weeds the rippling waves had washed stood like pikes in its dark gray shore; deep, blue-black lagoon crabs with gray legs and light blue and white claws emerged from their holes in watchful poses. They scuttled from side to side and retreated. Scores of rotting and hollow lagoon crab shells, lagoon snail shells, broken shellfish shells, and skeletal remains of tilapias littered the lagoon's beach. There were a few dead tilapias floating –belly up, on the lagoon. The variety of skeletal remains and empty shells caused me to wonder whether the dead lagoon crabs and shellfish came to such a fate as part of nature's cycle of death and renewal or were victims of man-made ecological neglect.

"Stop!" Kobina Amuah ordered as we reached the habitat of the red crabs in the bordering bog and vegetation.

"Look," he anxiously pointed. We stopped to find out what was riling him only to find a big red crab wandering away from its hole.

"Keep quiet!" he commanded in a voice that reminded me of a visit to hallowed ground where signs of "Let the dead rest in peace," floated in the tranquil air.

Keeping quiet and still, we watched him gingerly set down the jute sack on the ground. He opened the bag and emptied several red-crab trap boxes into a heap. I picked out two of the boxes, scrutinized them, and returned them to the heap.

"Look, look at the leveret," Danger exclaimed. "Look at it bouncing up and down in the elephant grass strewed with shards of pottery."

"Let's catch it. It will taste good in somebody's soup," joined Kobina Amuah.

We ran helter-skelter to trap the young white rabbit, but it was much faster at evading capture than we were at trapping him. It made a leap over Kwesi's body as he lay flat on the grass after his futile attempt to grab it and bolted into its burrow before we could reach it.

We teased each other about how the small, white, furry-coat rabbit outfoxed three clever boys.

"You were running like a chicken," Danger said as he hilariously pointed his finger at me and giggled.

"No, I wasn't," I protested.

"Yes, you were," Kwesi joined the teasing.

"And you were running like a turkey," Kobina Amuah said between laughter and a giggle as he looked in the direction of Kwesi.

"And so were you," Kwesi replied in kind.

"Let's get to work." Danger insisted after a few laughs.

We returned to the heap of crab traps to start laying them at the entry to their holes.

"How does it work?" I asked Kobina Amuah as we began to ready ourselves to lay the traps. He proceeded to give me a long explanation of its historical origins and how it worked. I didn't care for the historical nitty-gritty of the crab-trap. Despite my reticence, I recalled him saying that some of the boxes were U-shaped aluminum with wooden trap doors while others were totally constructed of wood. The traps measured about five inches long, three inches wide, and four inches deep and had small holes drilled close to the base of the back wooden frames. Either hard wood or a small nail was inserted into the hole and a piece of cassava attached at the end of the nail that entered the chamber of the box trap. The purpose of the cassava was to lure the red crab into the trap. A strip of inner tube rubber was attached at appropriate tensile strength from a nail in front of the wooden trap door to the protruding nail in the back of the frame. The set trap was placed a few inches away from the crab's hole and would slam shut when the crab entered the chamber and attempted to nibble or pull the cassava away from the nail inserted in the hardwood.

Kobina Amuah picked out the crab traps one at a time, opened the chamber doors, and pushed the cassava pieces into the holder. He pulled the inner tube rubber attached to the crab-trap door to set the trap, and distributed the readied crab-traps two at a time to us to search for crab holes, and gingerly place the open crab-trap with the chamber facing the entrance to the crab holes. Danger quickly caught on to the art and became proficient at identifying red crab burrows. Kwesi and I struggled with the idea until well into the project, and even after we had the hang of it, we still stumbled from time to time with the process. After awhile, I lost interest in my assigned task and began to watch the easy approach of our two country friends at the task I couldn't perform equally well because of a lack of opportunity.

"There is no crab living in that hole," said Kobina Amuah, as he observed me placing a readied crab trap close to a dry mound of untraveled in front of an apparently empty hole.

"Let me have it!" Kobina Amuah commanded, as he snatched one of the crab-traps from my hand and freed me to search for more promising holes. I found one, soon enough, and laid the other crab-trap I still had in my hand under his watchful guidance.

In my zest to carefully lay the crab-traps, I lost track of what the other boys were doing. I picked a twig and pricked open an ant mound and caused its residing Black ants to scramble out of their colony in all directions. I jumped to avoid their scramble and ended up slipping on the wet ground. Landing on all fours in a puddle of muddy water, I got up, looked around for any onlookers, and straightened my shorts, which were supple from the mixture of mud water and shredded green grass. I sat down in the soft green grass to recover from the incident and lazily picked up a dry, thick thistle resting nearby to bore a hole into the ground to pass time. A centipede happened to be crawling close at the spot I dug. I held on to one end of the thistle and used the other end to sever the worm into two parts. Then I watched the severed halves wiggle in the mud and gradually give up the ghost, and as if that was not enough to vent my hurt, I snatched an insect that was crawling on a leaf and methodically tore it apart wing by wing and leg by leg until it stopped moving.

I was engaged in the cruel decapitation when I heard a scream from a few yards away. I looked around and found Danger in the tufts of grass. I dropped the remainder of the decapitated insect I was holding and threaded my way through the swampland of broken twigs, hanging boughs, assorted tropical centipedes and other crawling insects to see what was troubling him. Kobina Amuah and Kwesi finished setting the traps they were holding and picked their way to aid our fallen comrade.

Danger was holding his left knee and reeling in pain. "Help! Help, somebody," he yelled mournfully.

Kobina Amuah and my elder brother knelt down beside him and asked in unison: "What is the matter?" with a ting of concern in their voice.

"It's my knee, my left knee," he replied between sobs. "Feel it, feel it!" he hysterically commanded, but I was too squeamish to touch it. "It hurts very badly," he moaned. "And now my whole day is ruined," he said with a sense of resignation.

Kobina Amuah bravely held Danger's left knee in the palm of both hands. He turned it around a couple of times from left to right, then right to left, and stopped and declared with pseudo-physician temperance, "He has no broken bones."

"Fetch me some shrubs," Kobina Amuah commanded.

My brother and I scrambled up and down the swampland and scrounged for vines, which he instantly used to bind Danger's left knee.

"Just stay there and rest," my brother Kwesi insisted.

The rest of us continued to scavenge the habitat for signs of crab burrows to set crab-traps after Danger calmed down from expressing his anguish. We gave each other a friendly slap on the back for a job well done after we were through. Kobina Amuah and Kwesi helped Danger to his feet for the homebound journey and offered to help him walk, but just a few yards into the journey he let go of their helping hands with the defiant words, "I want to walk by myself."

So, they let go of him, but the freeing of their hands did not speed up our progress because Danger interrupted our voyage with an unexpected request for support to ease the pressure and pain on his injured left knee. Once again Kobina Amuah and my elder brother went to his rescue. This slowed us down and tampered our enthusiasm. As a result, we were circumspect, subdued, and not as animated on our homebound voyage as we were on our outbound one.

We continued in this quite mood until we were reasonably far away from the crab habitat. Then, Kobina Amuah convincingly declared, "We will have a bumper red crab harvest. Just wait and see!"

We wearily trudged on and breathed a collective sigh of relief when we arrived at the edge of town and saw the townsfolk going about their early evening activities. We gave a social pat on each other's back to denote the end of the gang's adventure day and our commitment to meet again the next day.

"See you tomorrow," Kobina Amuah declared.

"See, you." Danger echoed as he walked away in a pathetic air of the disabled.

Kwesi and I hurried on after the goodbye and arrived at home just as the sun was dipping at the horizon to end its trip across the sky in that corner of the Earth where we dwelt.

The home looked empty and deserted like a ghost town when we arrived. So, Kwesi cried out: "Anybody home?" as we entered the compound.

Grandma's New Hampshire hen crackled a frightened response.

"Is anybody home?" I repeated.

The maid emerged from the shadows of the kitchen.

"Where is Grandma? Kwesi asked.

"She is not at home," she replied.

"We can see that," Kwesi responded with a bite of sarcasm.

"Did she tell you where she was going?" I continued with my line of inquiry.

"No," responded the maid.

"Do you think she will be back soon? I asked.

The maid did not know, nor did she have an idea when Grandmother would return. She informed us that our dinner of "*kotomble*" --a local stew made of boiled and slightly mashed cocoyam leaves, ground cayenne pepper, agushi, ginger, and mackerel in palm nut oil served over boiled unripe plantains and yams was ready. As Grandma was not at home, we took liberties and reversed the sequence of rituals leading to bed. We dined first and followed it with bathing instead of the other way around.

After that, we ventured outdoors to the open-air night market at a point where four dusty and unpaved roads met close to Grandma's home. A lamplighter stopped at the lamppost, switched on the lone fluorescent light that stood in one of the corners where four roads met and walked on with his long lighter pole in his left hand. We passed the town's only church, a nineteenth-century stone building with stained glass angels and a large wood crucifix atop its steeple. The church belonged to the Methodists.

Assorted short order cooks cooked ready-to-eat local foods, and fruit vendors were strategically positioned around the lamppost. Other cooked food and vegetable vendors that were positioned further away from the lamppost used the yellow flames of kerosene wicker lamps to identify their position and attract traffic. The air was filled with vendors avidly avowing quality of the wares they were selling in melodious voices.

As we threaded our way through the throng of marketers, we surveyed several ken-key and fish vendors, cooked rice and bean vendors, fruit vendors, and roasted plantain and groundnut vendors. I observed as a young woman in her twenties, a roasted plantain and peanut vendor, used the upper part of her two piece cloth to strap her baby to her back right under the lamppost. She shook her torso to adjust the baby's head on her back and resumed hawking her ware.

Farther away from the illumination of the lamppost, a woman in her mid-thirties who was selling assorted fried fish, anchovies, shrimp, octopus, eel, herring, red snapper, flounder, mackerel, and tilapia, repeated the same baby-carrying ritual. She had some of the same species of fried fish displayed on a large wooden tray of about twenty-four inches in diameter by size and price. Another female in her late teens was busy shaving off orange rind from a deep tray full of grapefruits, oranges, and tangerines.

A medium-built man of average height and weight, wearing a cloth and a pair of black rubber sandals made of car tire, stopped at the orange stand to buy an orange. He picked out an orange and gave it to the orange vendor to shave off the rind and ready it for him to eat. The vendor set aside a partially shaved orange she had on a cloth in her hand, and shaved the rind off the orange the man had selected. After shaving off the rind, she used the tip of her shaving knife to pierce and carve out a circle at the top of the orange and handed it to the man for payment. The man paid for it and melted away into the milling nighttime marketers, while merrily squeezing and sucking juice of the orange. One of the vendors was hawking "*kelewele*,' a ripe plantain that is sliced and seasoned in a mixture of ground ginger, cayenne pepper, and other spices and fried in palm kernel oil.

"Let's go and buy some," I urged.

"I don't have the money," Kwesi replied curtly, "besides Grandma has asked us not to buy such things."

I had no rejoinder to his response. So we continued walking with Kwesi, looking at things that interested him, and I doing the same.

Suddenly, a truck loaded with sugarcane, laboring up a hill to the market on the plateau, came to view. A mob of children was trying desperately to pull out sugarcane from the bed of the tired truck. Halfway up the hill, the truck sputtered, puffed and pulled off the road to a halt after a final gasp for energy. The children who were trying desperately to pull sugarcane off the truck melted into the encircling darkness that enveloped the town.

Suddenly, a sonorous operatic voice rang from afar and broke through the humming voices of the market: *"Mbor oshew nyio,"* which translates to, "Here is your warm, ready-to-eat ken-key." I turned in the direction of the voice for the source of the open-air announcement, but before I could set eyes on the source of the voice, the person behind it vanished into the cluster of thatch roofed houses like an apparition.

I continued to observe the goings-on and noted that the crowd was thinning out as the night got older. The stallholders began to pack up for the night. Kwesi tapped the hump of my left shoulder and signaled it was time to return home.

"Let's beat Grandma home," he said.

"Yes, indeed," I agreed as I wanted to remain in Grandma's good graces.

We left the market on that sneak preview for home and arrived before Grandma made it back. We gave a high five to each other and retired to bed without eating dinner. Looking back, my only regret is that I was unable to join the children welcoming the sugarcane truck or witness how the night looked after it closed. Perhaps there will be other chances, but I know full well that opportunities, like the clouds, do not repeat the same constellation.

Chapter 7

I found myself alone on the reed mat without a sign of either my elder brother or Grandma Elizabeth when I woke up. I wrapped myself in the solitude of the moment and let my mind drift freely from one thing to another until it settled on the silhouette of a moving woman I saw in my dream. I wondered whether that image stemmed from my recollection of my Grandma undressing in the wee hours of the morning or an impregnated phantom of my untamed imagination. I was just at the point of deciding how to approach Grandma with my conundrum when Kwesi barged into the bedroom and demanded, "Wake up, you lazy bum!"

I was not lazy and I was not a bum, but I did not want to argue the point so I tepidly responded, "I am wide awake."

I rubbed both eyes with the back of my right index finger, stretched my body, and slowly got out of bed. I folded the reed mat, placed it in the corner where we have been housing it during the day, and hurried downstairs to fetch a palm leaf stem broom from a corner of the kitchen to begin my morning chores.

I plied the broom open from the top where it was tightly bound with a twine to enlarge its base for sweeping. I swept the part of the compound that Grandma had assigned to me. I debated the virtues of the exercise when the end result was for the wind to blow over the tidy broomstick marks I had methodically left behind as I swept. Despite this misgiving, I completed the job partly out of respect for Grandma, and partly to honor the dignity of work.

While I continued with the work at hand, Kwesi came out of nowhere and impatiently implored me hurry up. "Get on with it slow poke, we have got to get ready for church."

I ignored his command and continued sweeping at the same easy pace to the very end.

I ate breakfast after completing the chore and thought about my ambivalence about church between mouthfuls. I concluded that, although I liked going to church and singing with the congregation for its therapeutic benefits, I resented the plethora of pretentiously polite interactions and the orderliness of worship rituals that were somber, stiff, and uninspiring. Above all, going to church while on vacation did not fit in with my idea of fun, which consisted of being on the open prairie, smelling the fresh air of the countryside, and listening to chirping birds and rustling leaves and the whispering wind. In addition, I saw staying away from church as my quiet way of rebelling against Grandma's notion of the church as a treasure-trove of truth and virtues. I did not want to hold the church in as high esteem as Grandma did but was afraid and too timid to air my true feelings to her. For starters, my life experience had not taught me that the church's moral teachings had positively impacted social morality. The religiously faithful, I found, behaved as if God had anointed them to represent His views on earth. They claim to know God's mind and the religious significance of world events and use their pantheistic frame of thinking to rank evil as venal, non-venal, and anything in between. To me, evil is simply evil; and sin is sin whether conceived and perpetrated by an individual or a mass of people in the name of an ill-defined altruistic good.

Evildoers and sinful people affect their victims in much the same way as large elephants do to the grass they crumble and trample during fights—both groups diminish the soul's harmonious relationship with the spirit and the world and demonstrate this bias with as much vim and venom as religious bigots' intolerance for Philistines. Evildoers and cohorts also tarnish and torment in much the same way as our misdeeds sentence us to a certainty of death that does not consider our good or evil deeds, reactions, or inactions. It is a certainty that dances to its own drums and does not heed solicited or unsolicited supplication for salvation. As planted seeds mature, bear fruit, and die, so do infants ready themselves for growth, maturation, and death. From my way of thinking, adults are nothing less than spent spindles teetering on a spool waiting to be felled at the dawn of death. I concluded that people acted more out of selfish motives than to fulfill a deeply held conviction, accede to some social dogma, or realize an altruistic goal.

Notwithstanding my ambivalence about religion and attending dogma, I was convinced that I had to go to church and behave like a good boy if I wanted to remain in Grandma's good graces, so I gulped down my breakfast, washed my porridge bowl, and turned it to drip off on the small soft wood table Grandma used when she dinned alone. I rushed upstairs to join my elder brother and Grandma, who were getting ready for church.

When I arrived, my elder brother was helping Grandma unload the stack of steel trunks containing scores of folded two–piece pairs of cloth and their complementary shoulder covers. As she went through the steel trunks, opening and closing them one at a time, I noted that she had starched, ironed, folded, and neatly arranged the clothing in layers and generously sprinkled camphor balls between the layers to protect them from molding or cockroach and moth infestations. She identified the clothing as she went through them, layer by layer, one trunk at a time. *Obra ye ko,* which means, "Life is full of struggles." *Obra nye woara abo,* which means, "Life is what you make of it." *Nsu annso eguar a oso nom,* which means, "If the quantity of water you have is inadequate to use in having a bath, it would at least be adequate for drinking." *Se aso awar a toto wo mperetse,* which means, "If you believe you are ready for marriage, then you have to buy your dishes to affirm that readiness." *Ehu mbobor fir nyame,* which means, "Grace is a gift from God." *Se ankaka mmpapa a nnkye mmpapa annnye krede,* which mean, "Let sleeping dogs lie." "*Awar nntse de nkatsi,*" which mean, "Marriage is not like a peanut whose husk you can crack, peel off the skin, and bite before deciding to chew or not." *Ma aye koom mo ro hwe nyame,* which mean, "I am patiently waiting on the Lord's directive." *Se eto okusinam a na wo dzi bo nam fir wo,* which means, "Your credit line is increased when you honor the obligations you assume for a low credit line." *Akyer Akyer biara wo naafi,* which means, "In the end, patience triumphs." Grandma debated which cloth to wear and settled on "I am patiently waiting on the Lord's directive."

"What do you do with all these clothes?" I asked as she went through the clothing from one trunk to the next.

"I wear them."

"But you cannot possibly wear all of them at once," I said quizzically.

"You are right, I can't. But I need them for special occasions," agreed Grandma, who continued, "Let me explain things this way. You see, in our culture, as in other cultures and customs, clothing is used as one of several social markers. That is why you generally see the rich and members of the royal families wearing the expensive Kente cloth on special occasions. The cloth visibly sets them apart by underscoring their social status and financial wherewithal from pretenders and the underclass.

"Our cultural heritage reveres age even when it is as slight as the difference in time of birth between twins born on the same day. This reverence and respect, which is not open ended, is based on the notion that, as a person grows up, he or she is exposed to more life experiences, matures by virtue of the exposure, and gains emotional insight and intellectual temperance. The old return the social acclaim by sharing their views and providing free counsel to the wider community on all aspects of life. They also share their collective experience to guide the young and mediate family squabbles and marital problems. Our elders tell stories and use several cultural constructs and rituals to boost their social position, set the tone, and manage the atmospherics for dispensing advice and giving counsel to the youth. The elderly lose respect and goodwill when there is social dissonance between their capacities to fulfill this role and cultural expectation. The wider society reduces its interactions with them and treats them with either benign neglect or total indifference. I entreat you to live within the norms of our cultural values and match your words with deeds if you want to avoid this social scourge. Live honorably and in dignity with those around you and have self-control and ample patience with all people, no matter their differences or stations in life. Keep your hands behind your back when talking to grown-ups, respond respectfully to your elders, and be a good moral example to the children around you.

Above all, point to the village where your parents come from, especially your mothers with your right finder, which is presumed to be clean, and not your left, which you are taught to use in cleaning after yourself. To do otherwise is to crassly violate a cultural taboo and disrespect your mother."

"Why should using my right or left fingers matter?" Kwesi impertinently asked.

"Because our culture considers mothers as 'special nurturers,'" Grandma answered derisively.

"And how about fathers?" I asked in an attempt to equal the plane of respect for mothers and fathers.

"Our culture does not presume fathers to be nurturers. You see," she continued, "the word we use to describe mother is *ena*. And when we use the phrase *oye na*, we literally mean that whatever we are talking about is rare. To use the phrase '*mena*' when talking about our mothers means, 'My rare and precious one.' We use the word *egya* to describe our fathers. The word is derived from *ogya*, which means fire. Our custom expects fathers to be strict disciplinarians and fiery. Children are expected to run to their mothers and not their fathers for nurturing. They are expected to respect both parents, but adore mothers because of the nurturing you receive from them. Therefore, pointing to your mother's village with the same hand you use to clean yourself is rude, and culturally discouraged."

Grandma told us that she wore either *Obra ye ko, Obra nye woara abo,* or *Se ankaka mmpapa a nnkye mmpapa annnye krede* when talking to wayward children whose parents brought them to her for counseling. She said, "I use the names of either cloth, depending on which one I am wearing, to set the tone for the conversations. I patiently listen to the children take on the 'infraction' under discussion and counsel them as appropriate.

"I use my life experiences and the wisdoms passed down to me from my forefathers to guide and influence the young ones in trouble. Some children, who come to see me, deny their part in deeds and mistakenly believe that most, if not all, adults are dumb, ignorantly stupid, and incapable of discerning truth from fiction or vice versa. They believe they have as much monopoly on virtue as adults do on stupidity. Children and often grownups are too mired in their pain to realize that the first steps to true healing start with the acceptance of their roles for their conditions. Adults, they mistakenly believe, are uneducated in the nuances of life. Somehow they assume that adults skipped adolescence and reached adulthood without experiencing the challenges they face. Consequently, they lie or take undue liberties with the truth and use trickery or subterfuge when talking to adults about issues. Interestingly, they turn to the same 'dumb' adults for refuge and explanation when faced with new or unexpected phenomenon.

"I wear the cloth to remind these wayward children that nothing happens in a vacuum. They are part and parcel of whatever happens to them. In that vein, I ruefully remind them to identify and accept the parts they play in what happens to them. At the end of the sessions, I tie a penny in a corner of a kerchief and return the kerchief with the penny to them. Then, I ask the children to untie and narrate what happened at the session to their parents when they arrive back at their homes, thus, jogging their memories on what led to the tying of the knot in the first place.

"I wear *Se eto okusinama nna wo dzi bo nam fir wo* when I am talking to financial leeches. Sooner or later, dead beats who borrow money without intending to repay their debts are found out and lose the honor and goodwill they enjoyed. They become pariahs whose social toxic odors precede them. Citizens make denigrating remarks and shamefully talk behind their backs when they depart from a gathering. I earnestly hope that neither of you is faced with the unpleasant prospect of choosing between your family's name and reputation or personal financial gain.

"I encourage you to strive for independence and self-sufficiency and promptly repay your debt with interest if it becomes necessary for you to borrow and be indebted. Heaven knows, you may need help from the lender at some future date. He or she will remember, and extend more credit to you. Your repayment of debts shows good faith, propriety, and recognition of kindness in time of need.

"Listen to me, my boys," Grandma said. "You listen to me," she anxiously repeated as we began to fidget, "I need to tell you this incident," she said with a voice of urgency.

"What incident? Kwesi inquired with a sense of curiosity.

"You see," started Grandma, "one day I was called to settle a marital dispute between the town's blacksmith, Kwesi Akobra, and his wife, Abena Abakan. I wore my *Awar nntse de nkatsi* to set the tone for the meeting and send a subtle message to the distressed couple that marriage is not like a peanut, which you can take out of its shell, bite into, and decide either to chew or spit out when you do not like the taste. It is a long time commitment and that is why we call it *awar*, which literally translates to mean, 'the unending committed relationship.' That is also why people like to know about the origin of families before marriages are consummated. Talking more of marriage, I would like you to bear this in mind to commit to a marriage only when you are sure your potential partner is equally committed to a matrimonial relationship. Never marry out of sympathy or to appease a nagging fiancée. A marriage premised on that proposition has shallow roots and will fall apart with the test of time like friable rock. You should not depend on your wife or vice versa, that marriage would be akin to a dead tree leaning against a live tree. The live tree will buckle under the stress of the dead tree and cause both trees to fall. Recognize and celebrate each other's uniqueness; be independent and interdependent; draw on each other's strengths; and support each other's foibles and frailties. A marriage built on love, trust, self-sufficiency, and healthy interdependence has a fairer chance for success than one that is not," concluded Grandma.

"And what should I do if the woman I marry is not good.... I mean, if she is cruel and inconsiderate or self-centered?" I inquired.

"You must identify something good in her and love that good. Over time, your love will grow to overcome her cruelty and inconsideration.

"And now let me share this story with you before I forget it," she continued. "You see, Kwesi Akobra met his bride at a park. The woman was beautiful and a stranger to the village. He was so taken in by her beauty that he did not spend enough time to know her family. They eloped and married in the capital city. After the marriage, he brought his young wife to our church for the minister's nuptial blessing. That could have been the end of the story, but it was not. The couple kept having children, one after the other. The children were beautiful, congenial, well behaved, served as good examples for the community, and were affectionately referred to as rabbits by townsfolk because of their close ages.

"One day, his wife killed him while he was asleep by savagely stabbing him. The police arrested the wife and prosecuted her for the crime. Unfortunately, she could not remember the grizzly incident or offer any defense. The judge, hearing the case, sentenced her to life in prison without the possibility of parole. Tragically, the children did not have any relatives in town and were left without family support when the incident occurred. They were left to fend for themselves until the deceased man's sister, who was at the brink of poverty from alcoholism, took them in. The church chipped in for their support. This is one of the reasons why I want you to know the family of the woman you want to marry, because when it is all said and done, we marry into families. We carry the genes that form our being, as well as the moral values and worldviews that are instilled into us. It is these attributes that largely help define who we are and guide us through life. It is also these attributes that influence the choices we make and how we relate to the world."

Grandma paused, looked over her cloths, vacillated between *Ehu mbobor fir nyame,* "Compassion is a gift from God," and *Ma aye koom mo ro hwe nyame,* "I am patiently awaiting the Lord's directive." She settled on the latter, which had an intricate background design of green grass, flowers, and black and white birds perched on twigs. Her pretext for her selection was that the cloth was more appropriate for the occasion since the worship program of the day had scheduled Christ's Singing Band to sing an anthem. I decried her process, which was similar to what my mother did at home when selecting something to wear. I wondered whether the Creator, who brought us naked into the world, cared what we wore to give thanks or beg for forgiveness and guidance.

Suddenly, I heard the pealing of the church bell summoning the faithful to commune and worship. I called it to the attention of my brother and Grandma.

"Let's get going. I want to be there on time," said Grandma in a hurried tone.

On hearing that, my brother and I rushed to ready ourselves for church. Kwesi oiled his body from a Vaseline jar and gave it to me to so the same. We combed our hair, put on the Sunday best we wore during our inbound journey, and descended the steps onto the sandy compound of the house. We looked at each other without saying a word and gave the solidarity sign to affirm our readiness to face the spiritual people of grandma's church, but deep down, I knew we were as good as any heathens you could find anywhere in Ghana or other parts of the world.

Grandma powdered her face and straightened her head kerchief and the lower portion of her cloth as well as her chemise and asked if she was presentable, to which we both nodded to affirm that was the case. She glanced at the stacked steel trunks of clothing and said, "We will restack them when we come back from church."

We descended the staircase on that note and made our way toward the gate to walk up the hill to church. I waved at the maid as we stepped out and muttered, "See you soon."

She waved back.

I took Grandma's right arm and Kwesi took the left as we walked to church. Grandma said "hello" to the some of the townsfolk as we made our way to church. When we arrived, she introduced us to some of the congregation and ushered us to the middle mahogany pew to sit down. She instructed us to observe the church decorum and left to join the members of Christ's Singing Band, most of whom were already seated to the left of the preacher's elevated podium, waiting for services to begin. I bumped Kwesi. "Hush," he said, putting his finger on his mouth. I turned my head and picked out Grandma as she maneuvered her way through the throng of congregants to join her group. I noted that group was similarly clad.

The church's organist was playing cantatas as background music to a drone of greetings and exchanges of goodwill among the congregants. Small groups made up of five or six members of the congregation, who were conversing in the narrow nave and around the pews, dispersed and took their seats in the pews, as if on cue. The drone of conversation subsided into silence and the church choristers, who were dressed in black robes, strolled in, led by their female members and singing a hymn. They took their seats to the right of the minister's podium. The lady choristers sat in the first rows and the men sat in the back rows. After they were seated, I surveyed the seating arrangement and compared it to Grandma's group and was astonished that Grandma's group did not have any males. I looked around the congregation to verify its mix and noted that the females outnumbered the males. This made me question if men and infants did not need the Creator as much as women did. It also made me ponder what people of other faiths were doing at that hour in their mosques, synagogues, temples, and houses of worship.

Meanwhile, the minister walked to the altar, raised his hands, and summoned the congregation to worship with the words, "Let us begin our worship with hymn number 365."

The organist played the first bars and phrases of the hymn. The choir stood up and started singing. The congregation got up from their seats and joined the choir. As the choir and congregation sang, I took a closer look at the minister and noted he was of medium build, weighed about one hundred sixty pounds, and was dressed in a black suit. His white stiff, cleric collar reminded me of the white feathers that go around the neck of the African pied-crow that dot the landscape and fly away when you get close. He sang along and motioned the congregation to sit when the song ended with an Amen. "You may be seated."

The minister called on an elderly man in his fifties, who was wearing a gray flannel suit and was sitting in the front pew, to come to the front to read the announcements for the week. The man got up and stood in front of the podium. Then he pulled a piece of paper from his trouser pocket and announced the upcoming activities for the church. He also gave a progress report of the church's expansion project and information about church members who were sick and in need of prayers before returning to his seat.

"Let us pray," said the minister, after the financial reports and the announcements were read.

Members of the congregation responded to this supplication by getting out of their seats. They turned around to face the back support of the seats they were sitting in and knelt on the footrest. Then they clasped their hands and buried their heads in their hands for prayers. Kwesi and I followed the congregation's example. After the congregation was settled and the church was completely quiet, the minister continued the worship with prayers for world peace, the sick and bed-bound, the injured, the poor and non-believers, and continued prosperity of the congregation. "Lord," he continued, "turn the hearts of your children from Satan's evil hold to God's salvation. Save them from destruction as you saved Daniel from the Lion's den and turn them into vessels of Your will. Bless this congregation and show it the majesty of Your glory. Let there be harmony where there is disharmony, peace where there is war, love where there is hate, tolerance where there is intolerance, and compassion where there is dispassion. Bless this congregation to walk with the Lord and live in your light. Amen."

"Amen," echoed the congregation.

The congregation turned around and resumed their seats. The choristers sang another hymn while sitting in their seats. Then the minister called the leader of Christ's Singing Band to sing an anthem. The band got up, shuffled their feet and cleared their throats, and sang an anthem of Ruth's journey in alien lands. The congregation applauded after the song was over and the group had retaken their seats.

The minister stood up from his seat situated behind the altar and said another prayer for God's guidance for the day's church activities. Then he called on an elderly woman in her sixties, who was dressed in a blue western-style skirt and blouse, to read the day's text from the Bible. The reader stood in the front of the podium, as the elderly man before her had done, and read from Hebrews. She concluded her reading with the words, "Here ends the first reading of the Holy Word."

The minister asked the church ushers to pass around the collection plate from one pew to the next for the congregation to make their offertory to a son by Christ's Singing Band. The ushers stacked the plates on top of each other and gave the stack to the lead usher after the collection plates had made their rounds through the congregation. The ushers followed the lead usher to a gap between the front seats and podium to hand over the stack of plates containing the offertory to the minister, who had walked down from the podium and was waiting for them. The minister took the stack of plates from the lead usher, looked at the ceiling as if to the heavens, surveyed the congregation, and prayed over the collection. "Thank you, Lord, for the charitable donations from your servants. Guide us to use it to spread the Gospel and do good works that will glorify your Son. Return the donations three-fold—four-fold—to the congregation, as you multiply the seeds that are sown in good soil. This we ask in the name of the Lord and Savior Jesus Christ, Amen."

The minister handed over the stack of plates containing the offertory to one of the church elders, who was standing to his left. This leader, accompanied by two other elders, carried the collection out of the offertory into an anteroom. The choir got up and sang another hymn, which started with the following stanza:

"All things bright and beautiful;
All creatures, great and small;
All things wise and wonderful—
The Lord God made them all."

The minister returned to the podium as the choir sang and waited for the singing to be over. Then he asked the congregation to turn their Bibles to the New Testament and read the parable of the Good Samaritan, as recorded by Saint Matthew, and concluded his reading with the words, "May the Lord add His blessing to the reading of His Holy Word, Amen." The congregation echoed his Amen.

Still on his feet, the minister paused and took off his coat like a Roman gladiator readying for battle in an amphitheater against a formidable enemy. He surveyed the congregation, took a long deep breath, exhaled very slowly, and launched into a sermon about proaction as a prerequisite of good discipleship. "As Christians," he proclaimed to the congregation, "you must be proactive in your communities and daily lives; you must move away from your comfort zones and dare to do the ethically right thing. Along the way, Satan and his agents will tempt and challenge you. The challenge could take any form," he continued. "Remain steadfast in your faith as you face these temptations and challenges. Think about how Satan tempted the Lord in the wilderness for forty days and forty nights. Stand with Him, pray for guidance, and trust Him to point you in the right direction. Anchor your faith in the Lord and not on your own knowledge, because your knowledge, no matter how deep, is imperfect, incomplete, and just a drop in the ocean of the Lord's infinite knowledge. Submit your will to God and serve without reservation as the apostle Paul did throughout his discipleship. The Lord will protect and keep you safe. The Lord will bless your seed as He blessed the seeds of your forefathers." Then he concluded the sermon with the words, "Rest in the Lord even as the Samaritan surrendered in his faith to the stranger—for the Lord, who knows the grain of your hair and your days on this earth, will not let you perish even as He feeds the birds that neither plow nor sow. And when your time comes, He will take you to Glory as He guided the Magi through the open wilderness to the manger where Christ laid. Rest in the Lord and trust Him in all things, for He is always faithful."

Suddenly, a lady from Christ's Singing Band, who was overcome by the moment, began to sing. The minister paused from delivering his sermon as the congregation joined in the singing, and resumed when the singing was done. He elaborated on the theme of his sermon and concluded it with the Lord's Prayer. A few Amens rang from the congregation as the minister sat down.

The choir, that appeared to listen attentively to the minster, sang the last hymn and filed out of the church's sanctuary. Christ's Singing Band filed out after the choristers. The congregation trickled out of the sanctuary in small groups and began to descend the steps toward their homes. We waited for Grandma to join us at our designated meeting place near the atrium of the church for the homebound journey. She brought two members of Christ's Singing Band with her and joyously introduced us to them, as well as members of the regular congregation that straggled around the church compound. Then she introduced us to Auntie Adoma, who invited us to visit her before going back home to Mama.

"I will make sure they do," Grandma replied.

On that note, we took leave of the church and its congregation and started on our homebound journey under the tropical afternoon heat.

I was hungry, tired, and sweaty from the intense and unforgiving humidity-laden heat of the baking sun, and desired cold water to soothe my fatigue when I arrived home, but I had two pressing issues I needed Grandma's help to resolve.

First, I wanted to know the depth of our blood relationship to Auntie Adoma, since we address even unrelated adults as uncles, aunties, and cousins as a way of showing deference and discouraging inappropriate social interactions between children of all ages and non-relative adults in our part of the world. This social stance is reinforced by the notion that unrelated adult males and females were more apt to protect and maintain appropriate boundaries and moral relationships with minors who called them uncle or auntie than those who did not. Adults who broke this social construct incurred social condemnation and, in egregious cases such as child rape, public derision and outright banishment from the town.

Second, I wanted to know why the reputable minister of a church would dress like a pied-crow and go to those lengths to win converts and assuage his congregation.

"Grandma," I began, "how is Auntie Adoma related to us?"

"She is your father's sister," she calmly responded.

I accepted Grandma's description of our kinship to Auntie Adoma as gospel. Her calm, matter-of-fact response encouraged me to proceed with the second issue on my mind.

"Grandma," I continued, "please tell me why the minister in church was dressed like a pied-crow?"

"How dare you compare the minister of our church to a pied-crow? That is disrespectful," she retorted angrily.

"I am sorry," I apologized, and continued, "I did not mean to offend him. The fact is, I do not understand why a leader of a church should dress like a bird."

"Well, let me tell, you young man," Grandma said rather caustically. "That pied-crow is a very significant symbol for a large number of Akans on this side of the Pra River. Let me give you a brief history lesson, young man.

"A long time ago," she began, "there was a severe draught in Old Ghana. The ensuing famine was so severe that our ancestors lost herds of cattle, goats, sheep, chickens, and other domesticated animals in large numbers. To salvage what they had and assure survival, they organized the citizenry into groups according to family lineage, and the seven-clan relationships elected three elders—Oburmankoma, Odapagayan, and Oson—to lead them in the emigration to greener pastures. The elders selected Oburmankoma, a huge man in his seventies, for his understanding of stars; Odapagayan, an unassuming middle-aged man in his forties, for his knowledge of war strategies; and Oson, a young man in his late thirties, for his diplomatic and negotiating skills. The leaders organized the clans into three groups with symbols to represent each clan. They chose the pied-crow, because of its intelligence and ability to deliver messages over long distances, to represent the Anana clan. They chose the parrot, because of its ability to learn and communicate in many languages, to represent the Aboredzi clan; and the tortoise, for its self-sufficiency, to represent the Esumo clan.

"The elders and the selected leaders led the clans through inhospitable terrain, inclement weather, and wars against several hostile tribes to this land, which we now call home. Legend has it that one of the several tribes they encountered and fought was the Krews of Northwestern Africa. It is said that the Krews were notorious for their savagery and cannibalistic rituals. As our ancestors made their journey southward, from what is now known as Mali, they pitched camp in the thick forest of Krew territory.

"During the night, the guarding watchmen noticed strange movements in the bush surrounding the camp. Odapagayan sent scouts to investigate the movements and report what they found to him and the other leaders. The scouts reported they saw husky, bare-footed men, probably of the Krew tribe, in assorted roan sarongs carrying sticks and cudgels. The unknown men piled their impedimenta into a heap, slaughtered a bull with a giant knife, and drained its blood into a large wooden pail. Then they transferred the pail of blood into a large earthenware pot and set it aside. They arrowed an eland that had strayed to the camp, flayed its coat for future use and tied it down on a wood platform. One of the tribesmen used the same knife and slashed off the eland's head with one cut. Two others drained the blood from the eland into another wooden pail and emptied the pail into the earthenware pot containing the bull's blood. They cooked the mixed blood over a large open pit fire and dished the cooked blood into gourds and passed it around for each of the tribesmen to take a drink. Then they ran a long stick down the throat until it emerged at the rectum of both carcasses and roasted them over the open-pit fire. The tribesmen stamped their feet to bongo-drums while pounding the ground with their sticks and cudgels and singing war songs in circadian rhythms. They punctuated the end of the ritual with screams and screeches when the roasting was done, sliced the roasted meat, and stacked it into parcels. Then they strapped the parcels on horseback, put out the fire with dust, and vanished in the surrounding forest with hyena-like stealth.

"Odapagayan surmised his people were in danger of an attack from the cannibalistic tribesmen when he heard of this account. He sent a message by a pied-crow to clan warriors who were straggling down the trail to assemble. The clan warriors responded back to him through the pied-crow.

"Meanwhile, they sent doves to scout and report on the Krew tribesmen's whereabouts. Odapagayan used the information from the scouting birds to develop an appropriate war strategy. He organized his men into small groups and launched a successful attack against the Krews under the cover of night, conquering them. He indentured the conquered tribesmen to plant and sack corn, millet, beans, rice, and other dryable legumes. This planting and harvesting by the prisoners of war went on for three planting seasons. After harvesting the crops of the third planting season, Odapagayan ordered the captured tribesmen to build four large wooden wagons and load them with the sacked harvest. When the wagons were fully loaded, Odapagayan and the other elders organized the clans to resume their southward journey until they reached New Ghana at the Atlantic Ocean.

It is also said that, when they arrived at the Atlantic, Oburmankoma was mystified by the expanse of the sea and the cool 'boiling' waves. He touched the ocean to validate his perception and realized that the ocean did not emit heat. He tasted the brine of the ocean, and called it *Epo,* because it was salty and did not burn. He turned to the clans who remained and announced, '*Ha na ye be tsi na,*' meaning, 'We shall make our home at this place.'"

"Did the tortoise play any role in the war?" I asked Grandma.

"Yes, it did," she replied.

"What part did it play?" I inquired.

"I will tell you that another day," she replied.

After Grandma finished with the story, I ran upstairs to undress and cool down. I took my shoes off, crumpled the suit, and tossed it into our laundry wicker basket. I put on my knockabout shorts and short-sleeve shirt and rushed to the kitchen where I picked up the large earthenware cistern containing water, filled a large hemi-gourd with the water, and drank it to the last drop. Then I walked to "Mr. Rock," the rocks that were set behind the bathroom for us to use as a water closet during the day, and emptied my bladder. I returned to the kitchen to wait for the boiling peanut butter soup with chicken to finish cooking.

Kwesi followed suit and undressed, but unlike me, he helped Grandma restack her steel trunks of clothing before putting on his knockabout clothes. After that, he came to the kitchen. Grandma went through a similar ritual and returned downstairs with the clothing she had worn to church to air them on the washing line. She pinned them on the line with pegs and joined Kwesi and me in the kitchen where the maid was frantically peeling off and slicing a medium-sized tuber of yam and four fingers of plantains to ready them for lunch. I watched the maid as she washed the sliced vegetables in a small aluminum pot and put the washed vegetables in an earthenware pot. She filled the pot with cold water and put it on the hot charcoal fire to cook. Grandma asked me to fan the fire and bring the yams and plantains to a boil. My hunger pangs, which became acute as I contemplated the progress of the cooking vegetables, abated with my preoccupation with fanning the charcoal, but the pangs returned when the vegetables began to boil.

"I am hungry," I complained in a loud voice for the first time and put down the fan.

"Food will soon be ready," Grandma consolingly responded.

I returned to my seat in the kitchen and tried to strike up a conversation with my brother, but the pangs of hunger abated my attempt and sent me into temporary lethargy. I felt light-headed and decided to rest my head on my knees while I waited for the food to cook. Periodically, I lifted my head to spy on the progress of the cooking vegetables. On one of those occasions, I saw the maid pick up the lid and poke her right forefinger into it to verify its status. She jerked her finger and reflexively put it onto her lips and licked it. I saw her repeat the process two more times. She picked up the pot after the third attempt and drained the cooked vegetables in an earthenware colander. Then she emptied the vegetables from the colander into a large earthenware tray to cool.

Grandma decided to forgo *fufu* over peanut butter soup that day. Instead, she asked us to sit at the table and have a lunch of peanut butter soup and the cooked unripe plantains, cassava, and cocoyams. She dished my soup and a drumstick into a bowl. She did the same for my elder brother before dishing out a chicken breast and a thigh for herself. Finally, she dished out two scoops of soup containing a neck bone, liver, gizzard, and two chicken legs for the maid. She put the remaining soup in a pot on the charcoal fire and left it to simmer until most of the soup's water had evaporated and the soup was thick and usable as stew. We topped off our lunch with cooked tapioca over Carnation brand milk. As usual, the maid sat by herself in a corner of the kitchen like a spider and ate alone.

Lunch lured us into siesta. I slept so deeply that I did not feel the intermittent buzz that accompanied the ubiquitous mosquitoes as they landed and took off from the exposed part of my slumbering body. Eventually, one of them landed on the tip of my nose and woke me up as it used its proboscis to suck my blood. I tried to catch it with my left hand, but it flew away. I tapped on my brother's shoulder and woke him up. Grandma remained fully asleep after we woke up, so we snuck out to rendezvous with Danger and Kobina Amuah to retrieve the crab traps we set at the bog.

Kobina Amuah and Danger were already waiting at the rendezvous point. Both Kobina Amuah and Danger looked relaxed. Except for an occasional passerby, the streets were deserted and the town quiet. The solitude gave an eerie sense of impending danger, but there were no visible signs to confirm or repudiate our feelings.

We quickly got reacquainted and plunged ahead on a different route to complete the task at hand. We came upon rows of dilapidated mud houses with showing wood structures that were either roofed with thatch or corroding corrugation. Goats and ewes were taking refuge from the scorching heat in the shade of the house and under nearby trees. A red and brown-feathered rooster ran out from a corner followed in hot pursuit by a silver colored one. Suddenly, the fleeing brown- feathered rooster stopped and turned to face the pursuing silver–feathered one. The two fowls circled around and gazed antagonistically at one other. They made pugnacious crackles. The plumage around their necks stood on end and so did the comb on their heads. They scratched up dust and got into a fight. We stopped to watch the spontaneous cockfight. After flapping their wings against each other a few times with *tout de force,* punctuated with vicious pecking on each other's comb and wattle, they began to bleed. The bleeding roosters paused momentarily, as if to heed the hurt, and resumed the fight on dispirited notes. I was appalled to see blood trickling down the combs and wattles of these beautifully feathered fowls, and was tempted to separate them, but they suddenly stopped fighting and parted before I could act.

We resumed our walk toward the marshes, horse-playing along the way, and soon arrived at a creek surrounded with foliage, hanging boughs, and reams of black dotted frog larvae. I dipped my hand in the water to scoop larvae floating close to a mossy stone that was partially submerged in the creek and missed. An array of water dragons took off and landed on the flowing creek as it wound its way to the black sandy shores of the gentle coastal lagoon. The air was cool, calm, and welcoming. A few gray and white lagoon crabs bobbed their heads above their holes and retreated when we got closer to them. For a brief moment I thought that nature was sharing the serene Sabbath with the townsfolk and the crustaceans.

We continued our journey on a footpath past the lagoon, and I was ruefully reminded of my folly when a twittering sparrow and two cooing cranes flew overhead. A pair of common bulbuls with brown coats landed on the branch of a nearby tree and flew away as fast as they landed. A butterfly, aided by the breeze, glided from one blade of grass to the next as it searched for an ideal landing platform. I looked at the grass and saw a large black ant crawling over the mound of dirt around the grass. It paused and exchanged a greeting with a brown tiger ant, the kind that was common around mango and guava trees. I looked down and saw a closed crab trap and realized we had reached the marshes where our crab traps were set.

We methodically searched the marshes for crab traps and assembled them in the opening as we did. After all the traps were located and accounted for, Danger and Kobina Amuah asked Kwesi and me to wait while they scoured for branch strands of the date trees in the area to tie the crabs together.

Hardly had they left when Kwesi took off on an expedition and left me to babysit the crab traps. A gray duiker unexpectedly emerged from one of the tufts of bush close to the bog. It was followed by a red-fronted gazelle. They looked surprised to see me sitting close to their habitat and retreated into the tuft they came from.

I was left alone and began to think of Mama and how much I missed her. I thought about how much I missed her tucking me into bed at night and telling me stories about things she used to do when she was a kid. I missed Papa and the smell of his court robe. I thought about the time I wore Papa's wig and looked like an old man with one foot in the grave, and how Kwesi and Mama teased me about my looks. I thought about my neighbor, Kofi Prah, a small boy of my age who lived across the street, and his brown and white pit-bull puppy Pogo. I could not help thinking about Pogo and how he would run to me to be petted, wag his bushy tail to denote excitement or pleasure, and growl to express displeasure or anxiety.

One day, as I recall, I was coming back from school after a particularly bad session. Mr. Atta, a rather harsh man who was my third grade teacher, had asked the class to garden. The garden was about a quarter of a mile away from school and close to the beach. I, along with two other classmates, skipped the assignment and went to the beach instead. Once there, we undressed, hid our school uniforms under a bush, and ran to the foreshore waters to play. One of the girls in our class squealed on us to Mr. Atta, who came to the beach and caught us at play. He commandeered us out of the foreshore, reproached us for endangering our lives, and punished us by asking us to write, "I will not play in the sea at any time of the day without adult supervision" two hundred fifty times.

I returned home after school in poor humor because of the writing assignment I had to do. I was also anxious about the explanation I would give when either one of my parents saw me doing the punishment. Pogo saw me coming home from school. He trotted, broke into a run, and slowed down to a stop when he reached me. He started wagging his tail to denote excitement. I knelt down and gently ran my fingers through the fur on his head and back. I stopped and decided to continue walking home, but Pogo jumped and put his fore paws on my left thigh as if to say "not yet." I instinctively took his paw, shook it, and let go of it. He lay on his back and lifted his forelegs and forearms, turned his head to one side, and began to whimper for more petting. I put the school textbooks I was carrying on a gutter ledge and began to gently rub his stomach and run my fingers through the fur of his ribcage. As I caressed his body, my fears and anxiety dissipated, and I began to feel that things would be all right.

Suddenly, Kwesi jumped out of one of the surrounding bushes and interrupted my solitude. "Look!" he screamed.

I turned to him and asked in a harsh irritated tone, "Look at what?"

"Look at these dates. They look delicious," he said as he pulled a date from a bunch for me to taste.

"Thank you," I replied with a bemused tone.

He pulled another wild date from the bunch he held in his hands, popped it into his mouth, and repeated, "They are delicious!" Then, after chewing on it for a few seconds, he handed me one and enjoined, "Try it." Then he popped another one of the brown dates into his mouth.

I gingerly put the one he gave to me into my mouth and scraped the tip of its hull with my front teeth. I cautiously nibbled away the remaining fruit, spat out the hard seed, which tasted like a smooth, stone pebble, and told him, "I do not find the date particularly tasteful. In fact, it is tart and not meaty."

"Indeed not," he contradicted, "they are delicious." "You," he continued while pointing, "do not like it because you have not developed the taste for exquisite fruits. I bet you will when you do."

Kobina Amuah and Danger returned with peels of the budding branches of the date tree. They cautiously set them on the grass of the opening and proceeded to take out the trapped crabs from the trap boxes one at a time. As Kwesi and I watched, Danger picked up the first crab trap, laid it on its back and slowly opened the front of it. He carefully inserted his hand into the trap and pulled out the live crab by holding its big claws firmly against its shell. Danger handed the crab over to Kobina Amuah, who used strands of soft date leaves to tie its claws and set it down on the grass. The two repeated the process until all the crabs were tied and on the grass. Kobina Amuah pulled out a vine and strung the crabs ten to a bunch and laid the tied bunches on the grass. When they were through with the exercise, Kobina Amuah said, "Now, you guys, let's stuff the trap boxes into the jute sack."

"Sure," we eagerly responded.

We loaded the empty trap boxes into the sack. Kobina Amuah strung his catch, tossed it on his shoulder, and we left the marshes for home. Kwesi, Danger, and I took turns passing the jute sack containing the empty crab trap boxes from one person to the next to haul over our shoulders until we reached town and decided to part company.

It occurred to me, as we parted, that in the morning when Kwesi and I were probably asleep, Kobina Amuah would be peddling his crabs at the roadside to make money and help his parents. His parents were poor and poorly educated. Their earning power was small, as compared with Papa's and other educated people. And so, like many children from economically disadvantaged homes, he was doing his best to support himself and increase the standard of living for his family through enterprise.

Chapter 8

The need to live and support oneself or one's dependents motivates breadwinners from all walks of life to wake up at odd hours, and to make and keep appointments. I was a child, who was not similarly yoked. I had the good fortune to live in the heart of a small town and enjoy the solitude that was typically reserved for forested hamlets and bungalows, but these privileges did not protect me from the needs of daily, loving discipline from my parents and the attention of doleful adults.

"Wake up!" Grandma screamed while sprinkling water on me.

I felt the droplets of water on my face and woke up from the flimsy reed mat to face her towering presence over my small-framed one. She had a pewter jug in one hand and was dipping her fingers in it to sprinkle water over me with the other. I jerked out of bed in near hysteria and reflexively folded the reed mat. I saw a ray of light piercing through a crack in the sash-window to our bedroom and realized that another day had dawned.

"Wake up! You have your chores to do," she said, and continued, "you have been sleeping like a well-fed python in hibernation."

I did not like the comparison Grandma made between me and the snake or its reference of laziness.

"No," I protested softly, and looked at her face to glean whether she heard my protest. But she remained stoic and impassive. So, I repeated my disavowal, "I am tired from what we did yesterday," I added, more to soothe my bruised ego than to escape doing my assigned morning chores.

"Nobody sent you," she replied, as she took a few steps backward to sit on her bed and fold her arms across her chest to indicate her mind was made up.

I ignored her insensitive and apathetic comments and continued rolling up the reed mat. I stored the mat behind the door after and inched out of the bedroom toward the staircase.

"Hurry up with your chores and eat your breakfast. We have to go and see your Auntie Adoma; otherwise she will feel badly," Grandma pleaded as I rushed downstairs.

I trotted to Mr. Rock, who was perennially present beside the corrugated outdoor bathroom, and emptied my bladder. I hurried though my morning chores, picked up my chewing stick from its holder behind the dining room, softened it in the usual manner, and brushed my teeth. I went to the kitchen and enjoyed a breakfast of quick-cooking oats, two pieces of toast with orange marmalade and butter, scrambled eggs, and a medley of mild tasting tropical fruits. I returned upstairs, folded my sleeping cloth, and put it at the foot of Grandma's bed. Then I hurriedly put on a pair of casual khaki pants and a red shirt and joined Kwesi and Grandma who were sitting on carved, softwood stools waiting for me in the shade cast by the house.

"Let's go," I mirthfully said upon arriving in the shade.

"Okay," replied Kwesi.

Grandma held on to both knees with her hands and slowly rose up from her stool. She appeared to be in excruciating pain.

"Grandma, what is the matter?" I asked in a concerned tone.

"Nothing," she replied nonchalantly.

"Really?" I said in disbelief, since her facial expression conveyed pain.

"Well," she reluctantly replied, "it's these arthritic pains in my joints. They sometimes hurt like hell when I walk. The pains get really bad when it rains or the temperature drops. Perhaps old age has already ensnarled me in its reaching tentacles."

Kwesi and I looked on with dreary helplessness as Grandma struggled to take the first steps of her walk towards Auntie Adoma's home. To me, she epitomized the insidious snares of advancing age that living beings must face sooner or later. I wanted to suggest we skip the visit and stay home, more out of empathy for Grandma's suffering than to satisfy a personal need, but I did not want to air my opinion on the subject because I surmised Grandma was fully grown, knew her body, and was quite capable of making decisions that served her best interest. As I was preoccupied with the thought, Grandma rose from her stool and strolled to the southern wall of the house facing the sunrise. She put both hands high above her head on the wall, placed her legs slightly part and away from the wall, stretched for a few seconds, and invited us to come along. "I am ready. We must go," she resolutely declared.

She walked to the gate with Kwesi and me trudging along. I waved good-bye to the maid and exited to the unpaved brown dusty street that lay in front of the house for the walk to Auntie Adoma's home.

As we walked down the street, Grandma, who appeared to be talking more to herself than to us, decried her condition. "I wish these arthritic pains would go away," we overheard her moan, but walked on quietly because we were concerned that any unwelcomed comment from either of us could aggravate her pain and sour her poor mood even further. Her pace gradually quickened as we got farther into the walk. The cloud of pain that hung over the first few steps of our walk like a bad omen gradually dissipated. Her intermittent moans, which marked the steps she took at the start of our walk, were replaced with frequent, facile smiles and returned to full life with the bellow, "Look at that house with the caved in roof and falling wood frame, windows, and doors! See how deserted it looks?" she pointed.

"Which house?" asked Kwesi, who was unable to identify the house from a clutter of crumbling houses with the hallmarks of a ghost town.

"The one to your left across the partially dirt-filled gutter," she replied.

We tracked her direction to a covered house of overgrown weeds and shrubs. The branches of a big tall tree standing in front of the house gave it an ominous foreboding look.

"That house over there?" both Kwesi and I asked in unison.

"Yes, that house," she affirmatively replied.

After a short pause that seemed like an eternity, she added, "That is where your grandfather lived when he arrived in this town."

"Can we go inside and take a look?" I asked, more out of an intense burning desire to know everything I could about Grandpa than to visit the dilapidated and decaying building.

"Yes, you can," she replied, and added as an afterthought, "look out for snakes, scorpions and other slimy creatures."

"Thanks, Grandma," I responded.

I accompanied Kwesi to explore the abandoned and falling building while Grandma took refuge under a neem tree adjacent to the house. We cautiously trod through piles of garbage and strewed chewed sugarcane fibers, rotting orange and mango skins, and black and shriveling banana peels that filled both sides of the footpath to arrive at the abandoned house. We came upon broken coconut shells containing standing rainwater as we trod our way up the path. I picked one of them up and emptied it, saying, "That could be a good ground for breeding mosquitoes." Then we carefully ducked our heads under a collapsing door resembling the entrance to the one-story mud house, and realized that wooden beams supporting the roof of the house had buckled under its burden of dirt like a thunder-struck tree in the middle of nowhere. We picked our way through the remaining rooms of the crumbling house, whose walls were green and black from live and dried algae. Two brightly colored male agama lizards with rusty red heads, bluish-black bodies, and orange tails were chasing a dark brown and white spotted colored female of the same specie across one of the crumbling building walls. One of the male agama lizards stopped its chase and bobbed its oval-shaped head as if to say, "Progress made so far is so good." It continued the chase and disappeared around the corner of one of the walls.

A smooth-bodied green gecko slithered along the ground and vanished under the green vegetation covering. I heard the soft landing of a swarm of black and bright yellow-spotted butterflies fluttering on the scattered wild flowers. A column of dark brown field mice made merry over rotten orange rinds and dashed for cover under the assorted foliage of creeping plants growing out of the buckled and cracked asphalt floor when they saw us. Howls of happy cats filled the air. We tiptoed over the soft moss that covered the floors and crumbling walls of each room and corridor, from one end of the house to another. We returned to the front of the house where a smell of pestilential ammoniac fumes, reeking from the four corners of the room closest to the front of the house, bid us adieu as we left the crumbling home to continue our journey.

"How did you find it?" inquired Grandma as we approached her.

"As fine as most abandoned buildings go," replied Kwesi.

For a moment, Grandma looked lost in thought. That apparent loss of memory prompted me to ponder whether she was fighting the onset of the first bouts of forgetfulness that affects us as we age. But since I was neither a physician nor trained in the matters of brain function and memory loss, I abandoned the conjecture to focus on listening to Grandma's recollection of life in the crumbling house. "Grandma, please tell me, did you ever live in this house?"

She nodded, as if the emotion of the moment had choked her like a frog in froth. I repeated my question and, this time, she nodded in two rapid successions. She paused, looked down, and replied in a barely audible, whispering voice, "Yes," and paused again. Then, she added affirmatively. "Yes, indeed!" in a loud, happy voice.

She went silent after the bellowing and began to wax nostalgic. "It was a good life. Oh, yes it was! Life with your Grandpa got better after your father was born—and much better after your father's siblings were born. There was your father, Sakyi, and his siblings—Araba, Kuma, and Suma. I must tell you that those children, referring to Papa and his siblings, were not born in this house. They were born in the house I now live in."

She paused, pondered for a moment, and continued, "I remember white merchants from England, Germany, and France coming to this home with assorted presents for your Grandpa and the rest of the family. They stayed with us while their ships were loaded with cocoa from your Grandpa's farm and told stories about England, Germany, France and ports in countries where they stopped to trade cocoa and other merchandise. I remember one particular German, Mr. Karl Hindenburg. He was a handsome man, with hazel eyes and wavy golden hair, who generally came ashore in a black flannel suit and a pair of black shoes. He was plump and probably six feet four inches tall. He brought barrels of German lager and crates of whiskey from England to your Grandpa. They toasted to a story Karl told about German workers. 'In Germany,' Karl said gleefully, 'workers fully ascribe to long-term apprenticeship and artisanship. Sometimes, the desire to follow instructions is so uncompromisingly demanding that they stifle creativity. People who are innovative are either considered social deviants or accused of constructive sabotage.'

"'Workers in Germany are marked for conformity,' your grandpa remarked, and reciprocated with a story about Ghana workers. He said, 'Ghana workers do not have ownership of the work they do. They believe that they work for a foreign power or boss who is more interested in exploiting them and the natural resources of their country than advancing the welfare of native workers. They piddle around and work as inefficiently and ineffectively as their imaginations allow them to.' The two men argued about various aspects of human nature, factors that make labor more productive and efficient, creativity, and dogged submission to authority and human ingenuity. They agreed that workers everywhere needed some supervision from owners of capital and toasted to that agreement. Then, they toasted to their health, good fortune, and anything they could think of with one dram of whiskey after another. They drank kegs of lager between the drams when they could not come up with anything to toast to, and exchanged stories about their life experiences, trade, and politics. They debated and proposed all kinds of possible solutions to economic and societal ills of the world until the cows came home and mooed behind the windows. I was not interested in their ceaseless, self-serving chatter and hollow male chauvinistic talk, so I retired to bed and left them to the sonorous wailing of the bats and grinding cricket chirrs.

"I woke up after one of their all night binges and found both men deeply asleep with their faces buried in their own vomit. The living room furniture was scattered everywhere. I sprinkled water on both and shook them out of their sleep. They gradually woke up from sleep and blamed each other for the disarray, like two teenage boys caught in the commission of a crime. I turned my back, pretending I had not heard their squabble, and walked to the kitchen to prepare breakfast. When I returned, they had recovered sufficiently from their drunken stupor, rearranged the living room furniture, and were intensely discussing the positive benefits of education. I shook my head in total disbelief. Karl apologized for the incident and so did your grandfather. There were other drink-induced incidents, some of which got raucous and unpleasant, but through it all, they maintained their friendship and respect for each other.

Looking back, I cannot help but conclude that their friendship endured because they saw something good in each other, something endearing and intrinsically profound, which transcended the cultures that nurtured them as separate individuals and caused them to express their common humanity and admiration. Sadly, Karl died at sea on one of his journeys back to Germany. Grandpa was saddened to hear of it and named your uncle after him in memory of their friendship."

The pace of our walking had slowed as Grandma told the story.

"Let's pick up the pace because the rising sun and increasing humidity will soon combine to tire us and drench us in our perspiration," she said.

We quickened our pace and soon found ourselves winding through alleys of uninspiring one-story homes of weathered boards and mud. The houses were roofed with tin, thatch, or corrugated iron sheets. Those with exposed weathered boards looked abandoned and unoccupied. Foraging goats, sheep, pigs, chicken, ducks, and other domesticated animals mingled freely with people trekking the footpaths that wound through the alleys. An emaciated, skeletal brown-and-white-spotted bulldog crossed our pathway and disappeared into the surrounding tall and overgrown grass. A jet-black cat screeched in hot pursuit of a dog. Perhaps it smelled the opportunity for a meal. Grandma saw the cat and whimpered, "That is a sign of bad luck."

"That's an old wives' tale," I remarked hilariously.

"No, not at all," Grandma calmly contradicted.

"The cat could have been any color," I replied, "and would a white or gray cat carry the same interpretation?" I asked sarcastically.

"Look around you, and listen to folks as they talk about things that are black. You will hear people associate blackness with sinister and evil things. Indeed, it is not unusual for people to associate black clouds with ominous twisters, thunder, lightning, and rain. Yet without overcast clouds, we cannot realize the goodness of rain. You will also hear people associate night with lurking danger, murder, and nightmares, not to mention shadowy phantoms and goblins of haunted houses. Yet it is the darkness of the night that induces sleep to nourish our bodies for another day's labor and lets the earth rest from the sun's burning heat. Evil opens our eyes and hearts to appreciate goodness and courage exposes the weakness of cowardice. This does not deny that there is some hidden truth somewhere. Scratch deeper into any myth and you are likely to find something inspiring and real. The fact is that you don't need to fall to the bottom of a pit to believe it is cold down there or be victimized to understand another person's pain. Empathy is part of a truly developed mind. Selfish, immature minds tend to crystallize the world into prisms of their limited visions. Such minds do not appreciate the diversity of creation, culture, or human thought. Things are as true and real as they define them. Their reality is myopic and so are their lives—paltry, poor, and woefully wanton."

I wanted to ask her whether she felt there was something ominous about being black-skinned, and whether the Creator toasted babies into blackness prior to implantation in the womb as some of my friends had told me, but I decided to leave the superstitious hogwash about black cats, and the array of evil thoughts and deeds associated with the notion of blackness, alone.

We quietly continued walking toward Auntie Adoma's home. The density of houses thinned to unveil a clear sky and serene openness. Two bare-footed, teenage girls, who were wearing well-worn, wrap-around cloths and carrying trash in uncovered containers, passed us and left a trail of noxious odors. Kwesi and I looked at each other and grimaced. I momentarily pinched my nose to avoid breathing in the foul air, but Grandma did not show any discomfort with the teenage girls and their noxious decaying garbage. Perhaps she had grown used to the smell.

The girls passed by us again on the way back to their homes, but this time there was no evidence of noxious odors. Kwesi and I looked at each other and breathed a sigh of relief, only to encounter the smell of burning garbage coming from the direction the girls had emptied their trash. It was a large irregularly shaped dumpster with a smoldering garbage fire at one end. The indescribable stench of decaying food and assorted castoffs fouled the air. Heaps of piled rubbish covered the open plain of the dumpster. A middle-aged man in tattered, tan shorts and a short-sleeved shirt was holding a rake and standing over one of several small heaps of trash. He appeared overwhelmed by what he had to do to prevent the garbage from piling up and keep the dumpster suitable for continued public use. Vultures squawked over the heap to grab remains of dead animals, fish, and other meat leftovers. A few pied-crows casually passed up and down waiting their turn to pick on the garbage. Our footpath ran through a corner of the dumpster's open plain, which felt like a padded carpet of dry sugarcane shavings as I walked across. It disappeared into the surrounding tall grass. I looked back to see the direction we had come from and almost stepped into a pile of stinking garbage that did not reach its intended destination. In the process of regaining my balance, I saw the wind fan the smoldering fire to flicker, burn, and smolder again. Eventually, we emerged from the tall grass and arrived at Auntie Adoma's home after an additional half-mile or so of walking.

Her home was a simple and unassuming one-story house. It was constructed of baked mud-bricks in the front and mud at the back. It was graced with two intricately designed mahogany doors at the entrance. The panes in the windows were tilted to keep out insects and ease ventilation, and they had mosquito netting too. Grandma knocked on the entrance door with an exaggerated sense of urgency.

"Who is there?" a voice behind the door inquired. "I will be right there," the voice assured.

"Oh! That's you, Grandma, come in," she said as she opened the door. "And the boys are with you?" she continued without waiting for a response. "It's so nice of you to bring them over. Come in, you two," she said as she embraced Kwesi and me.

Auntie Adoma looked like someone in her late thirties to early forties. She was four feet ten inches tall and weighed about one hundred fifteen pounds. She was wearing a loose, blue, tie-dyed chemise and a pair of rubber slippers made from used and discarded vehicle tires. A petite woman, she had hair that was kinky and unkempt and light brown eyes deeply set in their sockets, looking unpretentiously earnest. She had a kind and disarming smile on her expressively kind face.

We trailed Grandma into the house. Auntie Adoma escorted us to her sparsely furnished living room with one sofa, a small center table, and two chairs. She went outside the living room and returned with two small softwood carved stools and offered them to us. We thanked her for the stools and sat down. She and Grandma exchanged greetings and tidbits about other family members and amicable discussion about the about the good and bad qualities of the members whose names readily recalled. They had different, yet complementary, recollections of scenarios about individual family members, and debated what those individuals could have done differently to succeed. They disagreed on their takes about a few and concurred that it took all kinds of people to make a family. I made mental notes of their perspectives for my future use.

In the middle of the pseudo-family reunion, Auntie Adoma asked to be excused and invited us out for the welcome ritual. We walked behind her to a rock under a mango tree near the entrance to her home, where she asked Kwesi to remove his dusty shoes and set them aside. She asked him to set both feet on the rock with the right foot first. Then she filled a cistern with water from a forty-gallon iron barrel, emptied some of the water into a gourd and used the water in the gourd to wash his feet. She dried his feet with a spotless white cotton towel and repeated the ritual with me. She refilled the same gourd with water from the cistern and poured libation to our ancestral spirits. She summoned our ancestral spirits to guide us in our goings-out and comings-in and pleaded with the goddess of land and travel to protect us on our homebound journey. She punctuated the pouring of the libation with the invocation, "God of the sky, who brings sunshine, the wind, and the rain, we beseech You to endow Your children with wisdom. Let them understand that You have the force to make good and bad things. Show these children Your good side all the time and let them appreciate Your wisdom."

She came to the end of the ceremony and drank the dregs of the water to close the ritual. "Come on, you two," she said, after putting away the emptied half-gourd. We walked behind her into her living room and resumed our stools. Once again, she excused herself, walked out of the living room, and returned with a large earthenware pot containing *ahey*, a local non-alcoholic beverage made from corn.

"Here is some *ahey* that I made with my own two hands," she proudly announced.

She set down the pot on a brown kitchen towel and used a wooden spoon to scoop out enough of the corn beverage to fill three half-gourds to the brim. She offered the first gourd to Grandma, the second to my elder brother, and the last to me, because I was the youngest. She filled up one half-gourd for herself and proposed a toast, saying, "To the prosperity of the two fine young men, Ato Kwamena and Kwesi Sakyi, and the health of Grandma and continuing good family relationships."

Grandma returned the gesture by proposing another toast, adding, "To the health and welfare of Auntie Adoma and her two wonderful children, Effie Mansah and Kwodwo Kuma."

The two grownups sipped the drink and continued to exchange small talk. Kwesi took a sip of the soft drink and said, "That's not bad at all. Indeed, it is better than good." He clicked his tongue and gulped the rest of the drink to the dregs. I followed suit. Then we asked for more, which Auntie Adoma graciously accommodated.

The grownups left us out of their conversation since we could not make any meaningful contribution to the topics they were discussing. We got bored and started fidgeting for lack of something to do. Auntie Adoma's two children, Effie Mansah and Kwodwo Kuma, who are our cousins, entered the living room. The girl, Effie Mansah, was eleven years old and closer to my age. Kwodwo Kuma, the boy, was seventeen years and a year older than my elder brother. Auntie Adoma saw them enter and directed, "Go out with your cousins and play." She added as we departed, "It's only through play that you can know and appreciate each other."

We went out and left the two adults to their nostalgic recollections and discussion of family vice and devices. Kwodwo Kuma suggested that we go to the nearby forest and hew soft-wood to build lorries. I had never seen that done and thought it would be fun. Kwodwo Kuma picked a machete from their kitchen and told his mother that we would be right back.

We hurried out of the house into the nearby forest to search for the softwood. As we walked, Kwodwo Kuma saw a guava tree with large ripe guava fruits. He hid his machete in the nearby grass, dashed by Kwesi, who was leading the pack, and climbed the tree with chimp-like agility. He invited the rest of us to join him when he was comfortably perched in the tree. "Come on, you two! What are you afraid of?" he urged. "There are no dwarfs to chase us. Let's gorge on some guava."

I did not want to fall into the same trap of Kobina Amuah after his infraction was reported to his mother, so I politely declined the invitation.

"No, thank you," I replied.

"Chicken," he teased.

I looked around for my brother Kwesi only to see him begin to climb the tree. Effie Mansah, who was as good a tree climber as any boy of her age, followed him. I felt ashamed and defeated as I debated the validity of Kwodwo Kuma's ascription of timidity. To prove my metal, I abandoned all caution and joined the two boys and the tomboy in the tree. I looked up at the tree and selected a y-shaped pair of branches to use as a seat. Unfortunately, I lost sight of it as I inched my way up the tree. I identified a different set of branches to serve the same purpose. I overheard Kwesi, Kwodwo Kuma, and Effie Mansah talking about my tardiness as I climbed the tree, and did not respond to their charge.

"We would have been here much earlier had it not been for his sleeping."

"When did he wake up?" Kwodwo Kuma inquired.

"At about eleven o'clock," replied Kwesi.

"You mean to say he slept until noon?" Effie Mansah asked with a sense of incredulity.

"Just about right," repeated Kwesi.

"We do not sleep that long in our home. In fact, we go to bed as early as eight o'clock and wake up just before dawn."

"Why that early?" I inquired.

"So that we can bathe on the rocks in front of our home before the neighbors wake up and the streets get busy with people."

"Does your Mama bathe there, too?" I inquired listlessly.

"Sometimes," replied Effie Mansah. "I go with her when she does."

"Really?" I said quizzically.

"That is rather infrequent," Kwodwo Kuma explained. "What happens is that Mama often bathes in an unfenced indoor bathroom with a receptacle to catch run-off bathing water. When she is finished, she calls either Effie or me to scoop the water run-off into a five-gallon aluminum bucket with a half-gourd and empty the dirty water outdoors. I do not like doing that work one little bit because I do not believe it is fair of her to ask us to clean up after her. But then, what can I do or say? She is my mother and all I have. And I have to help her sometimes."

"Sometimes," rejoined Effie, "my brother and I retreat to the top of the trees to escape the oppressing realities of our lives and Mama's unreasonable demands. That is simply unfair. "

Kwodwo Kuma's disgust over his living conditions assumed a special edge when he started talking about his father. "One day we got up and Papa was gone. He simply disappeared like smoke into the thin air. Sometimes," he continued, "I wonder whether he left because he did not love us or because we were too demanding of him. It's our fault, my sister's and mine. And now with Papa gone, we can no longer afford to do some of the things we used to do. Mama has to raise my sister and me all by herself on a meager income from her fishing enterprise. She finished building the house Papa started with mud instead of baked bricks and now she has such little money that she cannot afford to buy toys for either my sister or me to play with. I come here from time to time to chop softwood to make toys for my sister and me."

"Let's go and find the wood," Kwesi suggested.

"Okay," Kwodwo Kuma agreed.

We abandoned the gentle wind that wafted at us and hurriedly descended the tree. Kwodwo Kuma picked up his machete, which was hidden in the grass, and took to his heels with Effie, Kwesi, and me in hot pursuit. The distance between the boys and the girl widened as we chased Kwodwo Kuma.

"Wait for me, you guys! I cannot run as fast as you do," Effie Mansah complained.

"Let's run faster and leave her," said her older brother. "She will catch up," he continued, as he trotted ahead. "To the turn left," he exclaimed as he tried alluding capture.

We tried to follow, but lost him to the forest. We decided to wait in the open since we were not familiar with the area. He emerged from a different side of the forest and pointed, "There is the tree," Kwodwo Kuma shouted. We galumphed and sped with renewed enthusiasm. As we neared the tree, the distance between the boys and the girl widened some more. Effie Mansah pleaded, "Wait, you guys." Then, in a loud desperate voice, she cried out, "You must wait for me!"

"Guys, let's stop and wait for her. Anything can happen to her," I pleaded.

We stopped and waited for her to catch up with us.

"Hurry up," Kwodjo Kuma said harshly. "That is what you get for following boys," he added.

While we waited for her to rejoin us, I thought about the innumerable times I have heard females plead for help when males were around and watched them successfully carry out the same tasks when males were not around. I began to wonder whether females were as feeble as they appear or fake feebleness and faintheartedness to obtain sympathy of naïve and unsuspecting males that are eager to please.

"Now we can continue," Effie Mansah said when she caught up with us.

"Okay!" replied Kwodwo Kuma, who took a few steps toward the identified softwood tree and began to harvest part of its trunk with his machete. He tossed the hewed wood onto the open grassland and entered nearby shrubs to search for vines to tie and tow it. He emerged at the other end of the shrub with two winding vines and asked Kwesi to help tie up the harvested softwood for our homebound journey.

In the meantime, I started to talk with my cousin, Effie Mansah, about the changes that had occurred in her home since her sense of family was irrevocably shattered by unknown circumstances.

"I am miserable," she said with a tinge of drama as she sat on the grass.

"What do you mean?" I probed and sat down next to her.

"Well, things have been difficult for me," she sighed.

"How is that?' I asked as I looked into her eyes and attempted to understand what was going on with her.

She hesitated, looked down at the grass in front of her, and silently started to sob.

I reached out to wipe the tears off her face with my bare palms, but she gently lifted her arms and used them to stop my arms from reaching her face. I inched closer, looked straight down and waited for her to gain composure. She did and continued with her response in a whisper. "Well…" she paused and blew her nose with her forefingers as I patiently looked on.

"Well," she hesitatingly repeated, "let me put it his way. Things have not been the same since Papa left."

"In what way?" I inquired.

"You see, when Papa was home, we welcomed and hosted important professionals like lawyers, doctors, expatriate judges, school principals, and emissaries from village chiefs who came to see him. Some dignitaries waited for days for the audience and others stayed and dined with us. The house buzzed with activity. And now, with Papa gone, we have lost our appeal and slipped below the radar of the social elite. Some of the same people, who frequented our home and smiled effusively, see us differently because they do not believe we have anything meaningful or relevant to offer. Others wave at us when they see us or simply turn their heads in a different direction and pretend we do not exist. By and large, people have left us for richer pastures of influential people, who can better butter their bread and support their aspirations for social ascendancy. We have become part of the new poor— the cream of social scum – whose value and relevance has fallen into disuse. We have become that part society whom the rich spend energy to avoid. "

"But we are somebody, aren't we?" I protested.

"No, I did not mean it that way. You are relatives and supposed to visit."

"Then what do you mean?" I pressed on.

"I mean those people of power and influence who make things happen in this town do not come by any more," explained Effie.

"But that should not make you miserable."

"Perhaps not…. Perhaps, I am not being clear. You see, when Papa was home, he would sit me on his lap in his wicker rocking chair behind the open window at the end of the corridor and rock me to sleep. Sometimes he read to me as we rocked in the chair, and sometimes we just sat and had a nurturing daughter and father exchange. I remember Papa talking to me about how he and his cousins tied a hook to a rope and lowered it from a grapefruit tree in which they were perched to haul fried fish on display under the tree when the owner wasn't looking. I loved it when Papa came home, hugged and kissed me on both cheeks or gently ran the tip of his fingers through my disheveled hair, and gently tapped my ribcage to tickle my funny bone."

"Did you laugh when he tapped you on your side?"

"Of course I did. In fact, I looked forward to him coming home to do just that."

Her eyes brightened as she finished the sentence. For a brief moment, her youthful exuberance and vivacity shone through her eyes to mimic the illumination of a solitary star on a dark, moonless night. She paused and, almost apologetically, asked, "Does your Papa sometime tickle you?"

"Yes," I replied.

"And does he play with you?"

"Yes, but not as much as I would like him to."

"And do you miss him?"

"Sometimes I do and sometimes I don't. You see, my Papa is a lawyer. He works in his chamber, goes to court all day, and comes home at night and goes to bed. Sometimes I see him when he comes home and sometimes I don't if I am already asleep. And sometimes, when he comes home early, he plays military band music on a gramophone, bobs his head up and down, and whistles to the tunes. Sometimes, particularly on weekends when he is at home and not preparing briefs, he plays happy tunes on the piano for us to dance to. What did your father do?"

"I don't know," she shyly replied, but confidently affirmed, "One thing is for sure—whatever he did was important. It was important enough for people from everywhere to wait at his door, and for them to give him audience."

I wanted to continue with the conversation with Effie Mansah but was interrupted when Kwodwo Kuma announced, "We are ready to go."

I looked up from the grass and saw Kwesi holding one end of the rope he and Kwodwo Kuma had used to lasso the hewed softwood.

I got up from the grass and lent an arm to Effie Mansah for the walk back to Auntie Adoma's home.

Hardly had we embarked on our homebound journey when the sky grayed and roared with thunder and zigzagged lightning. A whirlwind of dust laden with rubble blew to announce the approaching rain that fell in torrents. We sought refuge under a large tree but had to abandon the shelter when the rain began to trickle through the foliage and fall on us.

"Let's take this path," said Kwodwo Kuma as we emerged from the tree and reached a fork on the pathway. "It is a shorter way to the house."

As we made our way to the house, my brother Kwesi stamped his feet in a puddle of water to splatter water mixed with mud on Effie Mansah. I thought that my brother's action was cruel and uncalled for, but I had seen him do other evil things on other occasions. I chalked it up in my memory. I stepped on the running water and felt it gurgling under my feet. I removed my feet from the running water, slipped, and nearly fell. I steadied myself and intermittently kicked the tall grass surrounding the pathway as I followed Kwodwo Kuma's lead. We soon arrived at Auntie Adoma's home, drenched to the bone.

"Where have you kids been?" Auntie Adoma asked as we needled our way between the two adults who were scouring around like two lunatics. They had pans and pots in their hands, which they set here and there to catch the pattering raindrops that dripped through the holes in the rusting, corrugated roof.

"Go and dry yourselves!" she said as we walked into the house, and instructed Kwodwo Kuma to fetch a pair of towels for my brother and me.

"Come on fellows, let's go," cajoled Kwodwo Kuma.

We followed him through the corridors to his mother's bedroom door, and stood in front of it.

"Wait for me. I will be right back," Kwodwo Kuma said, and disappeared behind the door's curtain.

In the meantime, Effie Mansah went by us on the way to her room and returned in another loose chemise. She passed by us and said, "See you guys soon," and disappeared.

Shortly thereafter, Kwodwo Kuma emerged from his mother's room in changed clothes with a pair of tattered towels in hand. He handed the first of the two towels to me, and the second to my brother Kwesi. "That is the best we can do," he apologized.

Kwesi and I took the towels and expressed our appreciation for his kindness. We removed our wet clothing, dried ourselves, and wrapped the towels around our waists to cover our genitals, wrung out our clothes, and hung them on an indoor line to dry.

Kwodwo Kuma continued his unsolicited apology more as an afterthought, "When things really get bad, I dry myself with a worn out flannel undershirt."

For me, that comment was as extraordinary as it was unexpected. I could not conceive of people in my extended family to be in such dire straits and in need of the basic necessities of life. I began to wonder whether Auntie Adoma was really a relation, as Grandma had said, and turned to my elder brother for confirmation. I surmised it would be insensitive to ask at the time and deferred the question for a more suitable occasion.

The pattering noise of the falling rain decreased in intensity and ceased. Then Auntie Adoma drew our attention and directed, "Take your clothes outside and spread them on the grass. They will dry faster under the direct sun."

We followed Auntie Adoma's instructions and took our shorts and shirts off the in-house line. Then we shook and stretched them out on the Bermuda grass lawn in front of the house to dry.

As we stepped out of the house, I noted that the gray clouds had dissipated and the sky was clear. The prevailing hot breeze that previously filled the air was replaced with a cool and clean-smelling one. The sparrows, whose melodious songs were drowned by the whipping, torrential rain, had resumed their avian quartets and duets with a vengeance, and tranquility had returned to Auntie Adoma's corner of the world.

When we returned to the house, I noticed that the pots and pans that Grandma and Auntie Adoma had placed at various points in the house to collect the dripping rain were no longer visible. Sunlight was streaming through the corrugated roof to mark where the rain had dripped through.

Kwesi and I joined Effie, who was already seated on a small hardwood stool in the kitchen, waiting for her brother to carve out a doll. Kwodwo Kuma joined us in the kitchen. He had a chisel and a hardwood hammer in his hands.

"Let's go out and build lorries," he invited avidly.

We followed him to the front of the house and watched him chisel and hammer the softwood for the lorries. Enthralled and fascinated with his creative abilities, I watched him chisel the wood and transform it into continuously flowing lorry bodies with awe. Then he mounted the bodies on hardwood frames, threaded a short stick through the front and back axils, and mounted spent thread spools as tires for the lorries to drive on. He cut a long stick with a y-shaped ending, trimmed its leaves and small branches, and used it to push and steer the toy lorry.

Then he carved a softwood cross of padded soft shavings into a primitive mannequin and gave it to his sister. Effie was as delighted with her present as any child is on Boxing Day. He suppliantly presented one of the lorries to me, and another to my elder brother. "I hope you like it," he added.

Auntie Adoma had cooked palm nut soup and pounded cassava *fufu* when we returned home from watching Kwodwo's carving activities. She invited us to dine with her and her family. I declined her offer when I saw Giant African land snails, black shellfish called *apoofii*, cheap, blue lagoon crabs, and dehydrated herrings somersaulting in the simmering soup. My brother Kwesi took one look at me and followed suit in declining her offer without a comment. "No, thank you," he said politely.

"Now," said Grandma, "let's go home if you do not want to eat your Auntie's cooking."

Grandma looked to us to take the lead out of the house, but we did not, so she did so, after some hesitation mixed with an apology and goodbye hugs. As she did this, she saw the lorries Kwodwo Kuma gave us and remarked, "I see you have carved toy lorries."

"Yes," I replied.

Grandma took my lorry, turned it up and down and side to side, and returned it to me. Then she looked admiringly at Kwodwo Kuma and said, "You are quite an engineer."

"I try," replied Kwodwo Kuma, as he attempted to be modest about his achievement. Then, turning to us, she said, "Your clothing must be dry now; get them on and let's go back home."

We left the lorries with Grandma, fetched our dried shirts and shorts, returned to the house, and changed into them. We tucked the toy lorries under our armpits and started our journey back to Grandma's home after hugging Auntie Adoma and our two cousins.

"We hope to see you during our next holiday," I told Effie as we departed.

The sun had set and the sky was still cloudless and clear as we left Auntie Adoma's house into the surrounding noise of pied bats, croaking toads, and cricket chirrs. The full moon's illumination was bright to light our footpath and would have been adequate for reading. The sporadic jetting light of the fireflies that followed the rain was visible everywhere on the terrain we were traversing. I tried to focus my attention on one of the fireflies but lost track of it as immediately as I conceived the notion. The moon's illumination and the foliage affected my view. I gave up the effort and inched toward Grandma to talk with her.

"Grandma! What happened to Effie and Kwodwo Kuma's father?" I inquired.

"He died of a heart attack. It is about time your Auntie went ahead and told those children about the circumstances of their father's death. It is not my place to tell them. To me, the longer she delays, the harder it will be on the children when they learn about it."

"Perhaps she does not want to hurt their feelings," Kwesi suggested.

"That is cruel. Children deserve to know the truth no matter how unpleasant. They are more resilient and capable of handling misfortunes better than adults. Children do not have the uncertainty of the future that make adults turn their hearts to the past."

"Talking of the past, was Auntie Adoma's husband also related to us?"

"Yes, by marriage," replied Grandma.

"This means Auntie Adoma is a real relative?" I asked.

"Yes, she is. As I told you, she is your Papa's sister." "You see,"

Grandma continued, "life is filled with changing circumstances. One day you are on top and the next you are at the bottom. Now let me tell you a story.

"There was a rich man who lived in a town far away from here. Because of his wealth, several townsmen turned a blind eye to his social misconduct and maltreatment of his servants until one day when he was caught breaking the law. He admitted his infraction to the police and expected to be fined a large sum of money when he went to court for a hearing. So, he carried fists full of large bills to pay any fines the court would impose. Sure enough, the judge found him guilty, fined him one farthing and instructed him to march directly to the court clerk's office and pay the fine or be jailed for six months if he failed to do that. He did not have a farthing in his pocket to pay the imposed fine and none in town would loan him one, so he ended up in jail despite his wealth."

"What is the moral of the story?" inquired Kwesi.

"That is for me to keep and for you to find out. Despite the taboo against talking bad about the dead, I can say this much—your Auntie Adoma's husband was a very arrogant man. People of this town didn't like him, despite protestations to the contrary because they thought he was arrogant and lived as if the world owed him everything. He forgot that the line between life and death was as razor thin as the line between breath and breathlessness. As often happens, people who are materially rich may be either ethically challenged or spiritually poor. Their private lives may be diametrically different from their public persona. The Creator, in His infinite wisdom, gave different talents to each of us. Therefore, it is important to recognize your own talents and admire the talents of others. Support others as they try to realize their dreams, no matter how unrealistic the dreams may appear to you. They will, in turn, support you, because life is filled with giving and taking; a circle of death and rebirth, whose beginning and end are embedded in one continuum."

She paused and added, as we stepped foot into her home, "I hope you learned from your Auntie's environment."

We dined under the glow of a lantern lamp and retired to bed.

Chapter 9

Grandma woke us up at the crack of dawn and announced, "Today is the coastal lagoon draining day, or the *Bakatue* Festivals, as the locals call it. You must get ready as quickly as possible so that we can walk and arrive at the site in good time for the opening ceremony."

On that announcement, Kwesi pulled me out of bed and ushered me towards the staircase. I grunted and moaned resentfully as I half-slept and half-walked down the staircase to empty my bladder at the heels of Mr. Rock. After that, I labored to the bathroom where Kwesi sprinkled cold water from a bucket on my face to awaken me.

We had a quick wash down, breakfasted, and returned to our room upstairs to change into our shorts and short-sleeve shirts. When we returned downstairs, Grandma was waiting for us in the kitchen and, as usual, chewing on her chewing stick and humming in cadences. She took the stick out of her mouth when she saw us and spat out the saliva that had accumulated in her mouth onto the dusty compound. She kicked some dust to cover the mixture of sputum and chewing stick. She placed the chewing stick in a cup holder and ordered the maid to return it to its normal storage place in the kitchen. Then she invited us to come along.

"Let's go!" she exclaimed, "we have to hurry."

We marched behind her out of the house. Once out, we walked past the market and took a path that led to the seashore. I began to question why she took that direction when the lagoon lay to the left of our home. Then it occurred to me that the lagoon was an orphan of the sea. Therefore, a journey towards the sea was probably the most logical path to its abode. I kept a tight lip and kept the pace, because talking, as I have learned, does not always demonstrate intelligence. To the contrary, it may show the depth of your ignorance.

As we progressed toward the site of the ceremony, the sun's beam gradually emerged from the horizon and lit the branches of the distant coconut trees with its soft golden glow. Its warmth heated the dew into massive cold vapors that rose from the foliage to fill the expanse between the seashore and the waking town. An owl led a group of roiled pied-crows and hooded vultures across the sky. An African house stork and a swallow flaringly swooped in the rear. Distant traditional drumming grew louder with each step to inform us of our progress toward the center of activity. A couple of full-figured women and a ragtag group of teenagers ceased chattering and slinked by us. Six haggard looking old men in knickerbockers with walking canes and two young women with babies strapped to their backs labored along. One of the older men, who walked with a slight limp, said, "Hello," as he overtook us. Kwesi looked as he passed by and sniggered a response.

"What are you sniggering about?" Grandma asked.

"Nothing," he responded evasively.

"You mostly respond 'nothing' when I ask you about what you are doing. Why don't you share what 'nothing' is with us? Your younger brother and I would like to know. Wouldn't you?" asked Grandma as she looked to me for confirmation.

"Yes, I certainly would," I affirmed with a slight nod of my head.

"Then share it!" Grandma urged.

"Well," Kwesi began, "I just couldn't help laughing at how that man was limping. He struck me as if he were over doing it to gain public sympathy."

"And so what if he was?" Grandma asked.

"I just don't think it is appropriate for people to use their handicap to obtain public sympathy through pretense," Kwesi replied.

"You are not in his shoes and can't tell whether he is or is not over doing it. Besides, as the Good Book says, 'Thou shall not judge,'" Grandma said.

"Such people should be kept away," Kwesi rebutted.

"And be kept where and away from whom?" Grandma inquired.

"Anywhere except a sane society," Kwesi replied.

"I don't think so," replied Grandma, who added, "The crippled, the maimed, and the infirmed are all part of the so called 'sane' society too, and have as much right as you and I have to be here. They test our capacity to love and our ability to embrace difference. When you see a child, a man, or woman who is sick and less able than you are, look at his or her life in the context of your own. Imagine what you would want or do in his or her position. Take a minute and compare the feathers around the neck of the hooded vulture with the pied-crow. You will soon recognize that the hooded vulture does not have as many feathers around its neck as the pied-crow, nor has it got the white collar of the pied-crow. Remember that the misfortune that befell the hooded vulture and caused it to lose its feathers around the neck could have possibly killed the pied-crow. Life's misfortunes affect us differently. How we choose to handle our staple of misfortunes makes all the difference between living productively with your disability and allowing your disability to shape the context of your living.

You must remember that, in a very broad sense, we are all disabled—we are all imperfect. We have different talents and abilities and it is these differences that coalesce to define who we are as human beings," Grandma concluded.

Kwesi did not respond to Grandma's oration. I began to wonder whether we would arrive at the seashore in good time to witness the ceremony. "Worry," I remember Grandma say, "is not known to solve problems—only actions do, after careful deliberations." I kept my continence and maintained a steady pace with Grandma and Kwesi. We finally arrived at the seashore to a melee of spectators jostling for vantage points in the horseshoe ring of celebrants. We joined in the melee and wiggled our way to the middle of the ring where the organizing officials were putting the final touches to the prelude of the ceremony.

The town's fetish priest rang a large cowbell to bring the crowd to attention. He pulled out a short knife and invoked the spirit of our ancestral leaders and gods that led them to their present abode. He filled a half-gourd with gin and poured libation to the gods of the sea, the land, the trees, the visible and the invisible powers that surround all living and dead things. He asked four fetish servants to bring forth a sheep they were holding to him. The men did as requested. The fetish priest lifted the short knife, looked into the heavens, and slit the neck of the sheep after invoking the spirits of the clouds, goddess of traditions. The sheep wiggled with pain and gave up the ghost. The four fetish servants that brought the sheep to its demise dragged its carcass and dangling neck off the stage. A fetish serf fired a musket to signal the fetish priest to begin shoveling the sandbar that sealed the lagoon's entry into the sea. The fetish priest took a wooden shovel from the fetish servant and started shoveling the sand line that would open a passageway between the lagoon and the sea. He passed the shovel down to the chief's linguist when he was done. The chief's linguist continued shoveling the sandbar and then passed the shovel to the clan's war strategist who repeated the process and passed the shovel down to the clan's next in command until the sandbar was swashed and adequately cleared for the lagoon to rejoin the sea. At that point, the chief fisherman took over the shoveling to finish the job. He asked the spectators to get away from the forceful downward flow of the lagoon into the ocean. The town's high priest to the gods cast a casting net in the lagoon to denote an end to the moratorium on fishing that was placed on the coastal lagoon three months earlier.

The fishermen paddled large dug-out canoes up and down the lagoon. They stood on the plank-strapped seats of the canoes, which also served as deck, and began to cast nets into the lagoon for tilapia, shrimp, and blue crabs. From time to time, they came to the shore of the lagoon to unload their catch for sale by the fishmongers who had spontaneously organized an open market. We accompanied Grandma through the hurriedly organized market to haggle over the prices of tilapia, shrimp, and blue crabs with the fishmongers. We did not have a container to carry the fish home, so a fishmonger, who knew Grandma and sold the catch to her, lent us one to carry our purchase home. The fishmonger would wait without despair for Grandma to return her container because to do otherwise was a cultural taboo. Besides, Grandma would have interpreted a failure to return anything that was loaned to her in good faith as theft by subterfuge and an immoral, despicable act.

"Hello, Grandma Elizabeth," someone hollered as we made our way out of the market and headed toward home.

Grandma stopped and turned around. She took a long hard look at the lanky young boy who hollered. He was casually dressed and appeared to be in his early twenties. He was rather nervous and perplexed that Grandma didn't recognize him instantly. Both Kwesi and I inquiringly rolled our eyes at him. Then the young man asked Grandma, with an air of incredulity, "Don't you remember me?"

Grandma continued looking at him quizzically. The young man noted her uneasiness and jogged her memory with the explanation, "I am Kobina Abofa, Mr. Minoo's last child."

My heart literally sank into my belly when I heard him mention Mr. Minoo's name. I did not know whether he was the Mr. Minoo whose orchard we looted at the beginning of our summer vacation or an entirely different and unrelated person. I looked at Kwesi and saw him quivering in his pants.

"Yes indeed," Grandma said, "I should have remembered that voice. Your Pa marched you to my home for several talking sessions."

"Yes, he did," Kobina Abofa responded with a sense of relief.

"And what are you doing in town?" asked Grandma as a matter of courtesy.

"I came for the *Bakatue* Festival."

Kobina Abofa slowed down his walking speed to lock step with ours. Grandma continued with her line of social questioning. "So what are you doing these days?"

"I am studying for the University of London Matriculation examination at Achimota Secondary School."

"And what do you intend to study after matriculating?"

"Engineering," he proudly responded.

"What is that?" Grandma inquired.

"I want to study how to fix things," replied Kobina Abofa with an air of confidence.

"Ah one of those," she responded off-handedly.

"Yes," he replied, before inquiring, "by the way, who are these young guys?"

"They are my grandchildren. They are here on vacation. They have a few vacationing days left before their father comes back to pick them up."

"Enjoy your vacation," said the young Minoo.

With that, he began to quicken his pace and separate from us.

"And what would you be doing in town?" Grandma inquired, as Kobina Abofa drew further away from us.

"I intend to attend the gala at the town hall. I have invited some colleagues to witness how we celebrate the *Bakatue* Festival in our town. We are supposed to meet at the post office on Main Street."

"Good for you," replied Grandma.

"By the way," Kobina Abofa shouted as he began to jog. "Will your grandchildren come to the gala?"

Grandma ignored his question and proceeded, "Please extend my greeting to your Papa."

"I will," he replied, and broke into a run to rendezvous with his friends.

"Did you hear what he said?" whispered Kwesi.

"Yes," I responded.

"Did you hear that there will be a gala at the town hall today?"

"Yes, yes," I repeated off-handedly.

"Well," Kwesi continued in a whisper, "we have to attend."

"Not a chance. I don't think so. Did you notice how Grandma ignored the young Minoo's inquiry about the gala?"

"That is no skin off my back. And now that we are at it, I want to know whether or not you have observed that Grandma sometimes does not respond to people."

"Yes of course."

"So?"

"Why do you say, 'so'? I believe she uses silence to avoid involvement in unpleasant or controversial situations with unpredictable outcomes."

"I wonder if that is a woman's thing," Kwesi replied.

"I don't think so."

"Well, what do you think about this," began Kwesi. "What do you think about sneaking out to the gala after she goes to bed tonight?"

"Not a chance," I repeated. "I don't want to be on her wrong side."

"She will not do a thing to you if you do," Kwesi replied with conviction.

"You may be right, but I definitely don't want to find out," I responded.

"Well, you only live once. We have not attended a gala before and may not ever, if we do not seize this opportunity. Remember what Grandma said. 'Strike while the iron is hot.'"

"This is not an issue about hot iron or cold iron," I quipped. "Besides, there is nothing to strike here. This is what I see: Papa entrusted us to her care. Therefore, we need to respect and ask for her permission before we go out. Short of that, you can go by yourself and I will stay at home."

"What are you kids talking about?" asked Grandma.

"Nothing," Kwesi replied.

"Yes indeed," she retorted, and continued sarcastically, "it is great when children open their mouths for sound to emerge and claim they are not talking about anything when asked. What a miracle." She concluded.

I wanted to tell Grandma what we were talking about but Kwesi stared me into silence.

"Nothing, really," I repeated tepidly.

"Hurry up. The sun is already beginning to burn. We have to be back at home before it gets really baking hot. Above all, we have to go home for the maid to remove the guts of the fish and ready it for either frying or grilling. Then there is lunch and dinner to cook," Grandma explained.

We continued walking steadily until Grandma's home came to view. Then Kwesi suggested, "You do not have to worry about lunch. We will go to the market and buy some roasted plantains and peanuts." He looked to me for confirmation.

"Yes, that will do," I affirmed.

So when we got back home from the festival, Grandma untied coins she had at the end of one of the upper corners of her cover-shoulder cloth and gave them to us for lunch.

"Here is some money for you to buy the plantains and the peanuts for your lunch," Grandma said as she handed five pence to each of us. "I expect you to come right back."

"Yes, Grandma," we responded in unison as we dashed out of the house and closed the compound gate behind us.

110

Once out, we bolted toward the market with the speed of escaping jail breakers who had pack of charging hyenas in hot pursuit. We ran until we were out of breath before stopping to catch our breath and half-walked, half-trotted the rest of the way to the market. We stopped at the plantain and peanut vendors' stalls and strolled from one vendor to the next in search of the perfect roasted plantains at the best possible price. We settled on a stall attended by a teenage girl in a bright yellow dress with a yellow and black striped handkerchief to match. She was bare-footed, like most of the women that hawked various wares in the market and, for that matter, most people that frequented the streets. She had a pleasant engaging smile, a set of bright white teeth and a pleasant demeanor to boot. She sold us two big fingers of well-roasted plantains and a generous serving of peanuts in exchange for our money. Looking back, I don't know how much her good looks influenced our decision to buy from her.

"Thanks," said Kwesi after the exchange.

"She is cute," he said as we walked away from her stall.

"I agree," I replied, and added after a brief moment, "I was taken in by her dimples."

"I was taken in by her soft voice," Kwesi replied.

"And I liked her engaging smile," I replied.

"That's all right for now. Don't get carried away," said Kwesi. "Besides, you are too young to notice these things."

"And so are you," I retorted.

"She smiled at me," responded Kwesi.

"I do not think so," I contradicted.

"I think she smiled at me. I know she thinks I am cute."

"How do you know? I did not hear her say that," I replied

"Indeed she did not. You see, women do not always explicitly express what they want or wish. The mystery lies in getting you to accurately understand and respond to what they mean when it is not said."

"I bet they don't have to express their wishes," I rejoined.

"You see, women tend to be shy, or at least pretend to be, and want you to make inferences from their conduct."

"And men are not sly or shy?" I quipped.

"Not as much as women are, particularly on first encounters. That is why men are supposed to make the first moves when it comes to starting boyfriend-girlfriend relationships."

"I bet. Personally, I do not see anything wrong with women initiating those types of relationships."

"Maybe yes, maybe no,' Kwesi replied. "As you know, I am more of a lady's man than you are. I have a girlfriend at home and you don't."

"Granted, then, you cannot have this one. After all, how many girls can you hold and kiss at the same time? Only one, if my observation is right."

"Maybe and maybe not," Kwesi replied.

I stopped pressing the issue when I realized he had reverted to his usual ambivalence when he was losing an argument. He, like most people, must have a way to save face and preserve their sense of being.

"Let's go and visit Ayah's stall. Perhaps we may see Kobina Amuah and Danger. We haven't seen them for a while," I suggested as a way out of his discomfort.

"Okay," he readily agreed.

We walked in uneasy silence to Ayah's stall where we saw both Kobina Amuah and Danger. They were sitting on folded empty jute bags in the stall having a repast of ken-key and fish. Ayah invited us to join them but we declined since we had just had lunch and were not hungry.

"Have you heard about the gala at the town hall?" Kobina Amuah asked between bites of ken-key and fried flounder.

"Yes," Kwesi replied.

"Then you are going?" Danger joined in.

"No, I do not think so. I do not think our Grandma would like us to."

"Have you asked her?" Danger inquired.

"We haven't," I replied.

"Then ask her,' suggested Kobina Amuah. "The whole town will be there. I do not see how she can deny you that opportunity."

"Just ask her. You will be surprised," Danger encouraged. "We will wait for you at the last stand of the open night market."

"Okay, we will," I responded hastily, without thinking of what Grandma's response was likely to be when asked or of the consequences of breaking my promise to our friends if we were denied the opportunity.

We left them on that note and headed for home.

"We will ask Grandma," Kwesi echoed as we headed home. "She must agree," he said repeatedly, as if doing so would transform his wish into a reality.

Upon further reflection, I began to second guess my initial promise. Indeed, knowing what I knew of her during our short time with her, I was reasonably sure she would not grant us permission to go out at night without an adult's supervision, and I was not about to find out if her response would be different from my presumption.

"Well," I said, "you may have to ask her when we get home because I will not."

"I will, I will," Kwesi exclaimed with an edge in his voice, but he did not ask her when we arrived home. Perhaps he did not ask out of an innate instinct to protect his fragile ego. Like most children, his acute senses, which enable him to adapt to new phenomena, directed him to prefer the predictable safety of the known to the unpredictability of the unknown.

We washed down our lunch with water and joined Grandma, who was comfortably seated in the kitchen supervising the maid. The maid had finished removing the scales of the tilapia and was putting the final touches to ready it for the next day's dinner.

"Add a little more sea salt to the fish and dab it dry with the kitchen towel," she said to the maid, who followed her instructions without making eye contact. In fact, since our arrival, I had not observed the maid make eye contact with Grandma at all.

"Then drip two droplets of water in the cooking oil on the charcoal pit fire to check if it's hot enough for frying the fish," Grandma directed.

Once again the maid obeyed her instructions and did as told. "It is hot enough for frying the fish," the maid affirmed to Grandma. Then, the maid placed the pieces of the fish that were cut in threes or halves into the hot shallow oil of the skillet to fry. She turned the fish from one side to the other after probing it with the edge of the knife to confirm the half that was submerged in the hot oil was cooked through to the bone, and repeated the process until she was through frying that portion of the fish. Then, she dried both sides of the portion of the fish earmarked for grilling with a kitchen towel and grilled it over a mildly hot charcoal pit fire on a griller made from metal strapping. I watched her and picked up a few tips about cooking for future use.

"I am tired," Grandma announced as she got up from her seat. "I am going up to take a nap. You kids can go and play, or do what you will, to entertain yourselves... You can either play with the lorries that your cousin Kwodwo Kuma gave you or create your own toys to play with."

We were at a loss for something to do. I decided to sit in the shade of the house and enjoy the dry afternoon breeze. After sitting for a while on the softwood stool, my bottom began to hurt. I got up and went upstairs to fetch the reed mat we slept on at night from its holding place behind Grandma's bedroom door. I tiptoed around the room to avoid detection and allow Grandma to enjoy her sacred siesta, but despite my efforts, she heard my movements and woke up.

"Where are you going with the reed mat?" she asked as I stepped out of her bedroom and began to close the bedroom door behind me.

"I am taking it downstairs to rest on it in the shade of the house."

"Remember to return it."

"I will," I promised.

I took the reed mat downstairs and spread it in the shade of the house. I removed my undershirt and sandals and lay down with my back on the mat to rest. Two houseflies buzzed in one of my ears and landed on my head. I tried to snatch one with my hand but both flew away. Another housefly landed on the tip of my nose. I tried to kill it with a clap of the hands with exactly the same results. I gave up, and allowed the soothing breeze to coax my senses into sleep. I looked at the sky and listened to the noises that filled the air around me as I waited for sleep to envelop me in its bosom. The afternoon sky was clear, with strands of cumulus clouds strolling to an unknown destination, and the air was serene and unusually quiet. Billows of blue smoke rose up from the next-door neighbor's home and dissipated into the air. Two pied-crows flew across the sky. A gray and white-feathered mother hen crackled a warning to its yellow-furred chicks that were scavenging over leftovers to take refuge from a chicken hawk that was hovering in the sky. But the chicken hawk swooped down from the sky, snatched one of the chicks in its talons, and flew away before the mother hen could mount any defense. A black and brown-feathered male mallard that was lounging around the sandy compound squeamishly attempted to fly and fell, chest first, to the ground. I closed my eyes and slowly slipped away into a sweet sleep. My breathing quieted as the transient splendor of the afternoon passed away into the infinite, never to return.

The slanting light of the sun was about to make a final dip at the horizon when I woke up from the siesta. The tropical heat, which was unbearable at noon, had become as bearable as it was when the sun started its journey at dawn. The wind was calm and the birds were twittering merrily to mark the end of another day of unfettered freedom. The two nondescript houseflies that hampered the onset of my siesta were exchanging guard with the humming mosquitoes. They appeared to consult over which disease to pass on as day demurred into darkness. I heard a buzz in my ears but could not make out which of the two distempering insects caused it and decided to ascribe the mischief to the mosquito, since its reputation for infecting humans with diseases was more dismal. A small sac spider dropped down from one corner of Grandma's home and began to build a web intended to harvest any insects that strayed into the trap. The fruit bats began their evening wail and the domesticated fowls huddled under coops and pens to sleep away the night.

Grandma was already up from her siesta and sitting in the kitchen. She looked at me and remarked, "It looks like you had a pretty good nap."

"Yes," I agreed, and nodded to underscore my agreement.

I stretched my limbs and got up from the reed mat, folded and returned it to its storage space. All of a sudden, it occurred to me that I had not taken my anti-malaria tablets according to prescription. I quickly fished two tablets from our traveling suitcase, which was also our medicine cabinet, took them with water, and returned to the kitchen.

"Where is Kwesi?" I asked Grandma.

"The maid told me he left to fly a kite on the hill behind the church."

"Okay," I responded.

"He will be back soon," Grandma confidently replied.

Grandma looked at me and noted, "You appear worried."

"No," I lied.

The fact is that I was worried, but could not admit it to her before consulting with Kwesi. I was becoming increasingly aware that the time I spent sleeping at siesta was gradually getting longer. I was not sure why and wanted to talk with Kwesi and obtain his assurances that I was well and healthy. I received that assurance sooner than I thought. Kwesi returned home in an unusually festive mood and dismissed my apprehension. "You are just fine," he said after talking to him about my fears. "There is nothing wrong with you—absolutely nothing!" he reiterated, and added, "Sometimes we all need a little more sleep than usual. Remember Papa saying that young, healthy, active boys and girls need more sleep than inactive grownups. You are young, active, and doing more stuff than usual. Therefore, it stands to reason that you will sleep more than you usually do. That is that, pure and simple."

"Then why do I also feel weak in my limbs?" I asked

"It's all in your head. I don't see anything wrong with you. You are just worrying about a little ache here and there. All of us get those from time to time. It is part of growing up. You will get over it. Just trust me."

I accepted his words of assurance without further question. After all, he was older than I was, and, as Grandma told me, it is imprudent to challenge the wisdom of the old. Their life experiences give them insight into life situations, which is beyond the reach of youth's intemperance.

But that night I lost my appetite. The fried tilapia and the warm ken-key, which Grandma served us for dinner, tasted more like paper than food. I looked across the dining table at Kwesi who was avidly munching his dinner. He methodically pulled bones from the stomach lining of the tilapia on his dinner plate with his right fingers. He pinched a piece of the ken-key and a piece of the fish, put both pinches together into a small ball, popped it into his mouth, and chewed it with relish as I listlessly looked on.

We retired to bed after dinner. Grandma told us a story about a man who kept secrets from his friends and family. "There was a public lamplighter, a loner, who lived in a small town of three hundred where everybody knew everybody and people were really open and friendly. He did not socialize because he believed he was better than the rest of the town's people since he brought light to them. Bluntly put, he isolated himself from society and lived like a hermit. The townspeople reciprocated in kind by looking askance at him and not inviting him to their homes or social functions.

"One day, he went to the market to buy foodstuff and stopped at a fish stall to buy fish. As he was haggling over prices with the fishmonger, a scuffle broke out in the next fish stall between the fishmonger and a male customer. The male customer knocked the fishmonger to the ground and made away with the fish without paying for it. Passersby stopped at the stall to witness the goings-on and render assistance. When the fishmonger got up from the ground, one of the passersby, who had been drawn to the scuffle, asked her to identify the assailant. She pointed in the direction of the next stall, whereupon the passersby pounced on the loner and mercilessly mobbed him. The police arrived on the scene, arrested, and took him to the station without questioning any eye-witnesses. At the station, he was held for petty larceny and taken to court for trial. During the trial, he rightfully asserted his innocence. The judge listened carefully to his defense and asked him to provide a character witness to buttress his claim, but nobody in town knew him enough to vouch on his character or innocence. As a result, the judge sentenced him to prison for an indeterminate period.

"What is the moral of the story?" I asked Grandma.

But once again, she did not tell me the moral of her story. Instead, she replied, "It is only a fool who wants to know the chapter and verse of what you say, desirous for an inclusive meaning behind and intolerant of ambiguity. His deftness for definitiveness is devoid of imagination, and his destiny is irrevocably sealed."

I drifted to sleep after Grandma had finished her narration and would have slept until the morning had Kwesi not woken me up as I was beginning to dream. He softly reminded me of the rendezvous with Danger and Kobina Amuah.

"We have to meet them," he insisted.

"Yes indeed, but not in my condition. Really, I do not feel up to it." I responded.

"But you promised, and a man's word should mean something to his friends," he said harshly.

"Not when I am sick or about to be," I protested.

I felt cold and chilly. Perspiration shone on my forehead like the condensation of cold water on a gourd and oozed down my nose. I was weak and overcome by the notion that I was coming down with some illness. A mixture of desires to save face and maintain good relationships with my friends goaded me to go to the rendezvous. Leaving my friends in a lurch would demonstrate bad faith. Above all, I did not want Kwesi or any of my friends to think I was an unreliable boy of questionable integrity. I wanted them to believe that I was an honest and trustworthy friend who follows through on his promises. But, try as I did, I could not remember promising a meeting with them.

"I do not recall that promise," I replied.

"Yes Ato, you certainly did," Kwesi reaffirmed.

Left without a scintilla of evidence to the contrary, I reluctantly accepted what Kwesi said as gospel.

"Come on, let's go," he said, as he started crawling out of the bedroom. I crawled behind him until we were totally out. We tip-toed down the staircase and descended the stairs with catlike care until we arrived on the ground floor. Kwesi gingerly opened the latch holding the door to the staircase, closed it and put a large rock to hold it in place, and waved at me to follow. We both emerged on the compound to a bright moonlight whose illumination gave us the needed light for executing the final step to sneak out of the house and partake in the evening dance of the *Bakatue* Festival festivities.

We removed our sleeping clothes and folded them. Kwesi climbed the neem tree and asked me to toss them to him. "Give me your clothes," he commanded with an edge in his voice. I threw them up to him one piece at a time. He shuffled his feet on the first rung of the branches as he searched for a suitable hiding place for the clothes. He threw down our folded clothes and tennis shoes, which he had earlier hidden in the tree.

"Catch," he said as he threw them down.

He cautiously descended from the tree and quickly got into his clothes. I followed suit and brought up the rear. We walked briskly to the gate to the compound where Kwesi unlocked the crossbars of the gate bolts while I watched. The crossbars squeaked when he slid them from their holder. Kwesi stopped and looked over his shoulder to see if somebody was watching. There was no one, so he continued to unlock the continually squeaking crossbars and intermittently paused to verify if we were being spied on. He kept working the lock to the crossbars until he opened the gate. We watchfully crossed the threshold of the gate and stepped into the road that was lit by moonlight covering the sleeping town.

"Let's find something to keep the door slightly ajar," I suggested.

We looked around the open gutter that ran in front of the house and found a rock that was big enough to do the job lying close to the gate. Kwesi picked up the rock and pivoted it against the gate, thus assuring it was not closed shut. A dog bayed at the moon to mark our exit from home and a rendezvous with our buddies for the dance.

Kobina Amuah and Danger had already arrived and were waiting for us when we arrived at the steps of the nearby church, which was our agreed point of rendezvous. We joined them and walked through underbrush to the town hall where the evening dance was being held. We passed by rows of houses roofed with new corrugated iron sheets. They reflected the soft rays of the moonlight in much the same way as they did to the sun, but without the heat. The dark blue sky, which provided a backdrop to the night, blurred the distinguishing features of the tree leaves that covered the landscape. I could not separate the shadow of mango trees from the orange trees, nor the lime from the lemon, and had to rely on the scent emitted from their flowers to establish the distinctive identities of the grove of trees we came upon.

When we emerged from the shadows of the trees into the street, we saw lovers strolling hand in hand.

We passed them and headed for the town hall.

"Let's go to the entrance to see if the gatekeeper will consider our youth and let us in," Kobina Amuah suggested.

The entrance was choked with ticket holders trying desperately to gain entry into the town hall. "Here is my ticket and another one for my wife," someone shouted.

Kobina Amuah scouted the gathering and suggested we take a different route into the hall since we did not have tickets.

"It appears there are a lot of people at the entrance. It will be better for us to take a different route." We slunk from the gathering and took a footpath that led to the back of the hall and came upon a high mound of sand and rocks piled close to the wall of the hall, and a tree close to a mound of dirt on the other side of the wall. Kobina Amuah climbed to the top of the mound of dirt. He held on to the branch of the tree that extended over the mound and used it to scale the wall, taking refuge in the tree's branches. I followed him, and Kwesi followed me, with Danger climbing last.

"Who is there?" somebody demanded when we were all in the tree.

"Hush," Danger whispered.

A police officer in a black uniform walked under the tree and looked up the branches. He casually inspected its foliage and walked back to his post. I felt like sneezing when he looked up, and pinched my nose. We waited for a while in the branches and scaled down the tree after a consensus that the danger had passed. We tip-toed over the grass separating the dance hall from the wall and used the shadow cast by the wall to snake behind the bouncers.

We entered the hall and wrestled our way behind a wall of Boy Scouts and Cubs in their khaki shorts and white shirts with white scarves around their necks. They looked like gray parrots that formed a human chain separating the dancing expatriates from the local on-lookers. We knelt down behind the line and stuck our heads between the legs of teenagers to watch the expatriates dance. Cigarette smoke hung immobile in the dimly lit hall like a trapped black cloud in the valley of the dead. The orchestra was seated on a dais, playing an unfamiliar piece of music. The white expatriates, who were not dancing, were seated in knots of four or five to a round table and chatting freely. Some of the male expatriates wore tuxedos and tailcoats while others wore dark-colored suits with kerchiefs sticking out of their breast pockets. The wives or lady friends of the males wore long, flowing evening dresses of varied colors with brooches pinned to their chests. A native man of medium-build in black trousers, a white shirt, and a black bow tie tended the bar. He was serving drinks to the expatriates at a movable bar on wheels. The rest of the natives in the hall stood and watched as the expatriates went to and fro to the bar for drinks, gulped them down, and returned for more.

During the interlude, the orchestra, which was made up of local and expatriate musicians, rested in their chairs on a wooden dais. Some expatriate musicians got up from their seats and mingled with their compatriots on the cement dancing floor. Others took advantage of the break and walked to the bar for drinks. They returned to their seats with drinks and shared them with their native-born orchestral members who were not similarly privileged.

The orchestra's conductor called the orchestra to attention after the interlude. The musicians stopped whatever they were preoccupied with and returned to their seats at the dais. They tried a few notes and phrases to test the pitch and re-tune their instruments. The conductor raised his baton, lowered his head, and looked to the percussion section of the orchestra. Then he turned around and looked at the dance floor, again at the orchestra, brought down his baton, and the orchestra started playing a waltz, fox trot, or something like that. The conversations ebbed and the expatriates rose up from their seats onto the cement floor and danced with their female partners. The females looked at the faces of the men they danced with as if they were entranced or hypnotized by them. A stuck note in the accordion modulated up and down to synchronize the shriek of a trapped cave voice.

After a series of waltzes, fox trots, and other dances, the orchestra played a combination of the first few bars of popular tunes to the delight of the expatriates who sang along. The men, and possibly some of the women, started whistling and caterwauling. A husky expatriate man with a lynx's whiskers and feline hair lifted a lanky lady he was dancing with and tossed her into the air. Other dancing couples cheered as he caught the lady in mid-air and gently set her feet down on the floor. The church bell pealed twelve times to indicate it was midnight. A clapping of hands and shoes and a final flourish of the orchestra announced the end of the gala. The expatriates stopped dancing and filed out of the dance hall with their stiff felt hats in one hand and lady friends or wives on the other. The human shield of local Boy Scouts that separated the natives and the expatriates collapsed. I looked at my brother and said, "It is time to go home."

"Not yet," replied Danger.

"No, not right now! You must wait for the real gala to begin. You do not see or truly partake in a gala until you have joined your own to celebrate a significant cultural event. It is in the celebration of these events that people create a common bond that identify the soul of their cultural heritage," Kobina Amuah encouraged.

"Yeah, yeah," I replied caustically because I was feeling really puny and wanted to be in bed. I was getting the chills and my teeth were chattering involuntarily from time to time.

"Yes, let's wait and celebrate our own culture," rejoined Kwesi.

While we were engaged in these discussions, the expatriate members of the orchestra left the wooden dais and departed with the expatriate dancers and their guests. Local musicians, who had been waiting in the wings, carried their native and foreign-made musical instruments and joined the local orchestral members who straddled the dais. A native drummer beat his homemade bongo drum and a trumpeter sounded his trumpet. A saxophonist, a flutist, and a zither player joined them. A garrulous guitarist picked at his Spanish guitar and the local conductor harmonized the sounds into an upbeat festive tempo of what the locals call "Highlife." The natives, who had earlier looked on impassively at the expatriate celebrants and their dancing partners, swarmed the dance floor. The tempo of the music and the festive mood of the dancers drew us in. We joined the crowd on the floor and found ourselves dancing to the two-step beat of the "Highlife" music.

I succumbed to a dance-induced sweat that dried when the first conventional currents of the sea blew through the hall and carried away the noxious hanging smoke. I felt chilly and unsure of my steps, so I retired to the sidelines to keep from falling and waited for Kwesi and my two friends. As I sat holding my head in the palms of my hands, a middle-aged man in his dashiki stopped on his way out of the dance hall and asked, "How are you feeling, young man?"

"Fine," I replied, more out of habit than to express my sincere feeling.

He walked away saying, "Take care."

"Thank you," I replied.

In the din of the dancing and music, the church bell chimed three to denote it was three o'clock in the morning. I returned to the dance floor for a second time in the hopes of finding my compatriots, but there was no sign of them. I despaired and walked out of the hall to search for a way back home. I sought directions from anyone who would help, since I was not familiar with the terrain. I came upon a young lady and her companion who were returning home after the gala. They were going my way and invited me to join them.

"Thank you," I replied.

We walked quietly under the bright moonlit sky and did not make the usual small talk to pass time. From time to time, the scurrying of small animals of the night among the surrounding vegetation broke the clap-trapping of our footsteps. I assumed from their silence that they wanted to be left alone and did not ask the usual social questions to pass time.

"There is your home," the young man pointed as we came upon it.

"Thank you for your help," I replied as I walked towards the gate.

"You are welcome," the young man replied, and walked on while holding the hand of his lanky lady companion.

I removed the rock securing the gate and entered the house compound. I climbed the neem tree to retrieve my sleeping cloth, and could not find it. I descended the tree and used the illumination of the moonlight to scour the leaves of the neem tree and the vicinity for my sleeping cloth without success. I began to wonder whether the wind had dislodged and blown them away and started to search the compound frantically for them. The church bell pealed again but I didn't count the number of peals because I felt rather disoriented. I looked up and started walking toward the staircase and to bed.

"Is this what you are looking for?" Grandma asked, as she handed my sleeping cloth to me.

Her voice simultaneously reassured and frightened me. I stood, petrified and immobile, like a pillar of salt.

"Where is your brother?" she continued.

"I left him at the town hall."

"You did what?" She asked in astonishment.

"I was not feeling well and had to come home."

"You should never, never leave him behind! You went out with him, so you must come back with him. It is much easier for one person to be harmed by a stranger than for two people to face harm from the same quarter. That is why elands travel in pairs," Grandma added.

"I am sorry," I responded tepidly. "Grandma," I continued, "I really feel weak and don't feel like talking. Can we talk about this in the morning when I wake up?"

"Sure," she replied. "Now come here and let me check you out."

Grandma held me in both hands. As she did, the church bell pealed five times to denote it was five in the morning. The moon disappeared behind a vale of tree branches. I heard the rooster crow cock-a-doodle-doo and passed out.

Chapter 10

Sickness has a way of bringing your vulnerability to the fore. That vulnerability legitimizes your dependence and permits caretakers to overlook your ineptitude or deviancies. It also reminds people of the fragility of life and the transience of the many things they take for granted in good and healthy times.

Except for occasional bouts with coughs and sniffles, I was an energetic, healthy child with a zestful life, and had not been subjected to these tendencies before. Therefore, the idea of being sick to a point of dreary listlessness and confinement in Grandma's bed was as alien to me as a land-trotting tadpole. Yet, here I was, sick, languid, and confined. I did not know how I got into that bed nor was I about to ask—at least for now—because for whatever reason, lying in that bed was comforting. It made me feel closer to Grandma and feel that I would come out all right. I turned to the window facing the bed and saw the shadow of the tall hibiscus tree behind Grandma's room fall on the windowsill to denote the sun was approaching the apex of its parabolic journey through the tropical sky. The room was quiet and calm, with silence reigning over it like the pall on a funeral burial. The cheeping and twittering canaries, finches, and other common birds filled the air with enchanting aviary melodies as they returned to that corner of the world to feed their wobbling fledglings with their catch. The undying wind joined the aviary melodies with variations on hissing melodies as it sped up and slowed down its movement through the mosquito net that covered the partially opened window.

An unexpectedly gentle tap on the door broke my enjoyment of the unchained melodies. I turned momentarily towards the direction of the tapping and heard an inquiring voice ask, "Are you awake?" I did not respond. Then, after a pause, the voice repeated the inquiry to the accompaniment of an urgent second tapping. "Are you awake?"

"Yes," I replied in a weak, whispering voice.

"How are you feeling?" asked the person behind the voice as it entered the room. I fixed my look in the direction of the voice and saw Grandma slowly crossing the threshold of her bed room, inching toward where I lay in her bed on account of my illness. Kwesi hovered behind her in the room and pulled out a stool that Grandma stowed under her bed and made himself comfortable. In the meantime, Grandma removed the mosquito netting and completely opened the window overlooking the bed. "Let's get in some fresh air," she said as she set the net down on the floor close to the window.

The soft sun broke through the window and gave her a better view of my prostrated body. She looked at me from head to toe and inquired, "How are you?"

"Fine," I said, despite a tingling sensation in my feet signifying the contrary.

"Would you like some soup?" she asked with a concerned look.

"Not really," I replied.

"Try it. It will make you feel better," she encouraged.

"All right," I reluctantly agreed.

Grandma helped me out of bed and, with Kwesi holding on one hand and she on the other to give support, I walked laboriously to the dining room and slumped heavily into the same chair I used on the first day of our visit when Papa dropped us off to dine.

Grandma left the room and returned with a pot filled with garden eggs soup and plates containing slices of boiled yam and toasted bread on a dining tray. Kwesi looked on as Grandma set the table and urged me to eat. I straightened up in the chair and picked up a spoon to stir the soup. It was watery and contained tomatoes, sliced onion rings, grilled red snapper, and shrimp. Grandma picked up a large serving spoon from the top dining room drawer and spooned soup into a colorfully painted Victorian porcelain bowl. She set the bowl containing the soup on a large plate, placed it in front of me, and invited me to eat. "Here is some soup for you. Enjoy it," she said indulgingly.

I slowly bent over the table and picked up the spoon to scoop the soup. I slurped a spoonful of the soup and immediately vomited it out. I reclined in my chair and, for the first time, felt defeated by the illness. Grandma removed the uneaten soup and set it aside. She reached into the bowl of fruits that was sitting on top of the cupboard, picked out a tangerine, and asked me to try it. "Eat the tangerine, it will help settle your stomach," she urged.

I arduously peeled the tangerine, pulled a sliver off, and ate it with a repeat of the vomiting episode. Grandma was not deterred. She gave me a carafe of water from a cistern and insisted I try sipping the water. I took in a few sips of the water with the same discomforting results. Grandma looked at me with a dogged sense of determination, which I did not share. I looked at her and shook my head. The vomiting had zapped my energy and rendered me weak and lethargic. I was tired and wanted out of the dining room.

"I want to go back to bed," I declared.

Grandma screamed for the maid to clean up the vomit. "Abena Atokyene, bring a bucket of water and an overused towel to clean up the vomit. Hurry! Hurry!" she exclaimed.

The maid hurried up the staircase with a bucket of water and a mop. She assiduously cleaned up the vomit from the hardwood floor under Grandma's watchful eyes. She left the dining room with the bucket containing the mixture of water and vomit to empty in the open gutter that lay in front of the house. I tried to push the table away from my chair and get up and walk back to bed, but could not. I slumped in the chair, exhausted from the effort, and looked at Grandma and Kwesi with a sense of anger tinged with despair. Grandma noted my anguish. She got up from the chair she had assumed to watch me eat, gently tapped me on shoulder, and asked me to relax.

"Take it easy. It will be all right," she assured me before leaving the dining room.

Kwesi helped me back up the stairs and into Grandma's bed. "Sit back and relax. Everything will be all right," Kwesi echoed encouragingly.

The quiet room began to depress me. I felt dispirited and doubted whether I would ever be well again or was at the end of my rope. I was on my way out of the world with an undiagnosed disease as the conduit. To me, all animate things, including people, were born to grow old, if they were lucky, and die. Otherwise, they either fall ill and die or simply die. The notion of people recovering from illness was alien. Death was an inevitable end, the final chapter to illness for all. Several conversations I overheard on the subject between Papa and Grandma and their friends or relatives confirmed this. "Such and such a person died after either a short, long illness or just died," they said. Therefore, I concluded that since I was human in the grip of illness, it was only a matter of time till the illness would end my life. My ability to overcome the illness, live, and talk about it, was out of the question and far away from my consciousness. I thought it was apt to close the final chapter of my life by resolving outstanding conflicts and asking for forgiveness from the people I have wronged. After all, I did not want to meet my Creator when I was filled with self-doubt and hate, or worse, teeming with sin. Consistent with this notion, I decided to begin the first step of this journey at home by resolving an ill feeling I had been nursing against my elder brother Kwesi. And since he was already in the room, I invited him to sit down for a talk.

Kwesi reached under the bed and pulled out the stowed stool. He sat on it and cast down his eyes like one who was avoiding contact with one infected with diphtheria or some infections disease. I took a hard look at him and noted he was wearing a pair of red and black shorts and a matching shirt. He seemed uneasy to the point of melancholy—He had lost his baby fat and assumed more matured facial features. He had bushy eyebrows, long eyelashes, and a cross between a European and African nose. His lips were not as thick as you found with most natives. His cheeks had lost their childhood puff and assumed a lean, adolescent freshness. His black hair was rough and unkempt. His chest was ordinary and unpretentious and his round shoulders gave him a tough masculine look beyond his years. His voice had lost its childhood soprano shrill and taken on a determined alto tone. He had also lost his childhood bulge, from the benign effects of kwashiorkor, and developed a flatter, muscle-bound stomach. I could not see the lower portion of his body because of my position in bed. These changes had occurred right before my eyes and I did not know when or how. Perhaps the graduated pace of the changes were too incrementally small for me to notice.

It also occurred to me that I had generally taken it for granted that he loved me just because I was his brother. He is blood of my blood and skin of my skin and, as it's often said, "Blood is thicker than water." This and other cultural axioms about family's solidarity and commitments led me to believe that his love for me and loyalty to me were true and unwavering. Nevertheless, I was unsure if this love was as boundless and borderless as cultural norms implied. I did not know where my sense of individuality ended and where his began. After all, as siblings, we had shared many things, including half eaten mangoes and the same piece of bubble gum. We were also schooled to care for each other through thick and thin. Anything short of that was considered a repudiation of the social norms that form the bedrock of our cultural system. He had shared my interests and protected me against playground bullies and rascals.

But something else was gnawing at me. I was not sure if we shared the same cultural ideals, and the best time to clear the air was now when we did not have a looming family crisis or interests to protect. I also wanted to know what motivated him when he gave me a viscous blow to the stomach for a minor tap on his one Easter Monday morning five or more years ago.

In fact, over the years, I had wondered whether he hit me out of frustration or to expunge pent up anger towards me. The more I pondered the question, the clearer it became to me that he held the best cure to my uncertainty about how I perceived our relationship.

I looked at him while searching for an appropriate starting point. Before I could open my mouth to begin the conversation, Grandma's maxim about forcing people to divulge information before they are ready to do so came to mind. "Let people alone to their privacy; it is their right. You will face the ghost of the dead when your apprehension drives you to peel off the glue that holds their eyelids in place." That was Grandma's way of saying not to ask people to reveal intimate details about themselves when you are not prepared to do the same. And I was not about to look a ghost in the face or go over my life in its minutia. At least, not in my condition, when death was looking down at me with its eyes wide-open, without mercy or ethical compunction. Nonetheless, I overcame my trepidation, reconciled my sense of truth with the reality of the moment, and took the first step expressing the confused thoughts and feelings with this tepidly benign observation.

"You have changed."

"No, I haven't," he said, and nervously licked his lower lip.

"You have," I earnestly insisted.

"Perhaps that is how you see me from your bed," he replied with a charitable glance, and inquired, "How are you feeling?" as he attempted to change the subject.

"I think you have." I insisted, and proceeded to tell him the changes I had noticed in his physical appearance. He confirmed my observation and expressed, "Some of our family members—Auntie Agoo, Cousin Bessie, and others, to mention a few—who have known me from childhood made some of the same remarks. I took them at face value and chalked them down as the cordial or complimentary statements of casual acquaintances. They are as echoing as the hollow noise made by an empty forty-gallon kerosene barrels rolling downhill. Your affirmation gives me some confidence in the veracity of their observation, he said. After a pause he added, "I must say, all of us grow older by the day if you ask me."

"So their comments do not mean anything to you?"

"Not exactly. Let me put it this way. I don't know how many of them are sincere and how many are not."

"Just like in most situations," I refrained.

"Yes," Kwesi affirmed.

"What would you think if Grandma had made some of the remarks they made?" I inquired.

"I would have accepted it as the truth."

"Why?"

"Why not," Kwesi replied, adding, "You see, Grandma is sincere in what she says and does. Above all, she means well."

"What do you mean?"

"Well, let me tell you," Kwesi began. "The other day when we went to the *Bakatue* Festival gala, I got lost and did not get back home until dawn.

When I wobbled into the compound, Grandma was sitting at the gate waiting for me. She opened the crossbars to the gate and whisked me into the house like a cagey feline. 'What do you find so attractive about the outside world?' She began.

'Nothing,' I replied.

'Then why did you stay out for such a long time?'

'Because I wanted to see the gala to its end. It was an opportunity of a life time, and I didn't want to miss it,' I replied.

'That is why you stayed out without permission?'

'No, I replied.

'Then why?' She reproachfully pressed on.

'Let me tell you, young man,' she continued, 'your parents entrusted you and your brother to my care. I cannot, and I will not, fail them. Neither you nor your younger brother will deter me from that. I will do my very best to keep you safe and secure. The time for escapades and getting lost is not now. Indeed, there is a time and a season for everything under the sun,' she said between a yell and a shout that was mixed with frustration. 'There is a time to wake up and a time to go to bed; a time to obey your parents and a time to disobey them. There is a time to study and a time to put your books away; a time to sleep and a time to wake up and do your chores. Wandering about at night, without asking me for permission, is not a good night out. It is against my wishes and that of your parents. It is simply improper and wrong. I don't want you to ever do that again. Is that clear?'"

"She did not wait for my response. She immediately directed me sit on a stool and kept me awake, despite my fatigue and obvious need for sleep, while she casually went about her business. She went to the extent of sacrificing her sacred siesta to make sure that I did not sleep."

"I bet you will not disobey her again," I commented.

"Not a chance after what I went through. Not a chance," Kwesi repeated. "I would be fool to," he concluded.

After he had finished narrating his reprimand from Grandma, I posed the question, which, in my mind, had hung over our relationship like an ominous cloud for years.

"Why did you hit me so hard some time ago for a tap on your stomach?" I asked

"When?" he asked with a sense of astonishment.

I reminded him of the time and the circumstance when the incident occurred, but he could not remember.

"Honestly, I don't recall," he proclaimed time and again.

Here I was, nursing ill feeling against him for an offence he did not recall.

Over the years, I had looked at our relationship through this lens of hurt without his knowledge or complicity. Perhaps, I thought, it would have been better if I had brought the incident to his attention at the time of occurrence and hashed it out instead of carrying that burden of hurt and anger for so long. I would have had a much warmer relationship with him and enjoyed the things we did with a much clearer conscience. It occurred to me that we are influenced by different expectations and fears. It also occurred to me that the sooner one airs his or her misapprehension about an event or situation, the better the chance for understanding and resolution. People, I concluded, tend to evaluate situations from different personal experiences and cultural perspectives. I resolved to continue the journey of asking for forgiveness by counting the sins I had committed in my lifetime against people I had encountered in my life's journey. I quickly recalled the first ten people I had wronged but lost track of the name and identity of the eleventh person. Above all, I couldn't judge how venal or common the sins I committed were and decided to evoke Moses' Laws to assist my classification and assessment of my sins.

The first of his laws that came to mind was, "Thou shall not steal." I knew for sure I had broken this law. I had stolen oranges, mangoes, and guavas from Mr. Minoo's fruit orchard; I had stolen coconut from the coconut plantation close to the seashore; I had aided and abetted other children to commit chicanery, mayhem, and pillage. In fact, I had watched out while Kwesi absconded with a poor widow's wig for kicks. I had earnestly prayed to the Creator for forgiveness. That He had forgiven me was attested to by my continued living.

"Thou shall not covet thy neighbor's wife or property." I knew I was both spiritually poor and poor when it came to property. I had not coveted anything belonging to my neighbors. I was not of legal marriage age to do that. Therefore, marriage was not within my reach. Then it occurred to me that I did not know, either physically or euphemistically speaking, who my neighbor was. I began to wonder whether this law referred to the people who physically live next door to us; friends at schoolyards; occasional acquaintances at parties and public parks; the wayward people of blind alleys who may maim us; or the Dangers and Kobina Amuah's of the world who, right or wrong, aid and abet us in whatever we did, or failed to do. I could not fathom the nuances of the law and concluded to set it aside for future consideration if I survived the illness and had more time. I decided to continue examining how I had fared with the rest of the laws.

"Take care of your parents in their old age so that your children in turn will take care of you." My parents were not old and did not need me to take care of them. It was entirely another matter altogether if Moses meant the parents of the world I had not met and did not know. Indeed, I could not take care of an elderly person in some remote part of the world I did not know. Besides, I was still a child and exempt from social obligation. I did not have any children. Therefore, I considered myself safe and free of that sin, at least for now. I pulled my right hand from under the sheet and chalked an imaginary figure "one" in the air for the winning column. "One for me," I said under my breath.

"Thou shall not kill." I came to a mental wall when I started pondering this law. How can Moses expect me to live without killing anything to eat? Was it because to kill without being killed was an illusion? I had to kill fish, catapult birds, trap rats, pluck fruits, and break off tree branches to roast my catch and eat them to survive. I had eaten ripe bananas and roasted plantains, not counting the peanuts, the huckleberries, and whatever fell between them. I was neither malicious nor cavalier towards the fruit I plucked, and ate the fruit or the game I trapped and shared it with my friends. Without killing, without terminating one life, without closing a chapter on one existence I couldn't sustain my life. I had seen animals kill other species to sustain their lives. This made me question whether hunters who kill the grazing gazelle or the well-mannered mandrill would see my killing differently. I needed to kill to live. Yet, here was Moses, a respectable leader and prophet, enjoining me not to kill. This Moses Law, I concluded, was impossible to live by. I gave up on recalling the rest of his laws or thinking about what I had already recalled. "It's useless and futile. I am a killer and doomed to die." I gave up all hope and sank into an uneasy siesta that was hosted by birds singing an unrehearsed requiem in rustically pleasing phrases, and the curtain fell to close the chapter on another ephemeral day.

The usual twittering birds on the hibiscus tree behind Grandma's window awakened me. I found myself alone and looked through the mosquito netting to connect with the outside world only to see a red-breasted robin bobbing from one branch to another. A light blue-feathered finch opened its wings and took a short flight closer to a brown robin that had just landed on a branch with open hibiscus flowers and boisterously pecked their stigma. The finch coquettishly stretched out its light blue-feathered wings and used its beak to preen them. The two birds, which were sitting on a floating bough, socially groomed each other with the tender care of lovers on honeymoon and bobbed to another flower to repeat the ritual, and flew away into the setting sun. I heard the nesting birds shifting and occasionally complaining despite the darkness. I closed my eyes and began to drift away. I reached for memories to fill the chasm my thoughts had created between life and death, but they danced away from me as soon as I went after them. A bang on the door broke the haze and brought me back to myself.

Once again, Kwesi trailed Grandma into the bedroom to help me to my feet. We made our way to the dining room and assumed the same chairs. Grandma provided a dinner menu of toasted bread and a cup of cocoa with lots of milk. I ate the toasted bread and drank the beverage and started feeling nauseous, but did not throw up. This success buoyed her to fill a tumbler with water and create her special concoction of lime, honey, and herbs. She picked two limes from the fruit basket, which was sitting on top of the dining room cabinet, and sliced them into halves. She squeezed the lime into the water in the tumbler and added a tablespoon of honey and the juice of blended ground ginger roots to it. Then she thoroughly mixed it and handed the tumbler and the mixed contents to me and directed, "Drink it!" I hesitated because of my previous experience of throwing up the soup, the tangerine, and the water. I was unsure if my stomach would be receptive to Grandma's concoction and took the tumbler from her without knowing whether to drink its contents without protest or politely decline to drink, but something told me to try it. I did, and it worked. I did not throw up. Buoyed by this success, she gave me four more quinine tablets, which I swallowed with water. They had a bitter aftertaste. Grandma concluded the quinine tablets were responsible for initiating my recovery.

I slowly got up from the table, reasonably sure that I could walk unaided to the bedroom, but my senses betrayed me. My legs gave in, I stumbled on my attempt, and began to fall. Grandma and Kwesi grabbed me by the arms before I could hit the hardwood floor. They helped me back to my feet and supported me as I took slow, heavy, laborious steps to bed, where I lay exhausted from the ordeal. Grandma tucked me in her bed, which, for all practical purposes, had become my infirmary bed. I regained interest in my body and began to listen intensely for my heartbeat. I used my middle finger of one hand to feel for the humming blood running through the arteries of my wrist with the other. I ran my fingers over my thighs, legs, and upper torso and realized that my body was riddled with bumps and invited Grandma to examine them when she came to check on me in the middle of the day.

"Grandma, look at these bumps," I pleaded.

"They are chicken pox. You did not have malaria as I thought," she replied after examining me.

Grandma had misdiagnosed my illness and treated me for something I did not have. I had lost invaluable vacation time. But then, who could fault her efforts? She was neither an herbalist nor an accomplished homeopathic practitioner. She was a grandmother, my Grandmother, who, like many loving people, was doing her level best to keep me alive and well. The fact that she made a mistake did not diminish her remarkable strength and commitment to see me through my illness and mitigate my suffering. She was mortal and prone to error. She cared for me on the basis of her experience, knowledge, and the best of intentions. That, to me, was sufficient.

I ate lunch and retired to bed, hopeful of continuing my recovery. When I woke up, Grandma was at the ready with calamine lotion. She poured a portion of the lotion into a small calabash and asked me to disrobe and lie on the bed. She dabbed a corner of a washing towel into the lotion and carefully applied it from my neck down to my toes. "It will stop further spread of the chicken pox," she said. Then she left for the post office to send a telegram to my parents about my condition.

Kwesi came to see me when Grandma left for the post office to send the telegram.

"Stay away," I warned, "chicken pox is highly contagious."

"Don't worry about me," he said with childhood bravado. "I will be just fine. I am not a weakling like you are. Chicken pox only affects children and weak grownups. It doesn't affect tough people like me," he said with finality.

"I bet not," I responded caustically, not knowing whether what he was saying was true or not.

"You bet wrong."

"I am not a weakling," I protested. "By the way," I continued, "have you seen the gang?" (Referring to Kobina Amuah and Danger).

"Yes," he replied. "They have been asking about you, especially Danger. He has been wondering how you are doing. He misses you and is eager for the two of you to get together again."

"I hope to see them soon."

Grandma's return coincided with the buzz of a hovering mosquito in my ears. It warned me of the impending change of the guard between insects of the night and insects of the day. I looked at Grandma and Kwesi and realized how alone and lonely I was despite their presence. I knew they couldn't share in my thought or pain. I also knew I had to face the challenges of my illness, including the prospect of death, all by myself, and that scared me. The malaise reminded me of one of Grandma's maxims. "It is only the person with smelly, cancerous sore that really breathes in its stench. Equally, it is only the injured that can truly understand the anguish induced by pain and its effects on the soul. Loved ones and relatives are limited to vicarious understanding of your hurt. The best they can do is to support your struggle to recover from your illness and desire to overcome your pain. The nitty-gritty of the struggle or recovery is always up to you, the individual. I committed myself to overcome my illness and get better.

"Grandma," I called, "I would like some more food."

"Sure," she replied, and got up from her seat. She went downstairs to the kitchen and returned with two slices of toasted white bread.

"Here you go," she said, and handed them to me with a little lilt in her voice.

"Thank you," I said, and started nibbling on the first one, and then the second. She gave me two more quinine tablets and a tumbler of water to take them with. I swallowed them one tablet at a time and had the same bitter aftertaste in my mouth. I felt good about the bitter aftertaste because I recalled Kwesi's previous proclamation that good medicine, the kind that really cured, always left a bitter aftertaste. I did not vomit and began to feel hopeful about my chances for recovery.

That evening my mother called to inquire about us, especially my health. Grandma received the inbound call from a bulky black telephone that sat on a small round table in her living room. That telephone had four wires attached to it. One of the wires was connected from the base of the telephone to the receiver; another was hooked from its base into a socket mounted on a wood panel that was nailed to the wall of the living room; and the remaining two wires, which looked flimsy, were submerged in a large colorless bottle containing an unknown liquid.

"Hello?" yelled Grandma as she picked up the telephone to talk to my mother. "He is doing fine," she replied. Then, after a pause, she added, "Both boys are doing well. They have been involved in the usual adolescent squabbles that children get into when they have nothing else to do. As you know, the devil works its evil with idle hands." Then, after another pause, she added, "I don't think the situation is serious enough for you to come down. I have it under control," she said, and returned the telephone receiver to its cradle with a belated, "goodbye," which was more to herself than to my mother.

The fact is that Grandma repeated the phrases "yes," "sure," and, "I agree with you," and yelled throughout her telephone conversation, as if doing so made what she was saying clearer to Mama. She used the same phrases and manner of speech to repeat the story when Papa called later that evening. I was troubled that her responses to my parents about my illness were not thoroughly candid for the following two reasons: first, she did not ask me about how I was feeling before reporting on it; and second, I did not know whether her diagnosis of chicken pox was as inaccurate as her first one of malaria. Therefore, I thought it was presumptions, if not downright disingenuous, to assert things were under control without valid proof of my recovery.

Since I had never used the phone and didn't know whether her yelling on the telephone enabled the person on the receiving end to hear her any clearer, but then she did not have a monopoly on this virtue because I clearly remember passing by the post office at home in Cape Coast where a man was yelling from a red-painted telephone kiosk and pounding its walls like a trapped gorilla in an ill-equipped zoo. "Do you hear me?" I overheard him inquire between the poundings. He came out of the kiosk after the conversation with his clothing glued to his skin with his perspiration, and limped away like a boxer who had just lost a fifteen round decision to a nondescript opponent.

I went to bed feeling hopeful. Unfortunately, I did not sleep well during the night. I hallucinated that witches in black drapes with fangs popping out of their ears had attacked me and drained my blood. Chills ran down my spine. I broke out in a cold sweat and screamed for help at the top of my voice.

"Help! Help! Help me somebody. They are sucking my blood!"

My cry for help woke up Grandma. She picked up the kerosene lamp, turned up the wick to increase its illumination, and rushed down the staircase. She returned with a partially filled bucket of cold water and a towel. She soaked the towel in the water and dabbed the wet towel from one limb of my body to the neck and over my back and stomach until she had touched my whole body with it. She repeated the process a few times. Intermittently, she touched my forehead with the back of her fingers to verify my body's temperature. She put her arms around me in a manner that was intensely maternal and protective. Then she caressed my head, tucked me in bed, and tip-toed to sleep on a floor mat next to Kwesi when she felt the danger had passed. I slept through the rest of the night without succumbing to another nightmare.

Grandma was not on her mat when I woke up. She returned to our room just as the sun was beginning to dry the soft dew that had accumulated on the hibiscus leaves behind the window. She pulled me out of bed with help from Kwesi. Together, they walked me downstairs, steering me to sit on a stool in the middle of the compound. Kwesi stood at guard while Grandma strode to the kitchen. She returned with a bucket containing simmering lemon, lime, orange twigs, and neem tree leaves. She covered me with woolen blankets to keep away the chill and to force my body to sweat to break the fever. I felt suffocated and sweated profusely. She removed the blanket after a few minutes and asked me to stand up. I tried to, and sunk back into the stool like soggy sisal hemp. I was weak, dehydrated, and beaten. Grandma and Kwesi dragged me back to bed. She and Kwesi left the room only to return shortly with a cistern of water and a glass. She filled the glass with water and urged me to drink it. I drank the water, returned the empty glass to her, and fell into a fatigue-induced sleep. I woke up with an equable sense of tranquility the next morning. I ate an early light breakfast in the kitchen and was able to hold down my food.

I was on my way toward recovery.

Chapter 11

To believe you are on the last leg of your life and wake up to another beautiful day is a tribute to a caregiver's selfless devotion to your recovery and unbridled support for your life's journey. And, in my opinion, Grandma was one such yeomen who wanted me to live by giving me two more quinine tablets to take along with another tumbler filled with her fresh cocktail of fruits, honey and root juices to speed up my recovery. After that, she applied more calamine lotion to my body and asked me to sit under the shade of the neem tree for some fresh air. The cool clean air ignited my desire for life. The cock crowed the passing of the hour. The pair of yellow fluffy chicks that were hatched two or more weeks ago and had begun to assume a permanent plumage of shaded browns with blacks, emerged from the shadows of the mango tree at the corner of Grandma's compound. The mother hen in her regalia of light brown feathers followed them. She and her growing chicks scavenged the compound dust for remnants of vegetables the maid had thrown away in the washed-off water she used. The mother hen cackled a find to the mad dash of her chicks. The flock searched under the table for breadcrumbs and other leftovers. The mother hen fluttered her wings and landed on top of the table to peck large crumbs of bread from it. She jumped back to the dusty compound and swiped her beak clean of food particles, as if to inquire of the earth, "What have you done for me lately?"

A dark brown dust mouse dashed across the dusty compound from a decaying pile of wood next to the corrugated kitchen. "Look, look!" I repeated with a pointed finger as the fleeing vermin caught my attention.

"Look at what?" inquired Kwesi.

"A dust mouse! A large, soft-furred mouse!" I replied excitedly as I pointed again in its direction.

Kwesi got up from his stool and attempted to stomp the fleeing mouse, but it was too quick for him. It rounded the corner of the two-story mud home and snuck under a stack of assorted broken furniture at the other corner of the compound before he could reach it. The mouse was home safe. Kwesi looked dejected from the loss and stubbed his feet in the dust to register that feeling.

"I missed it," he exclaimed in disgust.

Just then, someone shook the compound gate with a sense of urgency. Abena Atokyene, the maid, emerged from the kitchen where she was resting from her morning chores, and rushed to open it. She lifted the cross bar that held the gate bar together and gingerly opened it to a man standing on the other side of the gate and invited him into the house. "Come in," she beckoned as she held the gate ajar. We watched as the man entered the compound and began to stagger and totter his way to the shade of the neem tree to seek refuge from the heat of the rising sun. Once there, he cleared his throat, spat into the dust and kicked some dust with his right foot to cover the phlegm-mixed sputum. He spread his legs and desperately attempted to readjust his thinning and fading dark blue cloth, which had slipped from his left shoulder and was about to entangle his legs. He vigorously pulled the part of the cloth that was partially trapped under his left foot and fell flat on his face on the sand with a big thud. He struggled up from the ground, wrestled his cloth around his waist, and alternatively used both hands to brush sand off his face, cloth, and legs. He ran his fingers over his legs for cuts and found none. Then he clutched his fists and loudly carped about everything that came to mind for his misfortune. He took two staggering steps, paused to regain composure and punctuated his frustration with an inquiry on the whereabouts of Grandma

"Where is she?" he demanded in a loud feisty voice.

"She is upstairs," replied the maid from a safe distance.

"Well, tell her I am here," he yelled.

"Yes sir," replied the maid, as she made her way towards the staircase.

I waved the maid to come closer and, when she did, I inquired in a whisper, "Who is he?"

"He is your Uncle Kwesi Bota," the maid said with a sense of alienation and unofficially introduced me to him.

Meanwhile, Uncle Bota staggered his way to the kitchen and fetched a stool. He put the stool under the shade of the neem tree a few yards away from where I was sitting and took a thorough look at me with shaded eyes and commented, "You look majestic in your pink robe," referring to the spread of the calamine lotion on my body. "I wish the Pope could see you now!" He rambled on. Then he languidly inquired "By the way, how the hell are you?"

"Fine, I presume," I replied calmly.

"Where is your cassock?" he sarcastically continued.

His demeanor of continual cursing and hostile attitude put me off. I thought his remarks were inappropriate, disrespectful, and off the mark. I was neither majestic nor dressed in a cassock, and decided to make it clear to him that I did not find his crassly insensitive remarks one bit amusing. I was just an ordinary young boy whose grandmother was desperately nursing back to health from the snarls of malaria and chicken pox. What I needed for my recovery was understanding and empathy, not sarcasm or grotesque antipathy.

"Uncle Kwesi Bota, I really don't like that," I began in a harsh tone.

"I was only teasing," he slurred apologetically.

"Yes, indeed, but that does not give you the right to compare me to the Pope," I sarcastically rejoined.

"He was only teasing," echoed Kwesi, who noted the bite in my tone and blinked his right eye to signal I let go of the matter.

"Then how come I did not feel that?" I indignantly continued.

There was an uneasy silence, as neither Uncle Bota nor Kwesi wanted to respond to my biting inquiry, so I decided to drop the matter on the following two accounts: first, because I did not have the energy to sustain a fight; and second, because I knew Grandma was on her way and would not approve of a heated exchange between a young boy and an adult, even when that adult was inebriated, irrational, and out of line. My real intention was to push Uncle Bota for a rational explanation. But then, when all is said and done, what rationality can one exact from a drunk? Not much! There was also the potential punishment from Grandma for perceived impertinence and disrespect of customary norms that enjoin children to defer to adults even when the adults are wrong. I decided to forgo my desire to assert my rights and the potential punishment for doing so, and chose to celebrate the mixed blessings of his visit.

"How are you?" asked Grandma as she walked toward the shade of the neem tree from the staircase.

"Quite all right," replied Uncle Bota as he laboriously wobbled up from his stool and belched from the strain. His belch gave off an obnoxious odor of over-fermented *ahey, Akpeteshi,* and decaying teeth. For a moment, I thought his pores, mouth, and everywhere on his body with an opening reeked of alcohol. Grandma looked him in the face, shook her head, and simultaneously clicked her lips to underscore her displeasure.

"Are you drunk?" she asked with raised hands.

"No," denied Uncle Bota.

"Then why are you shaking like a bean stalk on stilts?" Grandma demanded.

"I am not drunk," Uncle Bota repeated his denial.

"I insist you are drunk. I know a drunk when I see one, and you look, smell, and behave in the same manner as one of many drunks I have seen in my life time," Grandma asserted accusingly, while wagging her index finger at Uncle Bota.

"I contend not," replied Uncle Bota, who appeared frazzled under Grandma's line of questioning. He paused, looked to the ground, shook his head, and sheepishly admitted, "I had a dram or two of *Akpeteshi.* Something small and not a whole lot—just one lousy shot early this morning just before I came here. I stopped at a friend's house and he offered me a drink and I drank it only to be sociable. I did not intend to come here drunk. I only took one little drink, and no more; nothing serious and nothing for you to worry about; just one little dram of alcohol," he repeated as he gazed the dusty ground to avoid eye contact with Grandma.

"And that is why you are drunk. One social drink turns into two, and then three, and before you know it, you, like many others before you, have become a full-blown alcoholic. You are not under any obligation to drink with anyone. Besides, you did not have to accept alcohol. You can always ask for a non-alcoholic beverage like *ahey.* And, if all else fails, there is always water. Good old water. From what I last heard, most people would willingly give you water, no questions asked. Above all, it is the best thing to drink," Grandma sternly chided.

"Just let it go," Uncle Bota pleaded.

But Grandma would not let go. She looked him over and contemptibly addressed him, "What are you doing to yourself?" she began, and paused for her words to sink in. "Are you either seeking the title for the best drunkard in this part of the country or preserving yourself in alcohol? You disgust and nauseate me with your drinking. How can you, in good conscience, come to this house early in the morning drunk as the palm bee? What respect do you have for yourself or give to your nephews? What example do you want to set for them? If your intention is to set a poor example, then I must say, you are succeeding at it. Bravo!" She clapped to underscore her derision, and continued, "But if you intend to gain their respect and influence them to become good and honorable citizens of this community, then in my estimation, you have failed miserably. Children behave as they see. You cannot expect people to admire you when they see you drunk, unkempt, and do not appear to have a scintilla of self-respect. In fact, people will talk condescendingly to you and dismiss what you say— even when it is pertinent and thoroughly thought out—as misguided, insignificant, meaningless babble of an intoxicated mind. Get out of here, you miserable wretch, with your stinking alcoholic breath and never come back!" Grandma ranted sententiously.

Uncle Bota stood still and listened impassively to Grandma's ranting. He took a step forward, stumbled on a small river rock wedged in the dust, and steadied himself from a possible fall. He glanced at me and shook his head in self-pity. My brother, Kwesi, took a few steps back and slunk away.

Silence gripped the scene and froze it for eternity, but silence couldn't hold the passage of time or Grandma's affection for her grandson. A falcon crossed the sky and landed on the spike of a distant telephone post. A pigmy falconer, who was chasing the falcon, fired a musket at the falcon and missed his target. A pair of African gray parrots flew by and vanished in the distance. Grandma broke the suffocating tension hanging over the compound and asked Uncle Bota if he was hungry in a voice tinged with pity and regret.

"Not really," he replied, and took a step toward the gate.

"Please yourself," Grandma said, and looked at him askance.

Uncle Bota took another step toward the gate, turned around in the middle of the third step, and solemnly asked me, "How are you?"

"Fine," I repeated in frustration, because I could not understand why he kept asking me the same question over and over again when one response, in my estimation, was enough.

"You know, your father told me that you were not well and that is why I came here. I wanted to see how my favorite nephews were doing. Think of it, I saw you two years ago in the company of your parents in this very house."

I began to wonder why I had not heard of or met him until now if I was as dear to him as he proclaimed. He did not send me cards on my birthday nor did I hear from him on special occasions. Yet here he was, proclaiming I was special to him. Perhaps I was special in a macabre sense, when I was sick and of no use to anyone.

Grandma interrupted my thought with her invitation.

"Then you are welcome to stay and visit with your nephews, and nothing else."

But Uncle Bota turned and took yet another step toward the gate, and stopped. He turned around and, out of the blue, admitted, "I am hungry." He ambled back to sit on the stool he had just abandoned under the neem tree.

As he resumed his seat, I began to ponder the many disingenuous excuses, outright lies, and half-truths adults use to get what they really want from other people. I clearly recalled a recent incident when a distant relative came to our home and begged for provisions from my parents to feed her children, who were supposed to be my cousins. I remember Mama going to her pantry where she stored provisions and packing a box full of canned sardines, corned beef, canned milk, butter, margarine, and a sack full of assorted candies for her to take home and feed her children. In my mind, she could not cook any of the provisions to feed her children without feeding herself. Therefore, I could not understand her rationale for the lie when life experience and history are rife with the futility of hiding truth from children, as well as the unintended consequences of doing so. Ultimately, children find out. And when they do, they lose confidence, respect, and trust in the adults involved with the deception.

In the meantime, Grandma directed the maid to set a table and ready breakfast for Uncle Bota. The maid prepared the breakfast as directed. She cut up tomatoes, peeled and cut up onions, nipped the stems off a handful of cayenne and bell peppers, ground them on a grinding stone, and scooped it all into a shallow earthenware bowl. She went upstairs and returned with a can of corned beef. She opened the can and emptied its contents into an earthenware bowl along with the mixture of ground peppers, onions, and tomatoes. She set it up on a small table under the tree in front of Uncle Bota and brought a ball of ken-key, which was still wrapped in the wet banana leaves for cooking, from the kitchen and put it and the condiments on the table.

Finally, she brought him a cistern of water, a bar of lavender soap, and a hand towel for him to wash and dry his hands. Uncle Bota pushed aside the cistern and the lavender soap and handed the used hand towel to the maid when he was through washing his hands. The maid received the towel and walked away to the kitchen to wait to clear the table after he had finished eating. Grandma invited Uncle Bota to eat when everything was ready.

"Thank you," replied Uncle Bota, who said a short, silent prayer.

"Amen," he said aloud after the prayer, and started eating.

Uncle Bota's "Amen" reminded me of people I had observed at public places, toting the Bible in one hand and waiting for an opportunity to proclaim their faith to any listener in sight. To me, it would be best for these people to keep their faith to themselves and let others be. A commitment to any faith or religion, as I saw it, rested more on how you live than your acclamation, and therein lay the rub. Therefore, I viewed the public purveying of religion as nothing more than an insincere, sanctimonious, hypocritical act fit for haven with Satan and not heaven with God. But, as usual, I kept my continence and counsel to myself.

Kwesi, who had returned to the shade of the neem tree, stood quietly by me. We watched Uncle Bota as he removed the wet banana leaves wrapped around the ken-key, rudely cracked his knuckles, and began to breakfast.

"This is really delicious!" he exclaimed after a few bites. Then, looking in the direction of the maid, he added, "You really did a fine job with the condiments."

The maid acknowledged his remark with a bow and looked away. The first few bites egged him to chatter, and, as he did, it occurred to me how people who feel down-trodden and forlorn search desperately for affirmation from the high and the low, including the ranks of those who are similarly situated. The drunks seek affirmation from their kind and so do artists from all walks of life. People, I concluded, have a need for belonging, no matter the circumstance or the place. Perhaps that explains why peer pressure can be profound and compelling, and why victims come to accept their prosecutors as fine purveyors.

"The peppers will help me cleanse my sinuses," he said with a sneeze.

"Let me help you," Grandma said as she got up from her stool, and used her handkerchief to wipe dripping mucus from Uncle Bota's nose, as she would for a child. "Just eat," she added, and returned to her seat to watch him.

Grandma chattered with Uncle Bota through his breakfast. They talked about one thing or another and changed subjects without missing either context or content. After watching and listening to the ebb and flow of conversation between the two, I surmised they shared a basic common knowledge—like old couples do—and like an old couple, they had a few disagreements along the way and spontaneously laughed at jokes that appeared humorless to me.

Of the many stories Uncle Bota told that day, only one has stayed with me over the years. It was a story about a notorious drunkard at the point of taking in his first sip of an alcoholic beverage in a drinking contest. "There was an alcoholic who lived in a village tucked away in the shadows of a big town by a river, with an embankment teeming with colonies of Patas and Diana monkeys. Most of the males in the village drank as a matter of sport. One day, the mayor of the town proposed a drinking contest to determine which of the village drunkards was best at holding his or her drink. Notice of the contest was advertised on talking drums throughout the village. A few 'brave' men took up the challenge. Each contestant had a mid-size calabash of palm wine, then a large cistern of corn wine, and a sizeable gourd of *Akpeteshi* to drink in five hours.

"During the contest, the men were asked to stand and tap the tip of their noses with either their left or right finger to confirm their sobriety. The winner was adjudicated as the most sober man at the end of the contest. The contestants who got drunk were carted away one person at a time until only one contestant was left. This 'professional drinker' went through the drinks without showing any adverse effects of the alcohol. When he got to the *Akpeteshi,* which was sitting on the saloon's counter, he admonished it with the words, 'As you sit in this gourd, you are gaudy, sober, and unruffled.

You do not pose danger to either me, the people around here, or threaten society. You have neither killed nor maimed, nor are you capable of these crimes. Indeed, you look motionless and harmless. After I drink you and you enter my belly, I want you to stay the same. I do not want you to get me giddy, slur my speech, or lose my balance. Above all, I do not want you to influence my thoughts and cause me to be stupidly brave or take unreasonable risks that would end in somebody's death or cause pain to the community. Indeed, I want you to control my tongue and make me behave like all sensible people do. I want you to help me to be respectful of other people, hold myself in the highest esteem, and continue to honor and respect my family and friends.'

"After that injunction, he drank the *Akpeteshi,* to the acclamation of the spectators, but the alcohol entered his blood stream and influenced his behavior in every possible way. He vomited in public and peed in his pants without knowing. He cursed and shamed his family and got into a fistfight where he grabbed a knife from a bystander and threw it, killing an innocent child of five. A jury exonerated him at the trial for his crime and misconduct because he was deemed too inebriated at the time of the crime. He was so overcome with guilt and shame for the unintended consequences of his action that he killed himself by tying a noose around his neck and hanging himself from a tree in the center of the village. His conscience, it appeared, was a better adjudicator for his senseless violence against the innocent than society.

"I do not want to end up like he did. That is why I come home to my family when I think I have taken in a little more than I can handle," Uncle Bota concluded.

"You do not have to take in a little more. You must leave the drinking alone or it will usher you to the same shameful end as other notorious alcoholics," Grandma Elizabeth suggested with an edge to her tone.

"Not a chance! Not as long as I live," replied Uncle Bota.

"Life is not forever. I may be here today and gone tomorrow. It is far more prudent to plan your life strategies on the basis of what you can honestly do for yourself than on the basis of what somebody is likely or not likely to do for you. Be your own coxswain and not a rower of boats, who relies on others for direction," Grandma Elizabeth warned.

"I will, I will," Uncle Bota repeated as he washed his hands and pushed the breakfast table away.

Something told me that he would not keep his word. His behavior reminded me of an addict, who continually broke his promises and vows to do better on the next go around. Addicts, I have heard it said, need to hit rock bottom and understand the pathology of their disease before they can achieve a semblance of recovery.

Uncle Bota got up from the stool on much steadier feet to leave before I could give him a piece of my mind. Once again he said, "Hello," but in a much clearer tone. His gait was more confident and respectable. He parted his legs and readjusted his cloth and, as he did, his calico knickerbockers came to view. He re-tied the string that held it around his waist for a belt and completed readjusting his cloth without another hitch. Then he started walking toward the gate.

"I have to go now," he announced, and added as he turned to us, "You kids must not drink as I do. You should stay in school and make something of yourselves."

"Come back again soon," responded Grandma.

They hugged on that note and walked hand in hand to the gate like two warriors after a truce. Grandma unlocked the cross bars to the gate and waved him goodbye, leaving me to wonder why she wanted him back in the house that soon after the tongue-lashing. Perhaps they were driven together by that special immutable bond between grandchildren and their grandparents—the kind of bonding that drives grandparents to support their grandchildren in the face of misconduct and overwhelming social odds.

Grandma did not return directly to her stool. Instead, she walked to the young mango tree at one corner of the compound to inspect it, and remarked when she returned to her stool, "It appears the young mango tree will bear a lot of fruit this year."

"I think so," I agreed, and added, "I hope we get to eat some of it before we return home."

"I do not think so," Grandma responded.

"I hope you are wrong," contradicted Kwesi.

Hardly had Kwesi finished with his statement when we heard another knock at the gate.

"I will go and check who is there," said Kwesi, as he started walking toward the gate.

"Who is there?" he asked as he went closer it.

"Me," replied the voice.

"Who is 'me'?" Kwesi inquired.

"It's me, Danger."

Kwesi unbolted the latch and found Kobina Amuah waiting with Danger. They stepped over the threshold onto the compound and strode to the shade of the neem tree where Grandma and I were sitting. They appeared to have grown a little lankier and taller since I last saw them. Kwesi ushered them into the house.

"You appear to have grown a little taller," I commented.

"Not really," they both denied.

I observed that Danger and Kobina Amuah had wrapped packages in their hands.

"This is for you," they said, handing the packages to me.

I took the packages and thanked them for the thought.

After they entered the compound, Kwesi looked to Grandma for her approval on allowing our friends into the house, but Grandma was preoccupied with her thoughts and had a belated reaction to his unspoken request.

"Who are these boys?" she inquired as she acknowledged their presence.

"That is Danger," he said, pointing to him, "and that is Kobina Amuah," he added, as he casually nodded his head towards him.

"How are you kids doing?" Grandma asked.

"We are doing fine," they responded in harmony.

Grandma directed Kwesi to bring a pair of stools for the visitors, which he did. The boys took the stools and sat at a safe distance from me. Danger ended his visual survey of the compound with the remark, "This is a big compound."

"Yes," agreed Kobina Amuah, who was busy nibbling on his fingernails.

"And right in the middle of town. Yet we've never been here," observed Danger.

"Because we have had no reason to," said Kobina Amuah.

"Not until now," said Danger.

"And to honor the occasion, I will show you around the compound," Kwesi offered, and got off his stool to show them the compound.

He began by walking them to the rusting corrugated iron sheets we use as an outdoor bathroom where the boys showered Mr. Rock with their bladder blessings. Then he showed them the outdoor toilet constructed of planks of assorted types of wood, the chicken coop on stilts, and the goats and sheep corrals. Both animal houses had the pestilential smell of urine and animal droppings. From time to time, the maid scooped the droppings that fell from below the stilts and mixed it with sand from the compound for grandma to use as plant fertilizer. They walked under the hibiscus tree behind Grandma's window where some sparrows busily chirped away.

They proceeded to the pile of assorted broken household fixtures and fittings, which Grandma and Papa had determined had outlived their usefulness. Danger and Kobina Amuah rummaged through the pile and found a three-legged mahogany table with chipped varnish paint and a mahogany drawer with a lost hinge. They set them aside to ask Grandma's permission to take them home. Finally, he showed them the young mango tree that was just flowering with a few budding fruits before returning to their stools.

In the interim, I opened the presents Danger and Kobina Amuah brought me. One contained a roasted finch; the other had a wrapped ball of ken-key, fried shrimp, and a serving of anchovies. I was torn between eating the presents for a potential relapse or drinking Grandma's garden eggs soup filled with grilled red snapper and herrings for continuing progress toward full recovery. I chose the latter.

Upon their return from inspecting the compound, Danger and Kobina Amuah gave us an update of what they had done since our last escapade. Kobina Amuah told a story of a poorly educated letter-writer who composed letters in English at the open-air market for the illiterates for a fee. "This stout man with cropped salt-and-pepper hair," he began, "came to town just when you were sick. He wore a black and white striped suit with a white shirt and a bow tie to match his hair. He pulled a bulky, old Olivetti typewriter in a wooden cart behind him. He had the typewriter prominently displayed on an oblong table under a large bushy vanilla tree in the rear of the market and announced his presence over a megaphone built of the day's newspaper. Word got around and the illiterates came to him with their stories for translation from 'Gunda,' their native language, into English, the *lingua franca*. The illiterates sat on a long backless softwood bench behind him in his open-air office under the vanilla tree and took turns sitting in a wicker chair close to his typewriter to tell their stories. The letter writer listened intently to the tales, clarified his understanding and typed the stories in triplicate—the original for the addressee, the second copy for the customer, and the last for his records. I found natives waiting in line to narrate their stories whenever I passed by his office under the shaded tree.

"One day last week, I think Monday or so, I saw a lady in her twenties coming out of his office with a letter in her hand. She was weeping. I approached her and asked, 'What is the matter?'

'There is nothing the matter,' she replied, adding, 'I have just finished bearing my soul to the letter-writer.'

'Then you should feel relieved,' I replied empathetically.

'But I do not feel that way.'

'Why not,' I inquired.

'Because his mannerism made me uneasy. Perhaps I am just paranoid or overreacting,' she hesitantly replied in a trembling voice.

'Why so?' I asked.

'You see, the man was snickering as he read the letter.' Then, after a pause, she added, 'Something tells me he did not faithfully translate what I told him.'

'Maybe not,' I replied.

'By the way, would you mind reading over it and translating it for me? I just need to be reassured.' After a pause she inquired, 'I bet you go to school?

'Yes I do. And I wouldn't mind reading your letter for you. Indeed, I would be delighted to do so,' I replied.

'Just look at it and tell me what it says,' she pleaded as she handed over the letter for me to read.

She agreed with most of the content until I started reading the part about her account of a church sermon. She abruptly broke into hilarious laughter. She explained to me that she told the letter-writer of an expatriate missionary talking of God as the only one who knew a man's soul. The letter-writer translated, 'only God knows,' to mean, 'only God's nose.'

'Is that why you are laughing?' I inquired.

'Yes of course,' she replied, and continued, 'considering that God covers the whole sky, His nose will be a gargantuan one. Besides, what does God's nose have to do with knowledge? I do not know how he could translate 'knows' to mean 'nose' when the two concepts have nothing in common.'

'I could not help but join in her laughter,'" Kobina Amuah concluded, and neither could we.

After much debate and discussion, we concluded that the letter-writer was tricked by the native phonological similarities between "knows" and "nose."

"Let me tell you a story that will top that," Danger began after the laughter had died down.

"What is that?" I inquired.

"You see, last week on Sunday, one of the rich cattle ranchers in town was buried at the local cemetery."

"What is so wonderful about that? We all have to die someday," Kwesi interrupted.

"Last week," Danger began again.

"We are tired of last week. Just get on with the story and stop going over last week like a broken record," enjoined Kobina Amuah.

"That is how I have to start," Danger insisted.

We kept quiet long enough for Danger to collect his thoughts and continue with his story.

"Last week on Sunday this rich farmer died after a short illness. His family wanted to keep the body and mourn him for the traditional three days. However, after two days of the body lying in a coffin mounted on a bier, it started to decay and stink. The mourning family carried his body to the burial ground and, as is the practice for non-believers, buried him under a tree after the three p.m. siesta call of the roosters. The mourners returned home and the widow prepared the ritual dinner, which, as you know, is the favorite meal of the dead while he was alive. The meal consisted of cocoyam *fufu,* palm soup with mutton, a large bowl filled with a medley of fruits, and a calabash of water. The widow loaded the meal onto a large, flat wooden tray to carry to the burial ground. Mourners from the family of her deceased husband followed her to the burial ground, where they helped her set out the food on the fresh dirt mound covering the deceased's grave. They did this to comply with the traditional belief that the deceased would rise up from the dead during the night to partake in a meal with the living, who would be watching over his grave. Two of my friends and I heard about the meal preparations through an acquaintance who lived in the house. We went to the cemetery and walked around the gravestone before hiding in the branches of the tree overlooking the grave to lie in wait for the meal. Some gravestones were inscribed with either biblical quotations, honors, or both. Others were overtaken with weeds, broken, leaning in one direction or the other, or badly in need of repairs. All the gravestone inscriptions ended with RIP, which I presume means, 'rest in peace.'

'Sure enough, we heard the gong-gong beat of the talking drum and saw singing women in precession. They were carrying food on their heads and inching their way towards the burial grounds. We waited for them to set up the meal on the fresh grave mound and walk away. We descended from the tree, searched for any person hiding in the surrounding bush, and found none, so we made short work of the meal and started back to town. Just as we passed the archway to the cemetery, we saw a group of the town's elderly men, possibly four, who were clad in black cloth, walking toward the gravesite where the food was supposed to be. We veered into a ravine and took cover behind a large hedge to watch what the men would do, but the blanketing darkness and the distance made it difficult for us to discern exactly what they were doing. However, we did overhear them cursing the person or persons who had cheated them out of a scrumptious meal. 'May his or their souls rest with the dead,' we heard one of them yell. 'They are nothing more than a bunch of marauding hooligans who are up to no good, I wish the dead would rise up from the grave and smack them where it hurts the most!' said another. And yet another argued, 'I bet the people who ate the meal were the young boys we saw on our way here.' Be it as it may, they pouted over the lost meal and the ensuing obfuscation of traditional values. We counted our blessings for a delicious meal and the narrow escape. We looked at each other and broke into uncontrollable laughter for our triumph over moral decadence after we saw them pass on their way back to town."

"Will you do it again?" I asked

"Why wouldn't I? After all, you know as well as I do that the dead are viscous, stagnant, and still—they are immobile and cannot rise up from the grave to partake in meals with the living. Only the living can. And no one can convince me to the contrary. Reincarnation is an illusion for the living, who are hooked on a spiritual spell of paganism or unrealizable myth born of religious dogma and the sense of a superior being."

"My turn," Kwesi said, who started scratching his head for a starting point in his story.

"Well, get on with it," Danger said. "We do not have all day to wait on slow pokes," he continued.

Kwesi scratched his head a few more times and cracked his knuckles to ready himself for his narration. He looked at the three of us with the approach of a surgeon at the start of a difficult operation or a magician in the middle of a badly rehearsed trick.

"Okay guys," he started. "Well, this is the story told to me by our driver, Mr. Kwesi Gyesi."

"What was it?" inquired Kobina Amuah.

"Mr. Kwesi Gyesi told me that once upon a time the fisherman of a village near El Puca, known for its slave port, wanted to do their part to stop the slave trade. The elders came together and decided to trick slave merchant ships to their port so that they could free the slaves. They voted to build a big bonfire on top of a hill near the village and douse and stoke the fire to mimic the effects of a rotating lighthouse. They engaged in this trick for several nights until one day, when the navigator of a merchant ship fell in the trap. He directed his ship in the direction of the flickering light, but his ship got stuck in the shallow waters of the coast. The captain of the ship honked the ship's horn repeatedly to indicate distress and have another ship come to his rescue. The fishermen, who had never heard of the distress honking, thought the ship was weeping. They responded in unison, '*Bosu ara ewu*', which means, 'you will cry unto your death,' each time the ship honked her horn, but no passing ship came to her aid. The waves battered the ship, breaking both her bower and kedge anchors. She snapped in two and took on water. The crew abandoned her and swam ashore. The fishermen, who had been singing the refrain and lying in wait at the shore, scrambled into their dug-out canoes and surfboats and paddled to the abandoned ship. They descended into her hull and emptied her of the assorted merchandise and cargo before the sea could. They returned to the shore with their spoils and congratulated each other on the clever trick.

"The government got wind of the robbery and sent investigators to bring the perpetrators to justice. The investigators arrived in the fishing village, eager to ferret out information about the incident from the villagers. After days of inquiry, they identified the fishermen who engineered the infamous looting of the grounded ship. The first of the three ringleaders they questioned about the incident proclaimed his innocence with the words, 'I am as innocent of this crime as a newborn baby.' The second proclaimed his innocence, saying, 'I am as innocent of this crime as a newborn leaf.' The third, who had been exposed to Christianity, proclaimed, 'I am as innocent of this crime as Jesus on the Cross.' The government's investigators concluded they could not penetrate the pervasive code of silence that veiled the incident, gave up, and returned to the capital of Cape Coast to report their findings to the Governor."

"What happened to the ship?" I eagerly inquired.

"According to Mr. Gyesi, the ship is still stuck in the shallow waters of the sea close to the fishing village. It is reasonable to assume that fish are using its submerged chambers for spawning," Kwesi speculated.

"Do you have a story to tell?" inquired Danger, who had been looking empathetically at me during the story-telling session.

"Not really," I replied.

"Do you mean you do not want to tell a story, or you do not have enough imagination that lends itself in that direction?" refrained Kobina Amuah.

"No, not that. What I meant to say is that I do not feel like telling a story right now. I will in the future when I feel well, and that is a promise," I replied.

"Telling a short story will not kill you. In fact, it may help you," encouraged Danger.

The other boys voiced their encouragement. I felt obligated to tell a story, and chose to retell another story that Driver Gyesi told me and

Kwesi.

"Well, here is my story," I began. "There was a fisherman, Kofi Abekan, who lived in a fishing village called Moree in Gunta. One day, the fisherman went fishing with a crew and caught eel, red snapper, mackerel, and herring. While at sea, the fishermen seasoned some of the catch with spices and boiled it over a charcoal pit fire, which they carried with them. They ate the fish with *gari,* (a local food made from roasted cassava flour) for lunch, and continued fishing. At dusk, they rolled in their line, sacked their catch, and headed for land. Once ashore, they unloaded their fishing gear, shared some of the catch among themselves, and sold the rest to the local fishmongers. Kofi Abakan's share was six large red snappers.

"Upon arriving home, he called his new bride, Aba Abonsu, and gave her the fish to use as the central ingredient in a soup. He recounted his maritime experience with the boiled fish and asked her to replicate it, saying, '*Nam no naano nsu ye dew,*' which literally translates to mean 'the locus of the fish's taste is in its mouth.' With the literal translation in mind, the new bride accepted the fish from her husband and prepared the soup. She cut each fish into two halves. She opened the mouth, scooped some soup with a spoon, poured soup from the spoon into the mouth, rinsed the taste from the mouth, and threw away the upper half of the fish with the head and mouth attached. She brought the cooked soup to her husband who stirred it and found it to contain only the lower halves of the fish.

"Mr. Kofi Abekan asked his bride for an explanation on the whereabouts of the upper halves of the fish. The wife explained what she had done, but her husband could not believe what he heard. He persisted in stirring the soup for the upper half of the fish. After several stirrings without finding any upper portion of the fish, he reluctantly accepted the obvious."

"That is the end of my story," I said

"What a dumb woman! Doesn't she understand a simple euphemism?" Danger exclaimed.

"Whom are you calling dumb?" inquired Grandma.

Kwesi recounted an abridged version of the story for Grandma and explained why he thought the woman was dumb.

Grandma, as always, saw a teachable opportunity, and said, "The wife cooked in the manner she understood her husband wanted. She could have asked for clarification but did not, and that is where she erred. The husband could have gone to the kitchen to see how the cooking was going, since his bride was new, and offer his help, but he did not.

"Therefore, in my opinion, both husband and wife share equally in the snafu. Passing blame would not correct the error nor redeem the folly. The most important thing is not what they did or did not do, but what they learned from it. This incident should instruct you to be slow to anger and condemning people. The fact is: it is imprudent to impugn people until you have walked in their shoes and experienced their pain. On the contrary, you should quickly empathize with those in trouble and be quick with your sympathy for the same. Remember that there is more blame to go around when things go wrong than meets the eye. Also remember that there are more people who are eager to claim credit when things go right than there are contributors to a worthy cause," Grandma concluded, getting up.

Danger and Kobina Amuah visited until sunset. We talked about the many things we would like to do and settled on visiting the site of the scrumptious dinner at the cemetery.

Grandma gave her approval for Danger and Kobina Amuah to haul home the things they dug out of the pile.

Grandma advised that I bathe with *Amoronkye samina,* a local soap made from palm oil and banana roots, because of its high potash content. "It will help the chicken pox sores heal faster and not leave traces of scars."

I felt a lot better that evening and went to bed with a firm belief that I could conquer the world. I woke up the next day and could not recall my dream.

Chapter 12

"Your Papa called last night to say he will be here today to pick you up," Grandma announced when we woke up.

"At what time?" I asked.

"Sometime after court. He says he is defending a man who was charged with petty larceny," Grandma replied.

"What is petty larceny?" Kwesi inquired.

"I don't have an answer to that question because I am not a lawyer. You may ask your father, who is. I am sure he will gladly explain what that phrase means to you. In the meantime, I want you to wash your dirty clothing and ready yourselves to accompany your Dad back home. Your school reopens this coming Tuesday."

Her last sentence effectively ended our vacation in Apam. We rushed upstairs and picked up the dirty clothing we had tossed into a corner of the room we shared with Grandma. Grandma gave us two matchbox lengths of bar soap to use for washing our clothes. "Draw water from the well and set up three sets of buckets for the washing. Use the first for washing the clothing, and the second and third for rinsing them. It is advisable to empty and refill the buckets containing the rinsing water since they will get soapy," she suggested.

Kwesi and I soaked the clothing in the first bucket of water and took turns washing and rinsing them by hand, starting with the light-colored shirts. We pulled the shirts out of the bucket, one at a time, and rubbed the bar soap at the yellow-stained armpits and the discolored collars and cuffs. We scrubbed these points vigorously and submerged them in the bucket of water to dissolve softened perspiration and dirt and increase lathering. Then, we washed the light-colored shorts, and ended with the assorted dark-colored ones. We wrung water out of the rinsed clothing and pegged them on a clothesline to dry. The day's humidity and continual rubbing of clothing combined to leech sweat from my weakened body and made me limp like a boiled cocoyam leaf. I was deliriously tired and hungry at the end of the exercise and wanted to eat and go to bed, but Grandma couldn't stand the thought of postponing personal hygiene to satisfy pangs of hunger or morning sleep when the day of sunshine lay in front of you.

She was unequivocally adamant on these scores, especially over cleanliness. "You kids must have your bath first. It is better to eat when you are clean than the other way round. Cleanliness is next to godliness, and God is ever present at all meals," she proclaimed.

Above all, I was hungry and needed food. Personal hygiene, as far as I was concerned, could wait. I could not see the connection between cleanliness and godliness when death could scoop me into its bosom whether I was clean, dirty, or hungry. Those notions were debatable points for people who were well fed and had the wherewithal to quibble about the importance of full bellies to any hungry child. What I really needed was food to satisfy my hunger pangs. Therefore, I could not understand Grandma's insistence when neither God nor death cared if I had a bath before or after breakfasting. Perhaps, I thought, she had a greater purpose beyond my comprehension of her insistence. After much soul searching, I concluded that any delay would not earn kudos with her or abate my hunger. Most of all, I was not eager to tear myself apart on the issue, so I drank water to soothe my pangs and signaled Kwesi to hurry for us to bathe.

Kwesi bathed with his usual cube of Lifeboy bar soap. I bathed with a balled fermented banana root, potash, and palm kernel based *Amoronkye,* soap Grandma gave me. She explained that the soap contained natural potash, soda, and other minerals that would hasten the healing of my chicken pox-induced sores without scarring. She added, "Use the soap with a soft wash towel instead of the usual loofah sponge."

I followed her instructions and used the soap as prescribed with mixed results.

We had a hurried breakfast of the standard staple of porridge, fried eggs, and medley of fruits and asked permission of Grandma to say an impromptu goodbye to Danger and Kobina Amuah.

"Do not stay out all day," she said as we lifted the cross bars holding the compound gate and stepped into the outside world.

We walked briskly to Ayah's stall in hopes of seeing our friends one last time, but they were not at the stall. "I have sent them out on an errand and they should be back soon." Ayah replied. "Fetch your stools and sit down and wait, both of you," she suggested as she turned to serve a customer at her stall.

We pulled out the pair of softwood stools we had been using during previous visits and sat down to wait. We were hardly seated when a pair of black-skinned dwarf goats with white hoofs emerged from the mass of milling marketers. They stopped at a mixture of sand and gravel mound of the unpaved corridor running in front of Ayah's stall and readied themselves to ram their horns. The first ram that arrived at the mound was from a small goat about a foot and a half tall that weighed about thirty pounds and had an equally small goatee. He backpedaled to the top of the mound when the second, slightly heavier, goat imitated the antics at the bottom of the mound. They trotted *tout de force* toward each other with their heads slightly tucked down and bucked heads halfway up the mound. They stood on their hind legs and bucked heads again, but with less force, and locked horns on the third go around. They disentangled their horns, abruptly stopped the brutal exercise, and walked away in different directions with the same passivity that started the engagement.

A pair of short-horned forest goats pusillanimously imitated the rams with dismal results and walked away from nature's animal theatre like a pair of fallen imbeciles. As we sat discussing the mild display of primeval animal aggression we had just witnessed, the maid, Abena Atokyene, trotted to the stall to tell us Papa had arrived and wanted us back home at once. We got up from the stools, said a hurried good-bye to Ayah, and raced home.

We ran full force into Papa's opened arms for a warm embrace. "Slow down!" he pleaded as we approached. We slowed down and slumped into his embrace. He kissed both Kwesi and me on our foreheads and let go of us. We took a few steps back to catch our breath.

"How are you boys doing?" he asked, after we had caught our breath from the running.

"Fine," Kwesi replied, taking the lead.

"How is Mama?" I asked.

"She is fine. She is eagerly waiting for you to come home. She complains the house is like a graveyard without you to liven it," replied Papa.

Standing to Papa's right was Grandma, who was waiting patiently for the dissipation of euphoric energy brought on by Papa's presence. After we had calmed down, she directed our attention to the reality of the moment with a mixture of sadness and concern. "Check your clothing on the line to assess their dryness and pack them. There is no time to lose. Hurry up and leave before the evening falls and sunset ushers in darkness and the night. Heaven knows, I don't like you to travel at night into the boonies when you are far away from help," she added to underscore her concern over our safety.

We abandoned Papa's caressing hands and rushed to unclip our clothing from the clothesline. We bundled them in our hands and took them upstairs. Once there, we put them on Grandma's bed. Then we doubled them one piece at a time and stuffed them into our suitcases. We dragged the stuffed suitcases downstairs to the driver, who stacked them in the trunk of the car for the homebound journey. Papa gave Grandma a goodbye hug and started walking toward the car. We tagged along.

"Not so fast," Grandma protested. "You cannot leave without saying a proper goodbye to me."

On that note, Grandma grabbed Kwesi and hugged him. He did not resist her warm embrace. His suppressed smile and bright eyes underscored his delight. Perhaps, I thought, the days we spent with her had softened his initial hard feelings towards her. Grandma untied a nut at one corner of her covering cloth, pulled out a piece of folded paper held together by a safety pin, gave it to him, and let go of him with the words, "Open it when you get home."

Then, she grabbed and hugged me with equal passion before letting go of me. She untied the opposite end of her cloth, facing the corner from which she pulled my elder brother's, and pulled out a sealed envelope that she handed to me, saying, "Open it when you come of age."

"Thank you, Grandma," I said as I took the envelope. I stopped the driver, who was walking away with the suitcases, placed the envelope at the bottom of my suitcase, and asked him to proceed. As the driver continued his walk to the car with the suitcases, he sidestepped a mother hen and her chicks that were sauntering toward their coop after a day of scouring for food. He stacked the suitcases in the trunk and waited attentively for Papa to signal him to start the car for the return journey.

The driver ran through his routine of assuring that Papa, Kwesi, and I were comfortably seated. He inserted a long starter handle in an opening in front of the car, crank started the car, and returned the handle to the trunk of the car. He sat behind the steering wheel, revved the engine, and honked his horn to denote he was ready to drive off. The maid opened the gate and the driver pulled out of the house and onto the unpaved, dusty road. We waved to Grandma and the maid as we sped away in a plume of rust-colored dust. Looking back into the rear windscreen after traveling a few hundred yards, I saw the golden sun slowly dip its head at the horizon as it said goodbye to the day.

For a moment, I thought of Grandma and the pain of human loneliness that lay in store for her, and silently prayed for God's mercy in those hours. Dusk quickly succumbed to the blanket of night's darkness and the far away twinkling of stars that hovered in the sky. Gnats, moths, and other nocturnal insects smashed the car's windscreen and fell to their sudden death as they hit against the force of the moving car. Some of the falling insects left yellow and black streaks on the windscreen as they fell. Intermittent cricket chirring and naked-romped tomb bat wails punctuated the pattering sounds of the dying insects to denote there were other live creatures around. A pair of black-crowned night herons landed on the unpaved road and flew away as the beam from our car's advancing headlight sliced through the surrounding darkness like a surgeon's scalpel and shone on them. Our prattle with Papa gradually ground to a halt. Once again, the cool breeze and the rhythmic turning of the car's tires on the road soothed me into slumber. I slumped onto Kwesi's shoulder as I succumbed to sleep, only for him angrily to jerk me off his shoulder into partial wakefulness. He completed the cycle of breaking the hanging silence with a question to Papa. "What is larceny?"

Papa abandoned his doze and suddenly turned into a passionate lawyer pleading a case before a skeptical jury and an unscrupulous judge. "Larceny," he began, "is when a person takes another person's property without ever intending to return it to its rightful owner. The kind of things thieves do. It is against the law and deserves social condemnation and collective retribution. It is also an assault against hard working people, who get up every day to toil for a place to live and to put bread on their tables, only for thieves or knaves to conjure and steal their hard-earned property."

He went into lengthy explanation about the difference between petty larceny, robbery, aggravated robbery, and all kinds of legal mumbo jumbo that was lost on my youth and capacity of thought. He ended his long explanation with, "The sentence for any one of these offences is a jail term."

"Bravo!" I said to myself. I was totally taken in by Papa's knowledge of the law and decided to exploit his good humor with questions about Uncle Bota and the maid.

"Uncle Bota came to see us the other day," I began.

"Which other day?" Papa anxiously asked.

"A day or so ago," I replied nonchalantly.

"Be specific," he insisted.

"I cannot recall exactly which day," I regretfully replied.

"Think about it and tell me," he encouraged, and continued, "when did he come to see you and what was he wearing?"

He paused for my response, but I did not have any to offer because I simply did not pay attention to those details. Besides, I didn't understand Papa's obsession with details like date, time, and circumstance of his visit when they were not relevant to the questions I had posed. Therefore, I resolved to keep mum to avoid potential cross-examination without legal representation. To me, Uncle Bota's visit adequately denoted his thought and concern for us. That was enough. I closed my eyes and attempted to return to sleep, but Papa wouldn't let this sleeping dog lie. He broke the uneasy silence with a prompter.

"What did you say?" he asked in an insistent tone.

"Nothing that I can recall," I coolly replied, as I was beginning to get tired of the whole thing.

"The purpose of my line of questioning," he continued, "was to alert you to pay attention to things like time, place, circumstance, why, how, and when things occur. They provide the basic ingredients for cataloguing activities and establishing information retrieval points. Bear this in mind and don't let me catch you napping on those markers," he concluded.

Then after a pause, which felt like an eternity, he started again. "Uncle Bota is your uncle from my mother's side of the family. He was the first male born to the family and was raised by your Grandmother Elizabeth, who did not direct or discipline him for any childhood misbehavior. She gave him whatever his heart desired and adored the boy to no end. She did not set appropriate boundaries, structure, or give him any meaningful tasks that could encourage him to acquire commitment for performance and independence. She gave him unfettered liberties, access to money, toys, and whatever you can think off. She ignored his misconduct brought to her attention by other parents and playmates as misguided insults intended to embarrass and humiliate her grandson. 'Oh! Leave him alone. He is just a kid,' she often said when his infractions were brought to her attention.

"Sometimes she went to the extent of directly attacking the person or messenger who informed her of his misconduct for lack of sensitivity. Your Grandma used faulty logic to immunize and excuse all of Uncle Bota's inappropriate interpersonal conduct and deviancy. In short, to your Grandma Elizabeth, Uncle Bota was a living saint, and the only person who saw his faults and could chastise him with the right frame of mind and good intentions was your Grandma. Adults of the community had their hidden agendas when it came to him.

"As time passed, Uncle Bota grew up expecting the world to cater to his every whim and caprice. He did not respect other people's property or respect the rights of other people to live as they chose. He violated most of our unwritten rules of social intercourse with benign impunity. Sometimes he even broke the law and got away with it, if law enforcement officials were not present or in view.

One day, he broke into a neighbor's house to steal from him. The neighbor, who was a religious zealot, was traveling and expected to return in a few days. However, he returned home earlier than expected, and caught him in the act. Grandma pleaded with the neighbor to drop all charges in return for repairs to his broken windows and a handsome payment for his troubles. The neighbor refused her offer and pressed charges against your Uncle Bota. Uncle Bota was apprehended, prosecuted for aggravated robbery, and jailed for six months. He could not find employment when he was released from jail and resorted to drinking and conning family members for one thing or the other to survive. He called this 'living by your wits.' I call it downright abuse of family relationships and trust. I must admit that even I, with all my skills and training, have fallen for one of his shenanigans."

"This is what happened," Papa continued. "You see, on the 6th of March last year, he came to my chambers and informed me that he was going to Apam to visit Grandma. I gave him Grandma's living allowance, which I remit monthly through the mail, as well as a box of provisions containing canned sardines and mackerel, corned beef, assorted biscuits, canned butter, and milk to deliver to her. He told me he would be back in a few days and would relay how he found her. He did not. Indeed, the consummate scoundrel did not travel to see your Grandma as he had indicated. He spent your Grandmother's stipend on booze, cigarettes, and young girls and women who engage in commercial sex. He confessed to his crime and asked for forgiveness. I did not want to put up with the theft and was fully prepared to prosecute and bring him to court for justice, but your Grandma got wind of my intentions through your great grandmother, Akosuwa, with whom I discussed the matter. Grandma made a special trip from Apam to Cape Coast and admonished me for the thought. She said, 'Families are supposed to support each other and not wash their dirty linen in public with prosecutions, recriminations, accusations, and bad mouthing. The fact that you are a lawyer does not excuse you from this family edict because, as you well know, a divided family is soon finds itself torn apart one limb at a time or swallowed whole by a vicious public that smells blood or disenchantment.' I took her concern to heart and dropped the case. From what I hear, he continues to con other family members out of money, food, and anything else you can think of. I am confident he will con a jailer out of his keys if he lets him. He is a spoiled brat and an unethical, incorrigible crook that I do not care to be around, and he knows it."

"And what about Abena Atokyene, the maid? I noticed during our visit that Grandma treated her like a chattel."

"Well, son," Papa started, "the situation of Abena Atokyene is quite a different story. I will tell it to you tomorrow in my chambers after I am well rested. Right now, I am tired and need to rest. "

"Okay," I replied, and continued, "I may as well go to sleep too."

But before I could close my eyes, the continuous grinding road noise, which had characterized our travel on the dusty graveled road, suddenly stopped. We joined the main road, which was tarred. The driver pulled off the road. He pulled up the emergency brake and walked to the trunk of the car. He returned to the front of the car with a gallon container that was filled with water, poured some of the water on the windscreen, and used a soaped sponge to scrub off the debris of fresh insect carcasses that had caked on it. Then he wetted a dust rug with water from the container and rinsed off the mixture of insects, debris, and soapsuds from the glass. He wrung water from the dust rug and dried the windscreen and returned the cleaning gear to the trunk of the car. Resuming his seat behind the steering wheel, he continued the drive toward home. The ride on this part of the journey was smoother and more serene. I dozed off and fell into a sweet sleep, only to be awakened by Mom.

"Wake up sleepy head," Mama jokingly said as she opened the passenger door to the front seat.

I woke up, and noted the familiar surroundings. We were home. The driver unloaded the car. We had a late dinner and went to bed.

Chapter 13

There is nothing more exhilarating than waking up to familiar sounds and voices after holidaying away from home. I was delighted to hear chirping canaries, bobbing robins, weaver finches, and sparring sparrows that inhabited the nearby orange tree. I looked through the window overlooking the street and saw four pied-crows converging on an abandoned orange peel on the granite and bitumen tarred street that lay in front of the house on Beulah Lane. A vulture joined in the feast, whereupon the congregated birds scuffled and shifted positions for an advantage over the rotting orange peel. A passing mammy truck honked its horn to scare off the assembled flock. There was a brief silence. Then I heard Mama's voice ring through the house sounding sweeter than ever before. Perhaps, I thought, being away from her renewed my appreciation of what she really meant to me. The way she checked on us in the morning with her hellos and hugs and ineffable inquiries of, "How are you?" despite our listless responses tinged with desire to be left alone to continue sleeping. The way she continually asks us whether we were hungry and the steps she took to make sure we were secure and safe.

This time I was not overcome with the usual malaise. To the contrary, I got out of bed, eager to do whatever she asked without my usual nagging questions of why she did not ask the maid.

"Ato," she called, "come and help me fold these clothes from yesterday."

"Okay, I am coming right down." I replied and hurried down the mud-constructed stairs of the two-story building with deliberate speed to offer my help.

Upon arrival, I found her standing in front of a table with a large wicker basket filled with dried clothing beside her. I picked up a toasty bed sheets the tropical sun had baked, and started to fold it, but the sheet was too big for my small fingers, so Mama set aside a pair of shorts she was folding and helped me with it. We chattered freely as we folded the rest of the clothing. After we completed the task, she complimented me for the help and encouraged that I remain agreeable for the rest of the day. She also requested I stay away from hunting down the agama lizards that loitered on the walls of the abandoned building adjacent to our home. I had all intentions to remain agreeable. However, I could not see myself holding my distaste for lizards at bay in view of the part that they played in the development of my pigmentation. "I will try," I replied, and walked away.

Kwesi had slinked into Papa's chamber while I was engaged with Mama and was intently pouring through a sheaf of legal briefs and unopened correspondence scattered on his desk. He shuddered with surprise as I quietly entered the chamber and pulled his hands away from what he was snooping through. He turned and looked at me searchingly. "What are you doing here? He inquired in a hushed tone.

"I was looking for you," I replied nonchalantly.

"Well, you have found me," he answered in a voice that seemed to inquire what I wanted of him.

Because of what I detected in his response, I did not know how to proceed. I paused for a moment to search for the right words to continue our conversation. After a few moments, I continued, "Well...." I said tepidly, "I thought we could go and find out if the mother hen we found under the shrubs sitting on a clutch of eggs had hatched her eggs. I wanted to count how many chicks she hatched and pick up rocks to stone the lingering lizards on the walls of neighborhood houses. I also thought of visiting old friends and renewing acquaintances. You see, I just want to reconnect to the old and familiar things we left before going on vacation. Tell me, what do you think?" I asked apologetically, with a friendly pat on his shoulder.

"I have no opinion on the score," he replied, and casually added as an afterthought, "you can go by yourself. Besides, I want to wait here for Papa to tell me the story of Abena Atokyene's family lineage. It will be a treat to spend a little time with him since he is gone most of the time and busy reviewing briefs or preparing cases for court appearances when he is at home. For him it's work, work, and more work. He barely has time for the family."

I was pleased to see Kwesi show interest in something that did not advance his hedonistic ways, because, for as long as I could remember, he had tended to look at situations from angles that only benefited him. His selfishness paled in comparison to a cat's insatiable desire for caressing, and, along that line, I must say that he was arrogant and equally self-centered. He was concerned about how he dressed and the image he projected. For example, he washed his school uniforms and starched and pressed the pleats of his shorts from the waistband to the hem. He spent a greater portion of his weekly allowance on haircuts at the barber's and bathed daily, washed, dried, and patted his hair to a rounded evenness. He cut lemons in half and deodorized his armpits with them and faithfully, meticulously manicured his fingers and toenails with Papa's spent double-edged shaving blades on Saturday afternoons. He also spent untold hours vainly admiring the reflection of his physique in the mirror. "How do I look?" he would ask coquettishly after a spate of self-adoration. Not wanting to offend, I generally replied, "Quite all right," in a voice between affirmation and indifference.

I couldn't get over how much time and energy he spent on what I called "dead protein," by which I mean his hair and finger nails, because, as I saw it, he would have to trim or cut them down like dead wood no matter how much allowance he spent grooming his hair and manicuring his nails. In the end, I said to myself, his value as a human being will be measured by the quality of his relationship with others and not by his looks.

He was so adept at saying the right things and demonstrating appropriate deference that I began to believe he had absolute monopoly on social virtues. Indeed, I distinctly recall one occasion when Lawyer Blay, one of Papa's friends, visited us. "How are you?" Lawyer Blay asked.

"Splendidly well, thank you," he replied, in a gnawing Anglophone.

When I questioned him about this imitation, he explained he was speaking just like the expatriates did, which, as far as I could tell, probably represented his notion of ascendancy to the upper class. But then again, I knew he had several girlfriends and was simply practicing how he could use speech to impress the ones he had on his mind.

On the other hand, I could not be bothered with social decorum and all it entailed. I didn't care a whit about the look of my clothing or how I wore it as long as it was clean. For me, just having the basic things of life was enough. Indeed, I counted myself lucky to be alive when so many of my contemporaries had already succumbed to malaria, diphtheria, dysentery, or the effects of *kwashiorkor* and passed on. I was not interested in girls. Instead, I spent my spare time outdoor watching tadpoles swim upstream, mosquito larvae change into full-fledged mosquitoes and fly away from the stagnant water right before my eyes, a fluffy rabbit burrow into the ground, and houseflies buzz from one heap of filth to another or stop at patched places to rest. Sometimes I wandered off to the banks of the river running at the outskirts of town to mine worms, watch Diana monkeys socially groom their kind and trapeze from one treetop to another in a mixture of unbridled ecstasy and lunatic screams, or watch assorted butterflies flutter from flower to flower. At other times, I read a storybook—any storybook—or just lay on my back at sunset when the tropical breeze was cool and gentle and watched the cumulus clouds change shape and formations as they crept across the azure sky. On moonless evenings, I also looked at strips of sky festooned with clustered and scattered stars and did my best to count their twinkling. Otherwise, I just sat and listened to the surrounding silence and got startled when an unexpected noise broke it. In all, I delighted in the simple pleasure of life—the simple things that bring joy to the sick and laughter to children. I delighted in the things that kindle mischievous instincts in young boys and sweet remembrances for people engulfed in pain. I saw life to be filled with enchanted laughter and joy.

Kwesi's disinterest in my passions neither diminished my love for him nor dissuaded me from celebrating his success. I delightfully giggled when neighbors and unfamiliar people complimented him on his looks, and fiercely defended him when he was unjustifiably attacked. After all, he was my brother—skin of my skin and blood of my blood. I could not abandon him like I would a casual acquaintance or a man I asked directions of in the middle of nowhere. Blood, Grandma said, was thicker than water, yet sometimes I wondered how thick blood really was or what ends I had to go to defend him against public derision when he lied, cheated, and swindled me of my fair share at any chance he got.

"The mother hen and chicks, as well as the lizards, can wait. I will join you to listen to the story. I bet it will be a funny one," I replied.

Kwesi resumed his search of the papers on Papa's desk. A wax-sealed envelope embossed with a red monogram attracted his attention. He pause from the search and picked it up. Then with a puzzle look on his face, he asked, "Why do people use wax seals with personal monographs on envelopes?"

"To denote who sent it and make sure only the addressee opens them," I confidently replied.

"Hum," he acknowledged, and returned to his preoccupation with the papers. I began to read the titles on the spines of the collection of law books and novels arranged on Papa's bookshelf. Two of the books caught my attention. The first was entitled *The Philosophy of Lies.* The second was entitled *The Trial of Kennedy and Browne.* I thumbed through the pages of the first book and put it away because I did not understand what it was all about. Most of all, I could not fathom why lies should be philosophized into truth or vice versa. To me, a lie is what its name says: a lie is a misstatement of a material fact and unjustifiable under any circumstance. I thumbed through the second book in much the same way as I did the first. To the best of my recollection, this book told the story of two car thieves, William Kennedy and Fredrick Browne, who shot a police constable during a night of robbery and drunkenness on Essex Country Lane somewhere in England in 1927. Browne, I recalled, was the co-defendant who handed the gun to Kennedy to murder the constable. The most gruesome thing about the murder was that Kennedy shot the eyes of the constable six more times after he was murdered. Somehow, the two were caught and prosecuted. The question before the judge was to determine if both men were guilty of murder. Browne's lawyer advocated his client was not guilty because he could not know or anticipate that Kennedy, the co-defendant, would use the gun to commit the crime. Hence, his client did not have malice aforethought, an essential element for a murder conviction. However, the judge disagreed and found both men guilty of murdering the constable on the legal theory of principal before the crime. To the best of my understanding, this means Browne knew, or should have known, that Kennedy would use the gun to commit the murder.

As I got to the end of my musing, I heard footsteps approaching the chamber and stopped thumbing through the second book. I looked through the crack of the partially open door to confirm my suspicion and remarked, "It appears it's the Old Man." This was the name we affectionately called Papa when he was not around, and were careful not to use within his hearing for fear of incurring his displeasure. My hunch was that he had probably overheard us use the phrase and simply refused to react to it since that would normalize its usage, at least within our family circle, and denote acceptance or tacit recognition of his advancing age.

Kwesi paused from tampering with Papa's correspondence, to listen intently to the approaching footsteps and responded, "I am afraid you are right," in a soft voice. Then, he quickly thumbed through two or more pages of the correspondence, and took two sprightly steps, grabbed a chair that was leaning against the wall, and sat in it. I hurriedly returned the two books to the shelves, gently tapped them into alignment with the rest of the books, and resumed my chair. Our eyes met as we straightened ourselves in our respective chairs. We nodded our heads to denote acquiescence of each other's actions. I looked impassively at the wall facing us and assumed an air of false piety. Somehow, I assumed my lethargy would convey a sense of innocence and insulate me from any retribution, but I soon found out I was dead wrong.

The Old Man entered his law chamber, which he called his office, and quickly established control over the room with a thunderous greeting.

"Good morning! How are you kids doing today?" Papa asked, with a feigned gesture of surprise as he entered.

"We are fine," we responded in near harmony.

"And what brings you to my chambers?" he teasingly inquired.

"I don't know," I timidly replied.

"And what is the nature of the case?" Papa continued in the same teasing tones.

"We do not have a case," replied Kwesi in a stiff, imitative tone.

"Then why are you here?" continued Papa. "I am a lawyer and only deal with cases for clients, so you must go out and play if you don't have a case."

"But Papa, you know we do not have any case to bring. Besides, you promised you would tell us the story about Abena Atokyene and, now that we are here to listen to the story, you want us to go out and play. That is not fair." I pusillanimously protested.

"All right," Papa replied as he sat in the chair at his desk with his back toward us, and started rearranging the dockets and other correspondence that were piled on his desk.

"Who has been rummaging through my papers?" He angrily inquired.

There was a moment of awkward silence. I looked askance at Kwesi and turned my gaze to the cement floor of his chamber. Kwesi kept silent.

"Who has been rummaging through my papers?" Papa said in a strident demanding voice as he turned around his chair and faced us. The silence became grave and unbearable. Kwesi tilted his head slightly upward and took a sidelong glance at me. Then, gradually lowering his head, he turned toward Papa, and meekly confessed to his guilt. "I did."

Papa piercingly looked at him. He looked up to the ceiling, then at the floor, and back at him as if he were carefully measuring what to say. Then he gradually uncoiled his first finger, strenuously wagged it at him, and admonished him, "Don't do that again, ever," he yelled as he balled his fist and pounded it on his desk to underscore his displeasure. "Did you hear me? Ever!" Then, he released his clutched fist and continued softly, as if his anger had completely subsided, "Respect people, their properties and the boundaries they establish. An abuse of another person's boundary or property is an abuse of yourself. You cannot expect people to respect the boundaries you establish when you do not demonstrate that same respect for them." He concluded his admonishment with the reminder, "Charity, my son, begins at home and not in a barnyard of hooligans or the homes of ill-reputes and crooks. You will respect all people no matter their station in life or cultural heritage, and show deference to your elders, not only for today but at all times. Is that clear? "

Both Kwesi and I sat quietly as Papa ranted and raged. Then after the storm of his anger passed, he calmly continued:

"Now, you may sit down," he said as he formally invited us to his chambers.

"You are welcome in my chambers," he repeated in a friendly, disarming tone.

Since we were already seated, I could not understand why he kept inviting us to sit. Perhaps, I thought, he did that to reaffirm that we are in a place of business, but I was not about to ask for fear of rekindling his ire.

Papa methodically went through the sheaf of papers on his desk. He paused for lack of progress and added, "I will attend to them later. Now, let me see! Let me see," he said as he paused, clasped his fingers, which he momentarily unclasped on a deep inhalation, and changed course. He gradually exhaled and marked the end of his anger with the gentle question, "What did you say I promised to talk about?" he asked with squinted eyes to accentuate his recalling efforts.

"Abena Atokyene," Kwesi replied with a tinge of frustration in his voice.

"Oh, yes! Oh yes, Abena Atokyene," he jovially repeated, as if that was the first time he had heard of her. "Indeed, I promised to tell you the story about Atokyene, the abandoned child. Here we go.

"Sometime in 1764, John Newton, a British slave merchant, in an ironic twist of fate, was held in a Sierra Leone slave prison for six months to a year. I do not recall exactly how long. Be that as it may, he tasted the insidious evils of slavery and decided to end it after his release. He joined forces with William Wilberforce, a young Anglican parliamentarian, and Lords Granville and Bentham, who were similarly disposed to that goal. The four abolitionists tried to persuade British parliamentarians to change the British slave trade laws, but the British Parliament could not be persuaded because some of its influential members owned stock in the chartered East Indian Trading Company. This company and other trading companies used slave labor to operate and manage sugar, coffee, and tobacco plantations in the West Indies and other Caribbean counties. The income generated from these activities enabled Britain to establish its financial dominance and extend her commercial and political influence in the world. Above all, the chartered companies were not about to abdicate the benefits of slavery without a fight." Papa paused and looked at us.

"By the way, John Newton was born in 1725 and died in 1807," Papa added.

I began to wonder what John Newton, a Briton who died in 1807 and came from a country whose people benefitted from slavery, had to do with Abena Atokyene. I asked, "Papa, what does that Englishman have to do with her? After all, he is not her kin and does not come from our part of the world."

"Just be patient, listen, and you will learn and understand the connection," he replied.

I adjusted my seat and placed my elbows on my thighs. Then I opened my hands and rested my head in my palms to listen to Papa unfurl the historical mystery underlying the connection.

"Wilberforce, his cohort Thomas Clarkson, and his supporters then took their concerns to the newspapers with the same results. Unbeknownst to them, the British newspaper barons and the East Indian Trading Company, which was a major commercial enterprise, were in cahoots with some parliamentarians. Together, they controlled the world's trade and, in turn, the engines of the world's financial markets. But Lord Granville, who was in the House of Lords, was undeterred. He urged Anglican priests to preach sermons on the evils of slavery and the need to abolish it in their Sunday sermons. He and Thomas Clarkson encouraged other abolitionists to discuss the evils of slavery wherever they found sympathetic audience. Newton was invited to share his harrowing enslavement experience with churches and congregations. Newton obliged and told the congregations about his capture and showed them the marks he received from lashings during his enslavement. He also shared some of the pictures he painted of the squalid conditions of his confinement. He narrated the daily whippings meted out to the captured women, men, and children for talking to other slaves in the presence of slaveholders. He told the congregation about how slaves were numbered and chained in the ship's hull during their trans-Atlantic travels, the general abhorrent conditions of slave camps, and the meager gruel served to them. He adjured the congregation to consider the toll of the slave trade on the countries that sold slaves, the separation of families, and the decimation of cultural identities. He invited the congregation to join the crusade to abolish slavery in the name of Christianity and wrote a hymn called 'Amazing Grace' to mark his liberation from slavery, appreciation for freedom, and commitment to emancipate slaves.

"The congregation coalesced to support his vision. It gathered funds and mobilized grassroots support against the oligarchy that benefited from the dehumanizing trading of people for profit. The British newspapers and parliamentarians lent a reluctant hand. It banned the slave trade in 1807, and passed the Slave Trade Act of 1833 to emancipate slaves in England and its territories. The British Parliament also granted dispensation to the group to carry out its course. With that dispensation and the financial support of their congregations, the abolitionists bought boats and took to the high seas to track down and directly intercept ships ferrying slaves and free the slaves they were transporting. They boarded the slave ships; unchained and transferred the slaves, who were chained and pinned down in the holds of the ships, into their boats; and freed them at their ports of origin in West Africa whenever possible, or took them to Monrovia in Liberia or Freetown in Sierra Leone. Unfortunately, untold numbers of slaves died on the high seas during their trans-Atlantic journey.

"The interception and freeing of slaves did not end slavery in all its forms. The focus of the trade changed from trans-Atlantic to intra-country. Here at home, domestic slavery persisted partly because of continuing intertribal wars, and partly because of the economic value of slave labor to farming and the prestige slaveholders enjoyed in the wider community. The attitude of slaveholders, within countries on both sides of the Atlantic who had actively engaged in the trade, remained the same. In the Americas, slavery, I understand, assumed different forms. Here at home our kings and chiefs accepted the servitude of domestic slavery as a birthright and went as far as to have slaves buried with them. They did whatever they could to preserve the practice and dared any government, foreign or domestic, to oppose that right. In short, the official abolition of slavery remained a veneer.

"It was in this atmosphere that the British government legislated against the practice in 1833. Here at home, the laws were honored only in the capital and most coastal towns where the British government had a strong foothold. The foreign companies, including those registered in Britain that were doing business in the country, overtly supported the end of commercial slavery and demonstrated their commitment by refusing to partake in the open market for slaves. Covertly, they established trading posts in the hinterland where British law had negligible influence on local laws. They formed alliances with the kings, chiefs, and local aristocracy of similar mindsets to circumvent and undermine the spirit of the law through covert practices. The European expatriates and the companies they represent worked with the locals to redefine slavery to mean 'a person of the house'—an ex-slave who lived in the home of enslavement but remained in that home after he was granted freedom because no home was open to him. These slaveholders surmised that the freed slaves were better off in a home of enslavement, where they had a roof over their heads and left over meals, than to be outside braving the elements without a 'family' mooring.

"On the face of it, this redefinition was humane and noble. It gave the ex-slaves a home and complied with a *de jure* directive of the dominion's law. The effect was the *de facto* ignoble continuation of slavery. No matter how benign or well intentioned the redefinition, the slaves in our country were not truly free. They remained the possession of their owners and were used as property. Abena Atokyene's grandmother was one of such persons, a descendant of a person who lived in your Grandpa's house.

"You see, your Grandpa," Papa continued, "had more than twenty-five square miles of land on which he cultivated cocoa, and viewed slaves as a source of cheap labor and a way to manage his plantation. He cared for the slaves and treated them decently and humanely. In fact, the local slaveholders as a group treated their slaves humanely. To do otherwise was contrary to our established tradition and cultural norms. Abena Atokyene's grandmother was Odonko Nyi, a slave who cooked for the slaves that worked on Grandpa's cocoa plantation. She became romantically involved with one of the farmhands and had a daughter born under the benign slavery conditions. The daughter, Araba Atobra, had Atokyene, who, in our culture, is an *odonko nana*—a descendant of a slave. Atokyene was abandoned into your Grandmother's care when her mother learned that slaves of Ghana were truly freed following the April 12, 1927 trial of Hufuen Vardeen.

"You see," said Papa, repeating an old familiar phrase, "here at home, there were some European expatriates who were against slavery in all its forms and wanted it ended. They formed an underground network of clandestine operators with the natives and set up posses to fish for signs of slavery. They called themselves *'saabokyes*,' a possible mispronunciation of 'saboteurs.' These expatriates prevailed on other Europeans who owned slaves to abandon the practice and free their slaves. Most of them did so outright. Others converted their slaves into valets, maids, and domestic help and paid them meager stipends for their services. Still others magnanimously educated the freed slaves who remained in their homes. Over time, that education provided the ex-slaves with a true passage to freedom and the most important first step from the abyss up the social ladder of polite society.

"Some local kings and chiefs claimed slaves were spoils of tribal wars. As such, they had the same right of ownership to them as they had to any spoils of war. They believed it was inappropriate for foreign governments that knew nothing of inter-tribal conflicts or understood our local customs and rites to meddle with chieftain rights and privileges. These kings and chiefs went as far as having their slaves gagged, bound, and buried alive with them when they died. Natives who corroborated with the expatriates to stamp out slavery were summarily pierced with a poisoned arrow and hanged from a tree in the center of the village to deter others from doing the same. Yet, despite danger to life and limb, the *saabokyes* remained undaunted. They doggedly searched for signs of domestic illicit slavery in the colony and brought perpetrators to justice.

"On December 12, 1926, a group of scouts heard screaming behind the high cement walls of Mr. Hufuen Vardeen, a Dutch settler whom the locals called Mr. Weeden for short. Mr. Weeden lived in the European town of Sekunde. They scaled the walls and found Mr. Weeden mercilessly whipping a man who was stretched on a wooden rack. They reported the incident to senior local *saabokyes,* who, in turn, reported it to the authorities. The authorities investigated the report, arrested Mr. Weeden, and charged him with illegal slave possession and unlawful administration of lashes.

"On April 21, 1927, Mr. Weeden, was brought to court in handcuffs to defend himself against the charges. The trial became famous for its theatrics. It pitted local customs against crown law on one hand, and conscience against immorality on the other."

"What happened at the trial?" Kwesi inquired of Papa, who had been on a roll all morning and appeared to relish every minute of it. Here he was, with two of his own doleful children who worshiped the very earth he walked on and did not question him on any issue he chose to talk about.

He paused and asked me to fetch water for him. I ran to the kitchen, picked up a tumbler, filled it with water, and spilled half of it as I hurried back to the chamber. Papa took a sip from the tumbler. He pushed away some of the papers cluttering his desk, gently set the tumbler down on the desk, and resumed the story of the trial.

"The court opened at the strike of nine in the morning. A jailer in a pair of khaki shorts, a white shirt with a strip of medals pinned to the top of his left breast pocket, a well-polished pair of brown boots, and toting a double-barreled gun entered the courtroom. The barefoot prisoner, who was handcuffed and wearing rough-cotton prison shorts and a shirt, followed. Another jailor, who was similarly clad except that he was holding a long wood baton, escorted the prisoner. They entered the courtroom and quickly took the first row of seats that faced the left of the judge's bench. The prisoner's defense lawyer, Mr. Christian, followed. He exchanged greetings with the prisoner. The accused and his lawyer surveyed the courtroom and exchanged whispers. The lawyer sat on a chair behind a table situated in the center of the first row of seats. He started thumbing through a bundle of papers and files he had brought with him to the court. The prisoner and his jailors remained standing.

"Mr. Edwin Christian was an Englishman trained at Cambridge University in England. He was diminutive and appeared to be in his mid-sixties, was rather short at about five feet four inches tall, and weighed about one hundred and thirty pounds. He was also wearing black-striped trousers with a matching tailcoat, black shoes, and a black gown over the suit. He was wearing a white shirt with a stiff neck and a white periwig that was boiled into permanent curls. His eyes were dim and deeply impressed. This made me wonder whether he was dim-witted.

"The prosecuting lawyer, Mr. Wilber Green, a Queen's Counsel, followed. Mr. Green was also English and attended the Oxford University in England. He was five feet eight inches tall, weighed about one hundred sixty pounds, and was of medium build with a pudgy stomach. He arrived from Britain by sea just in time for the trial. He was similarly clad except for a red satchel around his neck to denote his admission to that order. He looked confident and took sprightly steps to the defense lawyer to exchange courtesies. He returned to his post and started to look through his briefing papers, which were lying on a table in front of him, and kept standing. Standing next to him was the Inspector of Police, a stout man of five feet four inches tall with a pot belly, possibly British, who was wearing a khaki short uniform with brown shoes and a plumed khaki helmet with a crown badge on the front of the helmet to mark his office. As if that were not enough, he had an array of medals pinned to the left of his chest. He consulted with the prosecuting lawyer and placed the papers he had in his hand on the table that was reserved for the prosecuting attorney.

"'Hear ye, hear ye, The Right Honorable Judge George Osgood,' the bailiff, who was a local man of about five feet nine inches tall, slim, in his forties, and with salt-and-pepper hair, announced in a raspy voice.

"The court observers and witnesses rose up from their seats on the announcement. The buzz of conversation that filled the courtroom decreased into a hum and ceased when the judge climbed up the bench and sat in his seat. The observers and witnesses returned to their seats after the judge was seated. The courtroom suddenly turned solemn and grave.

"The judge, who was also an Englishman, was wearing a heavy periwig, black trousers, a matching tailcoat and shoes, and a lace jabot with lilac facings under a black robe. He donned a red tippet over the left shoulder of his black robe to denote he was adjudicating a criminal case. He was six feet tall, weighed about two hundred pounds, and looked well-fed. He appeared mature and in his early fifties. He graduated from Gray's Inn, like I did, and had an imposing presence.

"The courtroom, which measured ninety-five feet long and twenty-five feet wide and stood on a hill, was filled to its capacity with visitors spilling over to its vestibule. On the front of the polished mahogany settee sat several Europeans dressed in assorted suits with long tailcoats. Some of them were holding tiller-felt hats with feathers stuck in their bands. Their wives and significant others wore long flowing dresses with medium-heeled shoes and straw or felt hats. Some of the men fanned themselves with their tiller-felt hats while others just held on to their hats. The ladies did the same with small folded fans, which they pulled out of their handbags and spread out for the purpose. One or two of the ladies turned their heads from time to time to survey the courtroom.

"Behind them sat several European newspaper reporters in assorted garbs who had swarmed the town like an invading army to witness and report on the trial. They lived with other Europeans that inhabited homes built on the cliffs close to the sea. A cluster of the local aristocracy and their wives, who were similarly clad and looked pretentious in their foreign-made clothing, sat at the back of the journalists. The few local kings and chiefs in attendance wore gold bracelets around their biceps and held a scepter in one hand and a curved gold-enameled cutlass in the other. Their advisors, some of whom were lawyers, flanked them on both sides and intermittently whispered translations of the proceedings to them.

"The buzz of conversation that had ceased when the presiding judge was seated began anew and broke the solemnity of the courtroom that hung like the end of a funeral procession. The court quieted down again and complete silence reigned when Judge Osgood started reading instructions on how he would conduct the proceedings. He closed with a rendition of the charges against the defendant. 'You are charged with four counts of illegal possession of slaves, inhumanely whipping a slave in your custody, and failing to free slaves as mandated by law. How do you plead to these charges? Guilty, or not guilty?' He asked the prisoner.

'Innocent,' pleaded Hufuen Vardeen, who was as ignorant of the court proceedings as a baby at a *Sanhedrin* hearing.

'Not guilty, your Honor' entered his defense counsel, Mr. Christian.

'So noted,' replied Judge Osgood."

I wondered why the defense lawyer addressed the judge as his Honor. After all, justice is presumed to be blind and impartial to either the prosecution or defense, yet here was the defense lawyer addressing the Judge as his Honor. The defense's prospect did not look good, in my way of thinking.

Papa proceeded with the narration, saying, "Mr. Weeden was a reputable, six-feet-four eligible bachelor who weighed about one hundred eighty pounds and had an imposing presence. He worked as an agent of a Dutch company that traded in timber and diamonds with our country. He lived in a two-story house close to the sea, where he threw lavish parties to punctuate his drab existence. He invited prominent members of the expatriate community to his parties and was affable, generous, and considered a ladies' man. He contributed handsomely to local social causes and attended church regularly, more out of a need to maintain relationships with both the expatriate and local communities than to nurture his spiritual growth. He was a shrewd businessman who viewed all interaction, both public and private, with the bottom line in mind. The moral teachings of the church did not influence him one whit. Things and people were good so long as they had utility and served the end he had in mind. Therefore, it was not surprising that he treated the 'persons of the house' under his care like house serfs or chattel to be used as he willed. In fact, he was deliberately cruel and treated his servants contemptuously. He was most cruel when drunk and would lash them without justification. It was during one of his drink-induced cruel dispensations that a *saabokye* overheard the wailing of the victim that ultimately led to his arrest and prosecution. And now here he stood, fragile and gaunt with hollow eyes deeply set in their sockets—a symbol of the elegant elite who lost his bearing with the law and was brought to an ignoble pass.

"Judge Osgood called the prosecution to begin deposing his witnesses for the case. Mr. Green called his witnesses to the stand one at a time. They swore to 'tell the truth and nothing but the truth.' He methodically deposed them to flush out the truth and boost his case.

'How long have you been living in this part of the country?' Mr. Green asked the leader of the *saabokyes,* Eva Gooden, who was a frail English woman in her thirties with a determined expression.

'I have been living in Sekunde for three years and am familiar with the locals and their ways. I also understood the laws of slavery and the British government's desire to abolish them.'

'On what day did you go to the house of Mr. Weeden?' Mr. Green asked.

'On the afternoon of December 24, 1926,' she replied.

'And what kind of day was it?'

'A dry day. The sun was high up in the sky, say about noon, and the wind came from the north carrying dust from the Sahara, and I remember I had the sniffles,' she replied.

'Objection!' interjected the defense lawyer. 'I do not see what her having the sniffles has to do with the case.'

'Sustained,' replied the judge as he nodded to the prosecution. 'Continue! Please stick to the facts,' pleaded the judge.

'And what did you see?' The prosecuting lawyer asked in a friendly tone.

'Well, nothing really,' she replied.

'Then why are you here?' inquired the defense lawyer.

'To narrate what I heard.'

'To tell us what somebody else had already told you,' the defense lawyer repeated with a sense of skepticism.

'Yes,' she repeated. 'Somebody has to say it. And I have chosen to be that spokesperson. The natives are not adept in legal proceedings. In fact, they are not used to our ways, so I or someone else has to speak out against their enslavement.'

"The defense lawyer got up from his chair at the table and was ready to cross-examine the witness, but the judge intervened.

"Please sit down, Counsel, and allow the prosecution to present its case. There will be plenty of time for you to cross-examine this witness."

The defense lawyer resumed his seat and the prosecuting lawyer continued deposing his witness for the record. The judge took notes on the entire proceedings.

"The prosecuting lawyer helped Ms. Gooden tell her story of how she became a *saabokye* through well-crafted questioning. Ms. Gooden detailed her Christian faith and personal conviction of the need for people from different cultural backgrounds to accept Christ and respect each other. She reaffirmed her religious conviction and legal ethics and explained her rationale for heading an organization that contravened the interests of some of her fellow Europeans. She concluded her testimony with an explanation.

'It is not the ethics of right or wrong that drives me. It is the ideals of self-respect, honor, and human decency that needle me like a conscionable criminal. I cannot claim the mantle of good Christian fellowship and either stand by unconcerned or condone the exploitation of one human being by another in the name of profits and to sustain a way of life. I cannot claim to be a good human being and be oblivious to the suffering and indignity of a fellow human being. To turn away from these indignities and lay claim to the mantle of human decency is to lie to my faith, the human spirit, and myself. A true Christian, in my opinion, does good work without expectation for the self. A good Christian does good work, and rights wrong wherever he or she finds it. He or she does not shy away from moral obligations because the price to family and friends is too high. He or she is proactive and not reactive, and that is why I submitted to the challenge of heading the *saabokye,* an underground organization that is totally committed to the abolition of slavery. After all, we are all God's children.'

"The prosecution called one of the scouts that scaled Mr. Weeden's cement wall. He was Kwesi Abohwe, a local boy of four feet six inches tall who weighed about one hundred fifty five pounds. He was bare-footed, like most natives, and spoke softly out of fright, but he was brave. He narrated his story through a local interpreter in his mid-twenties. Kwesi Abohwe described in exquisite detail how he and the other scouts scaled the wall to observe the goings-on on the other side of the wall, which was Mr.

Weeden's compound. He said, 'I was camouflaged in one of the branches of the banyan tree behind Mr. Weeden's house that was felled by rain against the eight foot wall. I laid my head on top of the wall and peeped into the compound. The leaves of the banyan tree gave protection and shielded me from discovery. From this vantage point, I saw a tall, husky man stretched on a wooden rack covered with cacti. He was pinned and held down to the rack with eight iron hooks, two on each limb. Mr. Weeden stood at ease and repeatedly lashed the man who was pinned down with a thick cane. The man that was stretched on the rack bled and cried out in agony with each lash. His cries turned into whimpers, and he became despondent. At one point during the whipping, Mr. Weeden asked one of his servants to pour water on the despondent man and revive him for more whipping. Finally, Mr. Weeden asked another servant to pour a mixture of sap and honey into the wounds. I presume he did this to attract ants to the bleeding man's wounds and exacerbate his pain.'

'Move to strike!' The defense lawyer yelled from his seat, and continued as he got up from his seat. 'His last comment is mere speculation and conjecture. I move to strike it from the record.'

'So noted,' replied the judge in a flat tone.

The Queen's Counselor, or QC, continued his deposition of Kwesi Abohwe with the question, 'How big was the cane?'

'About a quarter of an inch in diameter.'

'How many lashes did Mr. Weeden administer to the ex-slave?' the QC asked, as he took slow deliberate steps toward the witness.

'Fifty or, maybe more. I was too frightened to count,' Kwesi Abohwe replied.

'Continue,' urged the Queen's Counselor.

"He identified the wooden pegs, which were used to pin down the servant to the ground when they were presented by the prosecution, and reaffirmed what he saw on that fateful day over Mr. Weeden's bricked fence.

"The defense attorney incisively cross-examined the witnesses. He poked holes in parts of the testimony that witnesses for the prosecution gave to the court. He put up a brave and spirited defense, but in the end, the core of the testimony from the prosecution's witnesses remained firm and unshaken. The weight of evidence against the defendant was preponderant and was proven beyond a reasonable doubt. The judge was not persuaded by the rebutting testimony of witnesses for the defense and found the defendant guilty as charged. He paid particular attention to the heinous and abject brutality of the nature of Mr. Weeden's crime during his summation, and drew attention to what can, and does, happen when individuals are given unbridled power over others. Mr. Weeden possessed the mental capacity and the free will to do good or evil, to show compassion or cruelty, and to abide by the law or refuse to. He chose to appease his cruel nature instead of complying with the law, and now the law will mercifully sentence him to serve a prison term not exceeding fifteen years in jail to match the depth and extent of his cruelty to a fellow man.

"The verdict repudiated domestic slavery, undermined traditional laws, reaffirmed the British rule of law and its supremacy over our local customs and mores. However, the judge's verdict was not absolute in its affirmation of the British notion of the rule of law. It recognized that although there were distinct differences between the British and native legal proceedings, both aimed at searching for the truth. He resolved to use the traditional court's ruling to supplement British rule when it was expedient to do so.

"Abena Atokyene's mother heard of the ruling that abolished domestic slavery and took off, leaving her daughter behind for your Grandma to care for. That is why your Grandma did not want you to associate with her. Your Grandma did not want you to associate with her because of that lineage. She was, and remains, a house serf or 'person of the house' who was left as a legacy and a shameful reminder of your Grandpa's use of slaves on his plantation. She will remain with us as long as she wants and would never be cast out to the harsh elements of the world. I am confident that as time passes, you will come to find her beautiful in more ways than meet the eye.

"Tomorrow I will take you to St. George's Castle at Elmina where slaves were held while they waited for shipment to the Americas and West Indies. Go out and play with your friends," Papa encouraged, while he stayed in his chamber to catch up on his paper work and prepare for upcoming cases like he often did over the weekends.

We trouped out of his office to re-establish acquaintances and renew friendships with the neighborhood children of our age.

Chapter 14

I woke up ecstatic about the impending journey to the castle in Elmina. I rushed through my daily chores, breakfasted, and trotted downstairs to the veranda, where our family usually gathered to hatch its traveling plans. I was shocked to find Kwesi was already toileted and dressed in a pair of well-pressed brown khaki shorts and white shirt. He was strolling up and down the veranda to pass time while waiting for Papa. His hair was immaculately groomed. I was wearing a pair of faded gray pantaloons and a light gray shirt with a pair of threads hanging from the left sleeve. I approached him and inquired how he was feeling. "How are you feeling this morning?" I asked, and told him how excited I was about going to the castle without waiting for his response. "I am really excited about this visit. How about you?" I inquired.

"Yeah, yeah, I am," he replied offhandedly, and kept on strolling at a steady pace.

I surmised he did not want to be bothered with my babble and left him alone to continue walking up and down the veranda as I proceeded towards the exit to feed my eyes with nature's wonderment. I sensed someone was following me. I turned around to see who that might be and noted Papa coming toward the entrance of the veranda. I walked back to be with him, but he passed by me and walked towards Kwesi, who had momentarily paused from strolling up and down the veranda and was standing in a corner. I looked to the side of Papa as he passed by and noted he was wearing a black and white *kente* cloth over a pair of black pantaloons. He appeared cheerful and patted me on the head as he usually did. He reached Kwesi, who was standing, and softly asked him, "What are you doing?" in a manner that denied the obvious.

"Just trying to gather my thoughts," he replied.

"All right," Papa said, and joined him in the exercise.

I wondered whether I should also join them, but resisted the impulse and started pondering what had possessed Kwesi to gather his thoughts so early in the morning. I wondered whether he was planning some mischief or mulling over lost puppy love. Indeed, the idea of my elder brother spending a quiet time to reflect was novel to me because I have never observed him to be introspective over anything. To the contrary, I have known him to be gregarious, at times temperamental, and occasionally whimsical and unforgiving. I have also known him to be self-absorbed and engaged only in those things that attract his fancy, yet here he was calm, collected, and contemplative. Perhaps, I concluded, he was beginning to mature or was going through a growth phase.

Just as I reached that conclusion, Mr. Kwesi Gyesi, the driver, walked onto the veranda and announced he had finished washing the car and checking the oil levels and tire pressures and was ready for us to start the journey.

"*Masser*, we will need to top up the petrol," he informed Papa.

Masser, a mispronunciation of "master," was how Mr. Gyesi addressed Papa, and that is how he always will, because Mr. Gyesi did not have a formal education. In fact, he had never set foot in the classroom and did not intend to. School, he told me, was an aphrodisiac for the rich who do not have anything better to do with their lives. He had a family to support, and feeding that family took precedence over investing his hard-earned income in education with no guaranteed outcome. Education, he told me, was a waste of his time. Therefore, there was no possibility of increasing his limited proficiency in English, which is the country's lingua franca. He used a version of pigeon English, which had phrases like, "*I de go come,*" to mean, "I would be right back;" "*na him,*" to mean, "he or she is the person in question;" and "*them people,*" when talking about a group of individuals. I found it remarkable that his lack of proper diction and general appreciation of grammar and syntax had only minimal effects on his capacity to understand conversational English.

"Let's go!" bellowed Papa. "We will stop and buy petrol at the usual place," he said, more to the driver than to us.

We marched out of the veranda behind him and assumed our customary seating positions in the car. The driver started the car and set off for St. George's Castle in Elmina, which was fifteen miles or so west of Cape Coast, where we lived. We stopped at the petrol station, topped up the petrol, and drove off on the granite and tar paved roads of the town for two more miles after reaching the outskirts of town. Then we continued our journey on a dusty, unpaved road where the leaves of the small vegetation and germinating coconut trees fluttered their branches with the undulating sea breeze and wind left in the wake of passing vehicles. Above the low-lying vegetation, the rows of grown and matured coconut trees' leaves met over the road to form an elongated arch of dancing green leaves for cars and mammy trucks to drive under. The arch the leaves formed reminded me of what I saw at a military officer's wedding, where officers lined up on both sides of the pathway leading out of the church and drew their swords from their sheathes to form an arch for the newlyweds to walk under.

In addition to the dust, the road had a web of tattooed potholes, which marked it like a spectrograph. Drivers who frequented this road heroically swerved to evade the potholes. Sometimes their maneuverings landed the vehicles they drove and the passengers they carried in one of the two continuing gullies that ran on both sides of the road to channel rainwater downstream. In my humble opinion, drivers who engaged in such reckless road maneuvers can be aptly described as playing Russian roulette with the passengers' lives.

Our car swerved as driver Gyesi tried to maneuver around the potholes. This threw Papa, Kwesi, and me off our seats. Papa woke up from dozing and told Mr. Gyesi to slow down and drive more carefully. The driver immediately complied with the command. This acquiescence, to me, amply underscored what people meant when they said, "The person paying the Piper called the tunes." Here was the driver, a grown man older than Papa who was married with children, taking instructions from Papa, a young man, simply to earn income to house, feed and clothe his family. He could possibly be an *apparatchik* and sell his soul to achieve that end. I took one long look at him and mused how the power of money can easily influence actions of unconscionable men.

We rounded a corner and came upon adobe, hovels of wood and mud, weather boarding, woven coconut branches, and corrugated sheets scattered under a mangrove of coconut trees. Most of the hovels were roofed with thatch to provide an extra layer of protection from the intense tropical heat and the torrential rain. As we got closer, I noted that the ebb and flow of the wind caused the sunrays to dapple on the ground on which these houses stood like a blanket riddled with bullets.

The strew of houses became more clustered and the trees and groves became less dense and visible as we drove closer to Elmina. A few partially completed houses stood solemn, alone, and separated. They reminded me of relics of useless war machinery abandoned by a ransacked army in retreat. A bare-chested and barefooted young boy emerged from the back of one of the shabbily constructed houses. A girl, who was pursued by a young boy of about the same age, suddenly emerged from the same corner. Nungua black sheep and dwarf goats grazed on the open fields close to the homes. A hooded vulture landed softly on top of one of the coconut trees, flapped its wings a couple of times, and flew away. A pied-crow, which was pecking on a delectable find on the dusty road, abandoned its find and flew away as we approached it. We crossed a squeaking narrow wooden bridge, traveled an additional mile or so, and arrived at the castle.

The driver stopped the car on the lush and neatly manicured Bermuda grass that carpeted the front of the castle, got out of the car, and opened the door for Papa and us. A brown cock with strips of black in its feathers stopped pecking away at the green grass, and cried cock-a-doodle-doo, as if to welcome us. The church bell pealed ten times to announce the time of the day. We laboriously stepped out of the car and started walking towards the castle. I took a step or so, stopped, and stretched to regain flexibility from sitting in the cramped quarters of the car. Looking around as a matter of personal ritual, I observed four dugout canoes sailing up the bayou east of the castle where the lagoon joined the sea to form a natural inland harbor, and tapped Papa on the shoulder to draw his attention to them.

"Look at those canoes. Look at what the men are doing!"

"They are just paddling a canoe," Papa responded without a flinch.

I looked in the direction of the castle to survey its contours and saw a pair of coconut trees standing like sentries on duty in front of it. Pebbles astrolabe adorned the west corner of the lawn leading to the entrance of the castle. Kwesi, who was walking ahead, turned and signaled us to join him at a small mound that was a few feet away from where the driver had parked the car. We joined him and watched two coxswains jib their dugout canoes into harbor. The first of the two coxswains led a song, to the refrain of six fishermen, who were pedaling the canoe. The fishermen safely anchored their canoe and disembarked from it. Fishmongers, dressed in colorful wrap-around cloths and shoulder covers, accosted the fishermen to buy their catch for retail. They carried large, woven baskets on their heads to portage their fish purchases. Two more dugout canoes returning to harbor passed close enough to the mound for me to read the signs carved and painted onto their sides facing us. The sign on the of the first boat read, "All rivers end their journey in the sea." The second dugout canoe's carving, which was in the local language, read, "*Adom wo wimu,*" which means, "Grace comes from heaven."

"This way," Papa said in a tone reminiscent of a professional guide.

We left the driver to watch the car and strolled hand in hand with Papa to the castle. The castle was built like any of the ordinary castles of the Middle Ages. Nonetheless, it must be noted it did not have barbican to protect against enemies, since none were known. It had battlement with cannon gunnery mounted on it and a flanking tower. A rusting ball was lodged in the muzzle brake of the cannon gunnery.

We tiptoed across a small creaking wooden drawbridge measuring about four feet wide by forty-five feet long. This drawbridge crossed a moat, which joined the castle to land. Wooden planks fenced in the drawbridge on both sides to keep visitors from falling onto the cream-colored sand carpeting the bottom of the moat sixty feet below. Two-inch diameter iron strips moored the drawbridge on each side over a pulley to the castle's foyer. Papa told us that the sea used to fill the moat. A large bulb hung at the end of each line and was used as a lever to lift the bridge at night. An iron molding with the inscription, 'Genoa 1482,' was leaning against the wall of the foyer. From time to time, the sea breeze blew the peeling paint to twirl like a leaf trapped in a tropical whirlwind. A sac spider dropped from the ceiling of the portcullis and recoiled with all speed into safety before I could say, "Hello, Mr. Spider, how are you doing?"

The portcullis opened into an uneven inner stone floored ward. The wall of the ward was painted in flat white. I peeped into one of several holes that punctuated the wall of the ward and noted huge rocks protected the castle to the east, west, and south from sea waves that bathed the shore. Otherwise, the castle was wedged between the sea and land of the Gulf of Guinea, and tenaciously held on to its secrets of untold misery of man's inhumanity to man, like the last dying guard of the gulag.

I pointed to the inscription on the iron molding and asked Papa, "What is the significance of that?"

"It denotes a Portuguese trading post of that era. Perhaps Christopher Columbus stopped here on his southward-bound journey to the Cape of Good Hope and beyond."

"Does it mean that the Portuguese built this castle?" Kwesi inquired as he attempted to join the conversation.

"Probably," Papa replied.

"Why probably?" I asked, probing for clarification.

"Because nobody knows for sure, and I am not an expert in those sorts of things. One thing is certain: our country didn't work with iron in the fourteen hundreds. Therefore, it is more likely that the tablet was made around 1482 in Genoa and possibly left there by either Columbus on his way south, or by some undetermined Portuguese explorer. What puzzles me is how a castle that was supposedly built by the Portuguese came to be named after a British monarch when the British were the last to arrive in our country. I suspect they inherited it as their share in the 1843 Partition of Africa and changed its name from whatever it was to St. George to honor their monarch of that time. I based my supposition on the tried British mercantile practice of claiming colonies in the name of their monarchy.

"There is also an alternative story that the British won the castle in a fair-and-square pitched battle against the Dutch. According to this story, the British built that fort on top of the hill over there," Papa paused and pointed to a fort overlooking the castle, "with the help of locals, ransacked the occupying Dutch, who had beaten the Portuguese in an earlier battle, and took it from them."

We stepped deeper into the foyer of the castle and saw a slightly opened door with a crossbar dangling behind it. The gulf breeze, which rose from the sea to cool the land after sunset, had blown the door wide open. Papa drew our attention to it, as well as the two concrete steps that led away into the interior of the door. He encouraged Kwesi and me to walk the steps leading away from the door, one person at a time. He brought up the rear. When we got to the top of the steps, Papa asked us to peep into the two holes that were burnt through to the sliding wood window. We did as he had suggested and realized that it was a safe vantage point from which slave merchants could select slaves who were paraded through the enclosed walkway below. Papa showed us the kitchen with an iron cauldron and the inner ward with two heavy round balls, weighing about a hundred pounds each, embedded in the ground and told us that was where female slaves were coerced for compliance with owners' wishes, and male slaves were tethered as punishment for disobeying captivity rules.

I wondered what the wishes of the slave owners could be and did not ask Papa because I wanted my imagination to intrigue me. I did this in tribute to Grandma's admonition of peeling the layers of an onion to get to its core. Grandma told us that unmasking all lies to get at the truth can make you vulnerable to what you find.

We retraced our steps and made our way to the northern battlements facing the front of the castle, which Papa had pointed to earlier. Kwesi saw an old rusting cannon resting peacefully in a duck by the gunnery on top of the wall and asked Papa whether the Dutch defended the castle by firing it, but I interjected with my inquiry before Papa could point out another thing for us to observe. "So you are saying the British either had the castle outright or won it because they had the upper hand in the battle, if you consider that they held to the higher ground."

"That is true," Papa agreed, and continued, "either one of the two scenarios you have mentioned is possible. Unfortunately, our country, like other African countries, did not have trained historians to record events as they occurred during the formative years of our country. Our history was oral and largely unrecorded. Family members recounted significant events of their lives and passed them down from one generation to the next. They spruced up their narratives with anecdotes to enhance their roles, in myths, hearsays, or legends and to magnify what they thought was important. These narrative packaging, which were intended to enhance the roles of major players in our history, have distorted our earlier accounts and rendered them inaccurate and woefully inadequate. One thing is for sure: our history is rife with gaps, and may remain unfilled for years to come. It is a shame that some of our elders passed on without sharing their collective knowledge and life experiences. These elders, in my opinion, have robbed the next generation of invaluable information and left our country poorer than they found it.

Foreign nationals who wrote our early history have not been as assiduous and sensitive to our national identity or heritage as they could have been. They have taken undue liberties with facts, and shortchanged us every turn of the way. Unfortunately, they will continue do so for as long as they have the pen and inkwell in their hands and control the means of knowledge dissemination. Above all, their concept of human reality or historical relevance is different from ours and vice versa. Consequently, they cannot do justice to our cultural aspirations in the same manner as native-born historians. In my opinion nationals of a country are best suited to write its history because they tend to be truthful, more diligent, sensitive, compassionate, and understanding of the events and circumstances contributing to their own history.

Just envision hiring a professional writer to pen your biography without your input or encouragement. Or, for that matter, an occupying army chronicling the events that led to victory over the vanquished. Both narratives will tend to be unfaithful and biased. The professional writer will be influenced by his personal bias and so will the occupying force. History, in my opinion, is not as objective as people would have you believe. They are filled with few facts and riddled with opinions and unconscious bias. But the distortions tend to be minimized when it is left in the hands of caring, dedicated professionals with local sensitivities," Papa concluded.

Papa shepherded us to a seventy-five yard radius ward where slaves were held while they waited to board slave ships bound for the Americas and the West Indies. This ward, with a tall, white-painted wall and strategically placed opening, had a mosaic of cracks filled with moist vegetation and algae-induced greenness. A few wild plants hung from the cracks in the walls. Papa pointed to a flanking tower at the top of the southwest corner of the castle and told us that was where slave guards stood and scoured the gulf with monocular for incoming slave ships. The guards relayed news of the position of the ships to the ground guards who corralled the slaves and readied them for the outbound journey.

Next, Papa directed us to the shed that was used as both a kitchen and a holding area for slaves during inclement weather. Once there, Papa stopped and narrated one of the most horrific stories of the slave trade I ever heard.

"As the legend goes, in the latter part of the seventeenth century," Papa started, "an intertribal war erupted between the *Ashwazis* and the *Dagutas* over land ownership that lay between the two tribal enclaves. A severe draught turned the northern prairies, where the *Dagutas* raised their cattle, into a dry dust bowl. The sun had baked dry the lush green vegetation that covered the land the previous two summers and turned it brown and scarred. The Shea butter tree, which is renowned for its suppleness, was sapless and brittle. The northern wind had blown away the topsoil and laid the land fallow and unusable for either animal or human habitation.

"The *Dagutas,* who were nomadic, migrated south to search for greener pastures to feed their cattle and escape the scourge. They also wanted to protect their cattle, which were central to their customs and way of life from dying. They ended their search on land belonging to the *Ashwazis.* The *Ashwazis* failed to negotiate a peaceful withdrawal of the uninvited tribesmen on their land. A close review of oral history indicates that negotiations between the two tribes failed because the *Dagutas* customs did not recognize individual property rights.

"According to *Daguta* tradition, the Earth, and all that is in it, belongs to all. We came into the world naked and empty-handed, and leave it just as we came in. Therefore, nobody had individual right to any property. Children ensure the continuation of our species and should be celebrated for their beauty and the joys they bring to the community of their birth. The tribe killed cattle, drained the blood, and cooked the drained blood as part of their meal. As a result of this high protein intake, the *Dagutas* were tall and strong. The cattle ranchers, like most men in their community, wore sarongs around their waist and used arrowheads dipped in a concoction of crocodile liver and cobra poison to protect their cattle from other animals, and for hunting small game.

"The *Ashwazis*, on the other hand, believed in the private ownership of property. They believed that private ownership of property enhanced individual freedom and joy of life. This belief formed the central core of their way of life and provided the impetus and rationale for waging wars. In fact, other citizens in our country refer to this tribe as the bloodthirsty tribe.

"Adding to the difference in core cultural belief were language differences. The *Dagutas* could not understand the *Ashwazis*. Therefore, they resorted to war to settle differences emanating from both the language and 'unlawful occupation.' The *Ashwazis* faced the *Dagutas* with their traditional curved clubs and sticks in the famous battle at the *Opata* junction. The *Dagutas* hid among the branches and shot their arrows dipped in poison to kill or maim the *Ashwazis*. The traditional warmongering *Ashwazis* did not take the defeat kindly. They wanted to avenge the defeat at all costs and reassert their supremacy, so they sent an emissary to negotiate a peace treaty granting grazing rights to the *Dagutas,* in exchange for ten bulls a year. The two tribal leaders agreed to cease hostilities and end the war. Daunda Dagoda and his elders made a pilgrimage to sign a peace treaty. On their way back to their tribal enclave, the *Ashwazis* successfully ambushed and caught the elder *Dagutas* who had come to sign the treaty. They gagged, bound, and sold them into slavery. The *Ashwazis* surmised that selling their enemy into slavery was more humane and preferable to killing them in cold-blood. It earned them much needed gunpowder, barrels of whiskey, myrrh, incense, and rid them of their adversaries.

"One morning after the big rainy season," Papa continued, "Dagoda, who was a tall and feisty slave, overcame the guard who led him when he went to do his toiletries. He used the guard's key to unlock his chain and free himself, as well as other slaves. A mutiny erupted; reinforcement guards were called to put it down. The mutinous slaves tried to escape into freedom, but the guards raised and bolted the castle's drawbridge, which served as an entry door and thereby effectively stopped the slaves from escaping.

"During the melee, the guards fired their muskets and double-barreled rifles, killing five unarmed slaves and wounding several others. Most of the wounded wallowed in pain to excruciating death from their wounds. When order was restored, the guards loaded the carcasses of the fallen slaves onto a wagon drawn by a donkey and carted them to the entrance of the local chief's home. The guards returned to the castle and hanged Dagoda by the feet from up there," Papa paused and pointed to the ceiling, "and garroted him in front of the remaining slaves. The slaves hollered in horror as they watched their hero succumb to one of the most heinous practices of the slave trade. From then on, slave merchants branded monograms onto the chest of the enslaved with flaming irons to identify their holding.

"News of the aftereffects of the mutiny quickly spread through the community like wild fire. The local community became frightened of the death caused by the rifles and swore to stay away from the potential devastation it could cause. Legend has it that from that time on, slave merchants simply left double-barreled guns across the doorway of the rooms where prisoners of war were held while they either slept or took breaks." Papa then showed us the large cauldron used to prepare gruel for the slaves and walked behind the shed to look at a pair of mounted cannons with balls at the end of their muzzles.

We finally ended the tour by Papa walking us to what he called "The Tunnel of no Return," which was situated at the southeast end of the castle. "Tuck in your heads!" he yelled as we arrived at the entrance of the tunnel and started walking its length. We tucked in our heads close to our chests, walked on the uneven stone paving, and arrived at the exit where shackled slaves were dropped down and marched over the rocks toward boats to be ferried to slave ships anchored off shore for the trans-Atlantic trip.

"Why do you call this the tunnel of no return?" Kwesi asked.

"Because beyond this point, the slaves were severed from their cultural heritage and the soul of their forefathers and surrendered to a people who lacked the will and fortitude to fully appreciate the gamut of their humanity."

Papa turned and looked pensively at the sea. I followed his gaze and wondered about the lives that wallowed in indifferent death without consolation; the cries for help that the sea waves muted; the secret aspirations of my ancestry that were wrapped up in its waves and swallowed alive. I thought about the continuing struggle for a holding center among those who made it to the shore of the New World and began to sob.

"Why are you sobbing?" Papa asked.

"Because, I cannot understand why so much suffering and pain was brought by so few on so many in the name of commerce and profits."

"Look at your fingers," Papa commanded. "Look at them," he repeated in a high pitched tone.

I lifted my right hand and looked closely at each of my fingers for the very first time in my life.

Then looking tenderly at me, Papa said, "They belong to the same person and were born in the same day, yet they are unequal in length. For as long as human beings remain unequal, in one way or the other, slavery will continue in one form or another. It may continue as idol worshiping, adoration of superstars, or subjugation to another person because of some indeterminate influence. Slavery as an institution will transmute and survive because of the insatiable desire of some people to view themselves as superior or more deserving. That is the unfortunate truth and nature of the two-legged human beast."

We did not say much to each other as the driver drove us back home. Within few miles of the travel toward home, both Papa and Kwesi dozed off, but I could not doze off, much less sleep because I was in turmoil over what I had seen and heard from Papa about the inhumanity of man to his fellow man and the unfairness of it all. My spirits were at their lowest ebb and needed boosting. So, I said a quick "hello" to Mama when we arrived home and rushed to my room in search of the sealed envelope Grandma gave me as we departed, in the hope that it might contain something that would lift my spirits. I ransacked the bottom of my suitcase and found it exactly where I left it. After picking it up, I gradually and deliberately unfolded it, one layer at a time, and read this prayer, which St. Francis of

Assisi uttered several years ago:

> Lord, make me an instrument of thy peace;
> Where there is hatred, let me sow love;
> Where there is injury, pardon;
> Where there is doubt, faith;
> Where there is despair, hope;
> Where there is darkness, light; and
> Where there is sadness, joy.
> Grant that I may not so much seek to be consoled as to console;
> To be understood as to understand;
> To be loved as to love.
> For it is in giving that we receive;
> It is in pardoning that we are pardoned;
> And it is in dying that we are born to eternal life.

I went out to find someone in need of consolation and found none.
Perhaps, I was the one in need of consolation and not the other way around.

Stanley Sackeyfio was born in Ghana and lives in the United States. He holds a graduate degree in Business Administration from the University of Central Oklahoma and memberships in the International Honor Society in Economics and the International Business Communication Association. His hobbies are reading, traveling, and photography.

Gulf Coast Publications
Cover Photograph:
Stanley Sackeyfio

The author believes in continuing the Ghanaian tradition of teaching through story telling. He is available for discussion.

For more information, contact Stanley Sackeyfio
Songsofourfathers@Gmail.com

www.ingramcontent.com/pod-product-compliance
Lightning Source LLC
Chambersburg PA
CBHW072345090426
42741CB00012B/2925